A RESTATEMENT OF THE ENGLISH LAW OF UNJUST ENRICHMENT

A RESTATEMENT OF THE ENGLISH LAW OF UNJUST ENRICHMENT

ANDREW BURROWS

ASSISTED BY AN ADVISORY
GROUP OF ACADEMICS, JUDGES,
AND PRACTITIONERS

UNIVERSITY PRESS

Great Clarendon Street, Oxford, OX2 6DP,
United Kingdom

Oxford University Press is a department of the University of Oxford.
It furthers the University's objective of excellence in research, scholarship,
and education by publishing worldwide. Oxford is a registered trade mark of
Oxford University Press in the UK and in certain other countries

© Andrew Burrows 2012

The moral rights of the author have been asserted

First Edition published in 2012

Impression: 1

All rights reserved. No part of this publication may be reproduced, stored in
a retrieval system, or transmitted, in any form or by any means, without the
prior permission in writing of Oxford University Press, or as expressly permitted
by law, by licence or under terms agreed with the appropriate reprographics
rights organization. Enquiries concerning reproduction outside the scope of the
above should be sent to the Rights Department, Oxford University Press, at the
address above

You must not circulate this work in any other form
and you must impose this same condition on any acquirer

Crown copyright material is reproduced under Class Licence
Number C01P0000148 with the permission of OPSI
and the Queen's Printer for Scotland

British Library Cataloguing in Publication Data

Data available

ISBN 978-0-19-966989-9 (hbk)
978-0-19-966990-5 (pbk)

Printed in Great Britain by
CPI Group(UK) Ltd, Croydon, CR0 4YY

CONTENTS

Advisory Group	vii
Introduction	ix
A RESTATEMENT OF THE ENGLISH LAW OF UNJUST ENRICHMENT	1
COMMENTARY	23
Part 1: General	25
Part 2: Enrichment at the claimant's expense	41
Part 3: When the enrichment is unjust	63
Part 4: Defences	117
Part 5: Restitutionary rights	154
Table of statutes	179
Table of cases	180
Index	187

ADVISORY GROUP

Lord Rodger of Earlsferry (deceased June 26, 2011), Supreme Court of the United Kingdom
Lord Walker of Gestingthorpe, Supreme Court of the United Kingdom
Lord Mance, Supreme Court of the United Kingdom
Lord Justice Moore-Bick, Court of Appeal of England and Wales
Lord Justice Etherton, Court of Appeal of England and Wales
Mr Justice Beatson, High Court of England and Wales
Mr Justice Henderson, High Court of England and Wales
Justice Edelman, Supreme Court of Western Australia
Stephen Moriarty QC, Fountain Court Chambers, London
Laurence Rabinowitz QC, One Essex Court, London
Steven Elliott, One Essex Court, London
Andrew Scott, Blackstone Chambers, London
Professor Robert Chambers, University College, London
Professor Gerard McMeel, University of Bristol
Professor Charles Mitchell, University College, London
Professor Robert Stevens, University of Oxford
William Swadling, University of Oxford
Professor Andrew Tettenborn, University of Swansea
Professor Graham Virgo, University of Cambridge

INTRODUCTION

1 Why a Restatement?

A Restatement is a novel concept in relation to English law. In contrast, the Restatements produced by the American Law Institute are well known as non-legislative, but powerfully persuasive, statements of the law applying across the USA. While knowing what the law is in England and Wales does not raise the multi-jurisdictional problems encountered in the USA, there are nevertheless real benefits to be gained in setting out what the law is in England and Wales in as clear and accessible a form as possible. This may be said of more areas of the law than just the law of unjust enrichment, but it is believed that a Restatement of this area is particularly apt at this time for several reasons.

First, the law of unjust enrichment is a newly recognised subject. While the relevant case law is long standing, the subject was only 'officially' accepted in English law in 1991 by the House of Lords in *Lipkin Gorman v Karpnale Ltd* [1991] 2 AC 548 following the path-breaking work of Goff and Jones, *The Law of Restitution* (first published in 1966). Given its recent provenance, many lawyers have never studied the subject and, not surprisingly, find it an especially difficult area. A Restatement can help to make the law of unjust enrichment better known and better understood.

Secondly, some of the complexity is caused by the archaic terminology used and by the historic failure to provide a clear conceptual structure. Even the name of the subject has been a matter of difficulty, with Goff and Jones' favoured title (until the 8th edition in 2011) being 'the law of restitution' rather than 'the law of unjust enrichment'. A Restatement can remove, or at least reduce, those difficulties.

Thirdly, this area of English law has already benefited hugely from a close working relationship between academics, judges and practitioners. This Restatement project has provided the opportunity for a further strengthening of that collaborative relationship.

Fourthly, those working in this area in this jurisdiction have an expertise, and an interest in the subject, that is unrivalled across the world. It is important that this expertise is tapped while it exists.

Fifthly, there are signs from Europe that aspects of English law may be lost in an attempt to harmonise areas of private law across Europe. Particularly relevant to this project are the European model rules for 'Unjustified Enrichment' in Book VII of the *Draft Common Frame of Reference* (prepared by the Study Group on a European Civil Code and the Research Group on EC Private Law (Acquis Group)); and the proposed EU Regulation on a Common European Sales Law, which has some provisions on restitution after termination of a contract for the

Introduction

sale of goods. Whether one believes in European legal harmonisation or not, it is essential that the subtleties of English law are properly understood before there is consideration of whether they should be abandoned.

Sixthly, there is the inspiration to be gained from the recent US *Restatement Third, Restitution and Unjust Enrichment* published in 2011 after some thirteen years of work. This is a magnificent piece of work, led by the reporter Professor Andrew Kull. It is important to appreciate, however, that the approach of the US Restatement is rather different from that of this Restatement. The US Restatement contains a mass of detail with a compilation of all relevant cases from across the USA. This Restatement is more modest in its focus. It aims to stand back from, and to provide an overview of, the details of the English law on this subject. The result is that this Restatement is more conceptual, and less contextual, than the US *Restatement Third*.

It should be added that this Restatement project has provided a major intellectual challenge for those involved. This in turn has helped to enhance our understanding of this area of the law and it is fervently hoped that readers of this work will reap the benefit of that improved understanding. One cannot overstate the complexity and excitement involved in trying to 'hone down' what is essentially a common law area to specific and succinct rules and principles.

2 Type of Restatement

The word 'Restatement' might suggest that one is purely concerned to state the present law. That would be marginally misleading. What is being aimed for is the best interpretation of the present law. In some limited circumstances, this may clash with existing precedents so that one would require a decision of the Supreme Court to lay down the law as here set out. In other words, on some matters the Restatement takes a principled interpretation of the law that may be regarded as going further than the existing cases. The commentary makes clear where this is so. It may help to think of this as a 'principled' or 'progressive' Restatement.

It should be stressed that it is *not* intended that the Restatement should be enacted as legislation. On the contrary, the intention is for the Restatement to be a persuasive authority but non-binding; and it is envisaged that there may be periodic revisions of the Restatement to reflect new developments and thinking. It would be wholly contrary to the desires and aspirations of those who have been responsible for this project for the Restatement to be seen as working against the common law tradition. The idea, admittedly novel, is for the Restatement to supplement and enhance our understanding of the common law, and to make it more accessible, not to replace it.

Introduction

3 Type of commentary

It will be seen that the commentary attempts to state matters as succinctly as possible. Hypothetical or real examples have often been used in the belief that this is commonly the best way of understanding the law. The leading cases, but not all conceivable relevant cases, have been cited and the citation of academic literature has been kept to a minimum. The aim is to explain the Restatement, not to reproduce the textbooks in this area.

4 Intended readership

It is hoped that all lawyers dealing with issues in this area, whether as practitioners, judges, or academics, will benefit from this Restatement. Non-lawyers too may find it of interest and help, but the complexities are such that a degree of legal knowledge is likely to be necessary in order to understand all the provisions and commentary.

5 Working methods

Work started on this project in October 2010 and was completed in June 2012. Four five-hour meetings of the advisory group were held, three at All Souls, Oxford, and one at University College London. In advance of those meetings, drafts of parts of the Restatement and the commentary were prepared by Andrew Burrows and circulated electronically. Comments were then sent back, and revised versions of the Restatement and commentary were again sent out in advance of each meeting. Those drafts were then discussed at the meetings. They were further revised in the light of the discussions. While Andrew Burrows alone accepts responsibility for the Restatement and the commentary, and not all members of the Advisory Group agree with his version—indeed, it may be that each member would express matters somewhat differently throughout—he wishes to put on record the immense assistance he has derived from the Advisory Group, for which he is extremely grateful. The Restatement and the commentary seek to reflect the insights gained from the written comments and the discussions in the meetings. It has been a rich and rewarding collaborative exercise. Further invaluable assistance on drafting has been given by retired Parliamentary Counsel.

Andrew Burrows would also like to thank Norton Rose, who provided funding for this project, and those involved at Oxford University Press, especially Alex Flach and Emma Brady, for their enthusiasm for publishing this work and for their efficiency and skill in doing so.

6 Overview of structure and substance of the Restatement

The Restatement has five Parts. After the Introduction (which introduces the central ideas and provides an overview of what follows), the Restatement follows the conceptual structure for the subject that is now widely accepted. So it examines

Introduction

enrichment, at the claimant's expense (both in Part 2), the unjust question (Part 3), and defences (Part 4). Part 5 looks at the rights (or, as some might prefer to label them, the remedies) that effect restitution for unjust enrichment.

Some particular substantive features of the Restatement are worthy of mention at the outset.

(i) Restitution for wrongs, and other examples of restitution for reasons other than unjust enrichment, are outside the scope of this Restatement (s 1(3)).

(ii) In deciding whether an enrichment is unjust, the Restatement takes the 'unjust factors' approach (s 3). But it accepts that, in general, an enrichment is not unjust if the benefit was owed to the defendant by the claimant under a valid legal obligation (s 3(6)). This qualification suggests that the distinction between the 'unjust factors' approach at common law and the civilian 'absence of basis' approach to the unjust question is not as sharp as is often thought.

(iii) It is explained in s 3 that the unjust factors, which are set out in detail in Part 3, fall into two classes: first, those dealing with problems with the claimant's consent and, secondly, those dealing with other valid reasons why the enrichment is unjust.

(iv) The Restatement presents an integrated view of common law and equity within this area. Indeed, with one minor exception in s 30(8)(a) (dealing with the doctrine of laches) there is no reference in the Restatement to the historical labelling of common law and equity.

(v) Both personal and proprietary restitution are dealt with. While the standard restitutionary right is a personal right to a monetary restitutionary award to recover the value of the defendant's enrichment (ss 5(2)(a) and 34), other restitutionary rights (often referred to as 'proprietary restitution') are also responses to unjust enrichment (ss 5(2)(b) and 35). The role of subrogation (by operation of law) in effecting proprietary, as well as personal, restitution (and in preventing an anticipated unjust enrichment) is set out in s 36.

(vi) Much archaic terminology is cut through by referring to the standard award as a 'monetary restitutionary award' (ss 5(2)(a) and 34).

(vii) It is recognised that 'free acceptance' is a test of enrichment (s 7(3)(c)).

(viii) 'At the expense of' is analysed as meaning that the benefit was obtained from the claimant and, subject to exceptions, directly from the claimant rather than by way of a third party (s 8). Tracing within the law of unjust enrichment is explained as a means of establishing that the enrichment was at the claimant's expense (s 9).

Introduction

(ix) Ignorance and powerlessness are recognised as unjust factors but, where operative, a fiduciary's lack of authority is recognised as being the appropriate unjust factor, rather than ignorance or powerlessness (ss 16 and 17).

(x) Some uncertainties in the law are left open. For example, whether in the context of mistaken gifts there is a requirement for the mistake to be serious as well as causative (s 10(4)(a)); whether in the context of obtaining a trust asset from a fiduciary acting without authority the defendant is strictly liable (s 17(2)); and whether agency operates as a strong or weak defence (s 25).

The Restatement is based on the law as at 30 June 2012.

A RESTATEMENT OF THE ENGLISH LAW OF UNJUST ENRICHMENT

A RESTATEMENT OF THE ENGLISH LAW OF UNJUST ENRICHMENT

PART 1
GENERAL

1. Restitution for unjust enrichment
2. Enrichment at the claimant's expense
3. When the enrichment is unjust
4. Defences
5. Restitutionary rights
6. Prevention of anticipated unjust enrichment

PART 2
ENRICHMENT AT THE CLAIMANT'S EXPENSE

7. Enrichment
8. At the claimant's expense: general
9. At the claimant's expense: tracing

PART 3
WHEN THE ENRICHMENT IS UNJUST

10. Mistake
11. Duress
12. Undue influence
13. Exploitation of weakness
14. Incapacity of the individual
15. Failure of consideration
16. Ignorance or powerlessness
17. Fiduciary's lack of authority
18. Legal compulsion
19. Necessity
20. Factors concerned with illegality
21. Unlawful obtaining or conferral of a benefit by a public authority
22. Financial institutions and constructive notice

PART 4
DEFENCES

23. Change of position
24. Estoppel
25. Agency as a defence
26. Counter-restitution
27. Purchaser in good faith, for value and without notice
28. Illegality as a defence

29 Resolved disputes
30 Limitation
31 Special statutory defences: passing on and prevailing practice
32 Contractual or statutory exclusion
33 Affirmation

PART 5
RESTITUTIONARY RIGHTS

34 Personal right to a monetary restitutionary award
35 Other restitutionary rights
36 Subrogation

A RESTATEMENT OF THE ENGLISH LAW OF UNJUST ENRICHMENT

PART 1
GENERAL

1 Restitution for unjust enrichment
(1) A claimant has a right to restitution against a defendant who is unjustly enriched at the claimant's expense.
(2) A right to restitution is a right to the reversal of the defendant's enrichment.
(3) A right to restitution against a defendant who is unjustly enriched at the claimant's expense is to be distinguished from a right to restitution that exists for a reason other than that the defendant has been unjustly enriched at the claimant's expense, and in particular from a right to restitution founded on—
    (a) an agreement or promise;
    (b) a civil wrong (for example a tort, a breach of contract or a breach of fiduciary duty);
    (c) a crime;
    (d) continuing ownership.
(4) A right to restitution for unjust enrichment may be claimed concurrently with another claim (for example, for a tort or breach of contract) but satisfaction of more than one claim is not permitted where it would produce double recovery.
(5) This Restatement is concerned only with the law as it applies in England and Wales.

2 Enrichment at the claimant's expense
Part 2 contains provisions about the meaning of—
    (a) enrichment (see section 7), and
    (b) at the claimant's expense (see sections 8 and 9).

3 When the enrichment is unjust
(1) Part 3 is about when the defendant's enrichment is unjust.
(2) It deals with two classes of case—
    (a) the first is where the claimant's consent to the defendant's enrichment was impaired, qualified or absent;
    (b) the second is where, even though the claimant consented to the defendant's enrichment, there is a valid reason why the enrichment is unjust.
(3) In the first class are—
    (a) mistake (see section 10);

(b) duress (see section 11);
(c) undue influence (see section 12);
(d) exploitation of weakness (see section 13);
(e) incapacity of the individual (see section 14);
(f) failure of consideration (see section 15);
(g) ignorance or powerlessness (see section 16);
(h) fiduciary's lack of authority (see section 17).

(4) In the second class are—
   (a) legal compulsion (see section 18);
   (b) necessity (see section 19);
   (c) factors concerned with illegality (see section 20);
   (d) unlawful obtaining, or conferral, of a benefit by a public authority (see section 21).

(5) In this Restatement "unjust factor" means any of the cases mentioned in subsections (3) and (4).

(6) In general, an enrichment is not unjust if the benefit was owed to the defendant by the claimant under a valid contractual, statutory or other legal obligation (see sections 10(6), 11(6), 12(6), 13(4), 14(4) and 19(3)(c); but cf. section 15(5)).

(7) In the case dealt with in section 36(3) the enrichment is unjust because, if not reversed or prevented, the defendant would be over-indemnified.

4 Defences

(1) Part 4 sets out defences that defeat, in whole or in part, a claim based on unjust enrichment.
(2) Subject to subsection (3), the burden of proving a defence is on the defendant.
(3) The burden of proving that a limitation period has not expired is on the claimant.

5 Restitutionary rights

(1) Part 5 sets out the rights available to the claimant ("the restitutionary rights").
(2) The restitutionary rights are of two types—
   (a) a personal right to a monetary restitutionary award (see section 34), which is available whatever the unjust factor, and
   (b) depending on the unjust factor, one or more of the rights mentioned in section 35(1).
(3) A claim may be made for—
   (a) a restitutionary right based on more than one unjust factor (for example, mistake and duress), or

(b) more than one of the restitutionary rights, or
(c) subject to section 25, a restitutionary right against both a principal and an agent;

but satisfaction of more than one claim is not permitted where it would produce double recovery.

6 Prevention of anticipated unjust enrichment

(1) In limited circumstances, a claimant has a right to prevent an anticipated unjust enrichment of a defendant at the claimant's expense.
(2) In particular, subrogation under section 36(3) may prevent an anticipated unjust enrichment.

PART 2
ENRICHMENT AT THE CLAIMANT'S EXPENSE

7 Enrichment

(1) "Enrichment" requires the obtaining of a benefit.
(2) The benefits which may constitute enrichment include: money, goods or land; the use of money, goods or land; services; the crediting of a bank account; the discharge of a debt or other liability; the forgoing of a claim; and intangible property (such as intellectual property, receivables or shares).
(3) But a defendant is not to be regarded as enriched unless the claimant shows that—
    (a) no reasonable person would deny that the defendant has been enriched (as is normally the case where, for example, the defendant has obtained money or has been saved necessary expense or has turned a non-monetary benefit into money), or
    (b) the defendant chose the benefit (by, for example, requesting it, or demanding or taking it or, after a request for its return, retaining it when it was readily returnable), or
    (c) the defendant, having had the opportunity to reject the benefit, freely accepted it knowing or believing that the claimant expected payment for it.
(4) Subject to section 25, where an agent is acting for a principal, the enrichment of the agent is to be treated as also being the enrichment of the principal.

8 At the claimant's expense: general

(1) The defendant's enrichment is at the claimant's expense if the benefit obtained by the defendant is—
    (a) from the claimant, and

(b) directly from the claimant rather than by way of another person.
(2) In any of the following cases, it does not matter that the benefit obtained by the defendant (D) is from the claimant (C) by way of another person (X)—
   (a) where X transfers an asset to D but C has a better right to that asset than X;
   (b) where X transfers an asset to D but X was holding the asset on trust for C;
   (c) where X is acting as C's agent in respect of the benefit;
   (d) where X charges and receives from C an amount representing tax on X's supply of goods or services to C and pays or accounts for that amount to D (Her Majesty's Revenue and Customs) as tax due;
   (e) where C is subrogated to X's (or another's) present or former rights against D in a situation where the benefit was supplied to D by X;
   (f) where X was under a legal obligation to supply the benefit to C but instead supplied the benefit to D and—
      (i) the supply to D discharged X's obligation to C, or
      (ii) the supply to D was in breach of X's fiduciary duty to C but C's claim against X has been exhausted.
(3) In a contract for the benefit of a third party, the third party's benefit is to be treated as obtained directly from the contracting party who required the benefit to be supplied rather than from the contracting party who supplied it.
(4) Even if the benefit obtained by the defendant is directly from the claimant, the enrichment is generally not at the claimant's expense if the benefit is merely incidental to the furtherance by the claimant of an objective unconnected with the defendant's enrichment.

9 At the claimant's expense: tracing

(1) The defendant's enrichment is at the claimant's expense if—
   (a) the benefit obtained by the defendant is an asset ("the substitute asset") which under the tracing rules is treated as being the substitute for another asset ("the original asset"), and
   (b) immediately before the first transaction to which the tracing rules are being applied—
      (i) the claimant had a better right to the original asset than any person (whether or not the defendant) who was a party to that transaction, or
      (ii) the original asset was held on trust for the claimant.
(2) For the purposes of subsection (1), "the tracing rules" means the rules set out below.
(3) One asset is treated as the substitute for another asset if—
   (a) it is not a mixed asset, and

(b) under any transaction it was substituted for that other asset.
(4) An asset is a mixed asset if assets from more than one person have contributed to it.
(5) Subject to subsections (6) and (7), in the case of a mixed asset the proportionate share of the mixed asset is treated as the substitute for the contributing asset of the contributor.
(6) If—
   (a) the contribution was made by a person in breach of a fiduciary or other duty, and
   (b) part of the mixed asset has been dissipated by that person so that the mixed asset has declined in value,
   that decline in value is treated as borne first by that person.
(7) If there has been an additional contribution to a mixed asset, the substitute asset in respect of contributions prior to that additional contribution cannot be treated as exceeding the value of the mixed asset prior to the additional contribution.

PART 3
WHEN THE ENRICHMENT IS UNJUST

10 Mistake
(1) Subject to subsections (4) to (7), the defendant's enrichment is unjust if it is caused by a mistake of fact or law made by the claimant.
(2) For the purposes of subsection (1)—
   (a) the standard test of causation is the "but for" test which requires that the defendant would not have been enriched but for the mistake, but
   (b) there are exceptions to the "but for" test where—
      (i) mistake and another unjust factor were each independently sufficient to bring about the enrichment;
      (ii) the mistake was induced by a fraudulent misrepresentation, in which case the mistaken belief need merely have been a reason or present in the claimant's mind.
(3) The defendant's enrichment may be unjust under subsection (1) even though the claimant's conduct was negligent.
(4) If the enrichment is a gift—
   (a) there may be a rule that for the enrichment to be unjust, the mistake, if not induced by a misrepresentation, must be serious (as well as causing the enrichment), and
   (b) a mistake of law as to the tax consequences of the gift does not in itself render the enrichment unjust.

(5) The enrichment is not unjust if the claimant takes the risk that a mistake is being made; and the claimant is to be treated as having taken that risk if—
  (a) the mistake consists of the claimant's false prediction as to the future, or
  (b) the claimant is aware that a mistake is probably being made or recklessly fails to establish the truth.
(6) In general, mistake does not render the enrichment unjust if the benefit was owed to the defendant by the claimant under a valid contractual, statutory or other legal obligation.
(7) In the case of a mistake induced by a misrepresentation, the misrepresentation may be made by a person other than the defendant; but, if the claimant has entered into a contract because of the misrepresentation, the enrichment is unjust only if—
  (a) that other person was acting as the defendant's agent, or
  (b) the defendant had actual notice of the misrepresentation, or
  (c) the defendant had constructive notice of the misrepresentation under section 22.

11 Duress
(1) The defendant's enrichment is unjust if the claimant has enriched the defendant because of an illegitimate threat ("duress").
(2) The illegitimate threat may be express or implied.
(3) For this purpose a threat—
  (a) is illegitimate if the conduct threatened is unlawful (as in the case of a threat to the person or to goods);
  (b) may in some circumstances be illegitimate even though the conduct threatened is lawful (as in the case of a threat to prosecute, or expose the truth about, the claimant or a member of the claimant's family).
(4) But if the illegitimate threat is a threat to break a contract, the defendant's enrichment is unjust only if the claimant had no reasonable alternative to giving in to the threat.
(5) For the purposes of subsection (1)—
  (a) the standard test of causation is the "but for" test which requires that the defendant would not have been enriched but for the illegitimate threat, but
  (b) there are exceptions to the "but for" test where—
    (i) duress and another unjust factor were each independently sufficient to bring about the enrichment;
    (ii) the threat was to the person in which case the threat must merely have been a reason or present in the claimant's mind.

(6) In general, duress does not render the enrichment unjust if the benefit was owed to the defendant by the claimant under a valid contractual, statutory or other legal obligation.
(7) The illegitimate threat may be made by a person other than the defendant; but if the claimant has entered into a contract because of the threat, the enrichment is unjust only if—
    (a) that other person was acting as the defendant's agent, or
    (b) the defendant had actual notice of the threat, or
    (c) the defendant had constructive notice of the threat under section 22.

12   Undue influence
(1) The defendant's enrichment is unjust if the claimant enriched the defendant while under undue influence.
(2) A claimant is under the undue influence of another person if the claimant's judgement is not free and independent of that person.
(3) There is a rebuttable presumption of undue influence if—
    (a) the claimant was in a relationship of influence with the defendant or another person, and
    (b) the transaction in question was disadvantageous to the claimant in the sense that it was not readily explicable on ordinary motives.
(4) A relationship of influence—
    (a) is to be treated as existing in certain cases (for example, parent and child, solicitor and client, doctor and patient, and spiritual adviser and follower), but
    (b) otherwise must be proved on the facts.
(5) It is for the defendant to rebut the presumption mentioned in subsection (3) by proving that the claimant exercised free and independent judgement.
The defendant may be able to rebut the presumption by showing that the claimant obtained the fully informed and competent independent advice of a qualified person, such as a solicitor.
(6) In general, undue influence does not render the enrichment unjust if the benefit was owed to the defendant by the claimant under a valid contractual, statutory or other legal obligation.
(7) The undue influence may be that of a person other than the defendant; but, if the claimant has entered into a contract under undue influence, the enrichment is unjust only if—
    (a) that other person was acting as the defendant's agent, or
    (b) the defendant had actual notice of the undue influence, or

(c) the defendant had constructive notice of the undue influence under section 22.

13 Exploitation of weakness

(1) The defendant's enrichment is unjust if it is the result of a weakness of the claimant having been exploited by the defendant.
(2) The weakness may be—
   (a) a mental weakness (such as inexperience, confusion because of old age, or emotional strain), or
   (b) the difficult position that the claimant is in.
(3) The claimant's weakness has been exploited by the defendant if—
   (a) the transaction in question was disadvantageous to the claimant in the sense that it was not readily explicable on ordinary motives, and
   (b) the defendant knew of the claimant's weakness and that the terms of the transaction were disadvantageous,
   unless the claimant obtained the fully informed and competent independent advice of a qualified person, such as a solicitor.
(4) In general, exploitation of weakness does not render the enrichment unjust if the benefit was owed to the defendant by the claimant under a valid contractual, statutory or other legal obligation.

14 Incapacity of the individual

(1) The defendant's enrichment is unjust if the claimant is an individual who enriched the defendant while under an incapacity.
(2) A claimant enriches the defendant while under an incapacity if the enrichment is the result of a contract, gift or other transaction which is invalid because the claimant was under 18 when the transaction was entered into.
(3) A claimant enriches the defendant while under an incapacity if the enrichment is the result of a contract, gift or other transaction which is invalid because the claimant lacked mental capacity, or was intoxicated, when the transaction was entered into.
(4) In general, the incapacity of the claimant does not render the enrichment unjust if the benefit was owed to the defendant by the claimant under a valid contractual, statutory or other legal obligation.

15 Failure of consideration

(1) The defendant's enrichment is unjust if the claimant has enriched the defendant on the basis of a consideration that fails.

(2) The consideration that fails may have been—
- (a) a promised counter-performance, whether under a valid contract or not, or
- (b) an event or a state of affairs that was not promised.

(3) It is a question of construction whether the consideration fails; and, in deciding this question, if the consideration was a promised counter-performance—
- (a) failure of consideration does not require that none of the promised counter-performance has been rendered;
- (b) the consideration is not normally regarded as failing if the promisor has been, and is, ready, able and willing to perform the promise.

(4) If the consideration was a promised counter-performance under a valid contract and the contract has been terminated (for example, by acceptance of a breach or by frustration)—
- (a) restitution for failure of consideration may enable a party to escape from a bad bargain;
- (b) normally, a person who breaks a contract may not rely on failure of consideration as an unjust factor.

(5) Where a contract has been terminated (for example, by acceptance of a breach or by frustration), failure of consideration may render the enrichment unjust even though the benefit was owed to the defendant by the claimant under a contractual obligation that remains valid because termination invalidates obligations prospectively and not retrospectively.

(6) Where a contract has been terminated by frustration, the right to restitution for failure of consideration is governed by the Law Reform (Frustrated Contracts) Act 1943, unless section 2(5) of that Act prevents that Act from applying to the contract.

16 Ignorance or powerlessness

(1) The defendant's enrichment is unjust if the claimant—
- (a) had no knowledge of the conduct which enriched the defendant at the claimant's expense, or
- (b) was powerless to prevent that conduct.

(2) Subsection (1) does not apply if, in the circumstances, the defendant—
- (a) is entitled to cause loss to the claimant, and
- (b) is therefore entitled to be enriched without the claimant's consent.

(3) Subsection (1) does not apply if section 17 applies.

17 Fiduciary's lack of authority

(1) Subject to subsection (2), the defendant's enrichment is unjust if—

(a) the claimant's asset or an asset held on trust for the claimant has been dealt with by a fiduciary of the claimant without authority and without the consent of the claimant, and
(b) as a result of that dealing, the defendant has obtained the benefit at the claimant's expense.
(2) In the case of an asset held on trust for the claimant, there may be a rule applicable to the claimant's personal right to a monetary restitutionary award that the enrichment is not unjust unless the defendant knew, or ought to have known, that the fiduciary was dealing with the asset without authority and without the consent of the claimant.

18 Legal compulsion
(1) The defendant's enrichment is unjust if the claimant has enriched the defendant by discharging a liability of the defendant to another person (X) under legal compulsion exercised, or exercisable, by X.
The reason for this rule is the avoidance of the defendant's undeserved escape from liability.
(2) The following are examples of when the defendant's enrichment is unjust under subsection (1)—
(a) X is in lawful possession of an asset of the claimant, or there is an encumbrance over an asset of the claimant in favour of X, and the claimant discharges the defendant's liability to X to recover the asset or to remove the encumbrance;
(b) the claimant and defendant are under a common liability to X, which the claimant discharges, but the claimant's liability is secondary to the defendant's;
(c) the claimant and defendant are under a common liability to X, or are each liable to pay compensation for the same damage to X, and the claimant discharges the liability in circumstances in which the defendant should bear part of that liability.

19 Necessity
(1) Subject to subsections (3) and (4), the defendant's enrichment is unjust if the claimant, in responding to a necessity, enriches the defendant by—
(a) supplying or paying for goods or services, or
(b) discharging a liability of the defendant.
(2) There is a necessity for the purposes of subsection (1) if intervention is needed to preserve another's health or assets, especially against imminent harm.

(3) The claimant—
   (a) must be a suitable person to intervene, and
   (b) if possible, must make reasonable attempts to communicate with the defendant before intervening, and
   (c) must not be under a contractual or statutory duty to intervene.
(4) The defendant's enrichment is not unjust if the claimant's intention at the time of intervention was that no payment would be sought for the intervention.

20 Factors concerned with illegality

The defendant's enrichment is unjust if the claimant has enriched the defendant under an illegal contract and either—
   (a) the claimant withdraws from the contract before the illegal purpose is achieved and when it remains likely that it will be achieved, or
   (b) the reason the contract is illegal is to protect the claimant as a member of a class.

21 Unlawful obtaining or conferral of a benefit by a public authority

(1) The defendant's enrichment is unjust if the defendant is a public authority which unlawfully obtained the benefit from the claimant.
(2) The obtaining of the benefit need not be preceded by a demand.
(3) The defendant's enrichment is unjust if the claimant is a public authority which unlawfully conferred the benefit on the defendant.
(4) The question whether the obtaining or conferral of the benefit was unlawful is to be decided by applying the principles of public law; but there is no requirement that the claimant must proceed by first seeking judicial review.
(5) There are statutory provisions, especially in the context of tax and social security, that govern the right to restitution from or for a public authority.

22 Financial institutions and constructive notice

(1) Unless subsection (2) applies, the defendant is treated as having constructive notice of a misrepresentation, illegitimate threat or undue influence if—
   (a) the defendant is a financial institution with whom the claimant entered into a contract of suretyship guaranteeing a debt owed to the defendant, and
   (b) the claimant has a non-commercial relationship with the debtor and entered into the contract because the misrepresentation or illegitimate threat was made by the debtor or while under the undue influence of the debtor.

(2) The defendant is not treated as having constructive notice if, before the contract was entered into, it—
   (a) informed the claimant, by direct communication, that it required written confirmation from the claimant's adviser that the claimant understood what the claimant was doing, and
   (b) forwarded to the claimant, or the claimant's adviser, the financial circumstances regarding the debtor's loan application to it, and
   (c) received confirmation from the claimant's adviser that the adviser had provided the claimant with fully informed and competent advice.
(3) In this section "adviser" means a solicitor or other legal adviser.

PART 4
DEFENCES

23 Change of position
(1) The defendant has a defence to the extent that—
   (a) the defendant's position has changed as a consequence of, or in anticipatory reliance on, obtaining the benefit, and
   (b) the change is such that the defendant would be worse off by making restitution than if the defendant had not obtained, or relied in anticipation on obtaining, the benefit.
(2) But the defendant does not have this defence if—
   (a) the change of position—
      (i) was made in bad faith, or
      (ii) involved significant criminal illegality, or
      (iii) consisted of taking a risk with loaned money, or
   (b) the weight to be attached to the unjust factor is greater than that to be attached to the change of position (as, for example, where the unjust factor is the unlawful obtaining of a benefit by a public authority).
(3) In the case of a contract to which the Law Reform (Frustrated Contracts) Act 1943 applies, the defence of change of position is governed by section 1(2) and (3) of that Act.

24 Estoppel
The defendant has a defence to the extent that the defendant has detrimentally relied on a representation by the claimant that the defendant is entitled to the enrichment.

25 Agency as a defence

(1) The defendant may have a defence simply by reason of obtaining the benefit as an agent.
(2) In any event, if the defendant has obtained the benefit as an agent the defendant has a defence to the extent that the defendant—
   (a) has transferred the benefit (by payment over or otherwise) to the principal, and
   (b) has done so without actual notice of the claimant's right to restitution.

26 Counter-restitution

(1) The defendant has a defence if it is impossible for there to be counter-restitution of reciprocal benefits conferred on the claimant by the defendant.
(2) The defendant normally has a set-off defence for counter-restitution of reciprocal benefits conferred on the claimant by the defendant.

27 Purchaser in good faith, for value and without notice

(1) The defendant has a defence if the defendant—
   (a) is a purchaser in good faith of the benefit for value, without notice of the claimant's right to restitution, from a person other than the claimant, and
   (b) can rely on an exception to the rule that no person can give a better title than the person has.
(2) The defendant normally has a defence if the defendant has obtained the benefit from a person who satisfies paragraphs (a) and (b) of subsection (1).

28 Illegality as a defence

(1) The defendant has a defence if the claimant's conduct has been illegal.
(2) Conduct is illegal if—
   (a) it constitutes a crime or a civil wrong, or
   (b) it is contrary to public policy.
(3) But the defendant does not have this defence if—
   (a) the unjust factor is concerned with illegality (see section 20), or
   (b) the unjust factor excuses the illegality (as, for example, where the claimant was acting under duress or, because of a mistake, did not know of the illegality), or
   (c) the denial of restitution would be a disproportionate response to the illegality, taking into account in particular the following aims—
      (i) furthering the purpose of the rule which the illegal conduct has infringed;

(ii) avoiding inconsistency in the law;
(iii) deterring illegal conduct;
(iv) ensuring that the claimant does not profit from the illegal conduct.

29 Resolved disputes

The defendant has a defence if—
(a) there has been a judgment or contract of compromise which dealt with the unjust enrichment and has not been reversed or set aside, or
(b) the claimant is seeking restitution in respect of a payment made by the claimant to stop legal proceedings that were initiated against the claimant in good faith.

30 Limitation

(1) The rules set out in subsections (2) to (7) are largely derived from the Limitation Act 1980.
(2) Subject to the exceptions in subsections (3) to (9), there is a limitation period of 6 years to enforce a restitutionary right which runs from when the cause of action accrues.
The cause of action in unjust enrichment accrues when the defendant is unjustly enriched at the claimant's expense.
(3) If the unjust factor is mistake, the limitation period does not start to run until the claimant has discovered, or could reasonably have discovered, the mistake; but this postponement does not apply to the restitution of tax paid to Her Majesty's Revenue and Customs under a mistake of law.
(4) If any fact relevant to the claimant's cause of action has been deliberately concealed from the claimant by the defendant, the limitation period does not start to run until the claimant has discovered, or could reasonably have discovered, the concealment.
(5) The limitation period does not run where the claimant is under 18 or lacks mental capacity.
(6) If—
(a) an action in unjust enrichment has accrued to recover any debt or other liquidated pecuniary claim, and
(b) the defendant acknowledges the claim or makes any part payment in respect of it,
the cause of action is to be treated as having accrued on the date of the acknowledgement or part payment.

(7) There are statutory provisions which displace the 6 year limitation period to enforce a restitutionary right running from the date of the accrual of the cause of action.
(8) Under the doctrine of laches—
   (a) the enforcement of restitutionary rights which are equitable may be barred because of the prejudice to the defendant caused by an unreasonable delay of the claimant in commencing the claim;
   (b) there can be no unreasonable delay for the purposes of paragraph (a) until—
      (i) the claimant has discovered, or could reasonably have discovered, that the defendant has been unjustly enriched at the claimant's expense, and
      (ii) if the enrichment was unjust because of impairment of consent under any of sections 11 to 14, the impairment no longer exists;
   (c) the enforcement of a restitutionary right may be barred if—
      (i) a limitation period mentioned in any of subsections (2) to (7) has not ended, or
      (ii) there is no limitation period.
(9) In general (but subject, for example, to subsections (4) and (5)) the terms of a contract may govern—
   (a) the limitation period to enforce a restitutionary right, and
   (b) when that period starts to run.

31 Special statutory defences: passing on and prevailing practice
(1) Passing on of a loss by the claimant to a third party is not a defence at common law to restitution for unjust enrichment, but, in the case of particular taxes, there are statutory defences of a similar nature.
(2) In the case of a payment made under a mistake of law, payment in accordance with prevailing practice or the settled understanding of the law is not a defence at common law but, in the case of particular taxes, there are statutory defences of a similar nature.

32 Contractual or statutory exclusion
The defendant has a defence if the defendant's liability is excluded (in whatever terms) by a contract or by statute.

33 Affirmation
The defendant has a defence if the claimant has affirmed the contract, gift or other transaction under which the benefit was obtained.

A Restatement of the English Law of Unjust Enrichment

PART 5
RESTITUTIONARY RIGHTS

34 Personal right to a monetary restitutionary award
(1) A personal right to a monetary restitutionary award (see section 5(2)(a)) is a right, enforceable only against the defendant or the defendant's representatives, to recover the value of the defendant's enrichment.
(2) The value of the defendant's enrichment is normally the market value of the benefit at the time it is obtained by the defendant unless it is shown (for example, by the terms of a request) that a lower value is more appropriate.

35 Other restitutionary rights
(1) The rights referred to in section 5(2)(b) are—
   (a) if the benefit obtained is directly linked to an asset retained by the defendant, the right to have a monetary restitutionary award secured by a lien over that asset;
   (b) if the benefit obtained is the discharge of a secured liability of the defendant, the right to be subrogated to the discharged security;
   (c) if the benefit obtained is a right in property retained by the defendant, the right to revest, or to have revested, that right in property, by rescission or rectification of a contract, gift or other transaction;
   (d) if the benefit obtained is a right in property retained by the defendant, the right to be a beneficiary of that right in property under a trust imposed by law.
(2) The following restrictions on the rights mentioned in subsection (1) apply in relation to particular cases of unjust enrichment—

unjust factor	*restrictions on rights*
failure of consideration (section 15)	the subsection (1)(a), (b) and (d) rights are available only in limited circumstances
	the subsection (1)(c) right is not available
legal compulsion (section 18)	the subsection (1)(a), (c) and (d) rights are not available
necessity (section 19)	the subsection (1)(c) and (d) rights are not available
factors concerned with illegality (section 20)	the subsection (1)(a), (b) and (d) rights are not available
unlawful obtaining or conferral of a benefit by a public authority (section 21)	the subsection (1)(b) and (c) rights are not available

(3) The claimant does not have a right mentioned in subsection (1) if—
   (a) the claimant has, as part of a bargain, taken the risk of being unsecured or inadequately secured, and

(b) the right would give the claimant better security than the claimant bargained for,

unless the unjust factor undermines the consent of the claimant to the taking of the risk.

(4) In this Restatement, "a right in property" means—
   (a) a right in tangible property (whether money, goods or land), or
   (b) intangible property (such as intellectual property, receivables or shares).

(5) In this Restatement "rescission" and "rectification" include any consequential order necessary to revest a right in property, such as rectification of a register.

36 Subrogation

(1) Subrogation is the process by which, either by contract or by operation of law but without an assignment, a claimant may take over, or be treated as having taken over, some or all of a person's former or present rights against another person; but in this Restatement "subrogation" means subrogation by operation of law.

(2) In connection with sections 34 and 35(1)(b)—
   (a) if the defendant's enrichment is the discharge of a liability of the defendant to another person, the claimant may be treated as having taken over some or all of that person's former rights against the defendant, in order to reverse that enrichment;
   (b) if a liability of one defendant to another person has been discharged at the claimant's expense, the claimant may be treated as having taken over some or all of that person's former rights against that defendant in order to reverse the resulting enrichment of another defendant.

(3) If the claimant has indemnified the defendant against a loss under a contract of indemnity (for example a contract of indemnity insurance), the claimant may take over some or all of the defendant's present rights (or the fruit of those rights) against another person so that, in conjunction with that person's liability not being discharged—
   (a) the unjust enrichment, by over-indemnification, of the defendant at the claimant's expense is reversed or prevented, and
   (b) the claimant's loss is recouped.

(4) Subsection (3) is not exhaustive as to the situations in which the claimant may take over some or all of the defendant's present rights against another person in order to reverse the unjust enrichment of the defendant at the claimant's expense.

For example subrogation may be available where a claimant has not been paid for supplying goods or services to a business carried on by a defendant trustee.

COMMENTARY

PART 1
GENERAL

1 Restitution for unjust enrichment
(1) A claimant has a right to restitution against a defendant who is unjustly enriched at the claimant's expense.
(2) A right to restitution is a right to the reversal of the defendant's enrichment.
(3) A right to restitution against a defendant who is unjustly enriched at the claimant's expense is to be distinguished from a right to restitution that exists for a reason other than that the defendant has been unjustly enriched at the claimant's expense, and in particular from a right to restitution founded on—
    (a) an agreement or promise;
    (b) a civil wrong (for example a tort, a breach of contract or a breach of fiduciary duty);
    (c) a crime;
    (d) continuing ownership.
(4) A right to restitution for unjust enrichment may be claimed concurrently with another claim (for example, for a tort or breach of contract) but satisfaction of more than one claim is not permitted where it would produce double recovery.
(5) This Restatement is concerned only with the law as it applies in England and Wales.

1(1)

This central proposition was authoritatively accepted as part of English law in *Lipkin Gorman v Karpnale Ltd* [1991] 2 AC 548, HL. Commentators and courts (see, eg, *Banque Financière de la Cité v Parc (Battersea) Ltd* [1999] 1 AC 221 at 227, per Lord Steyn; *Cressman v Coys of Kensington (Sales) Ltd* [2004] EWCA Civ 47, [2004] 1 WLR 2775 at [22]; *Chief Constable of the Greater Manchester Police v Wigan Athletic AFC Ltd* [2008] EWCA Civ 1449, [2009] 1 WLR 1580 at [38], [54], [62]; *Investment Trust Companies v HMRC* [2012] EWHC 458 (Ch) at [38]–[39]) have broken it down into four elements which constitute the conceptual structure of a claim in unjust enrichment. Has the defendant been *enriched*? Was the enrichment *at the claimant's expense*? Was the enrichment *unjust*? Are there any *defences*? Along with clarification of the relevant rights (or, one might say, remedies), it is that four-fold structure that underpins the structure of the Restatement. Part I provides an overview of what is covered by the subsequent Parts which deal with, respectively, enrichment at the claimant's expense (Part 2), when the enrichment is unjust (Part 3), defences (Part 4) and restitutionary rights (Part 5).

1(2)

Although there do appear to be a few pockets of law exemplifying the prevention of an anticipated unjust enrichment (see s 6), rather than the reversal of an accrued unjust enrichment, the vast bulk of the law of unjust enrichment is concerned with the *reversal* of enrichment. Certainly the term 'restitution' only makes sense when confined to 'reversal'. This subsection makes a general definitional point about a right to restitution. Restitution is always about reversing (which includes 'giving up' as well as 'giving back') an enrichment in contrast to, eg, compensating a loss. In the law of unjust enrichment, restitution reverses an unjust enrichment.

1(3)

This subsection makes clear that, viewed at a high level of generality, one is concerned only with a right to restitution that has been created as a response to unjust enrichment of the defendant at the claimant's expense. Rights to restitution created by other events are outside the scope of this subject.

It can be argued that it is most helpful to view unjust enrichment as a *cause of action* rather than as a principle or concept. However, some might think there is a difficulty with describing unjust enrichment as the cause of action rather than the cause of action being more specifically, for example, restitution for mistake or duress or for a failed consideration. So, if one takes the analogy of tort, some might think it odd to describe tort as the cause of action rather than the cause of action being the specific tort such as negligence or nuisance or trespass to land. Cases on s 35 of the Limitation Act 1980 support the view that a cause of action, at least in that context, is thought of as being rather specific. Another possible difficulty with describing unjust enrichment as a cause of action is that some rights to restitution created by unjust enrichment arise without court action (eg the right to rescind a contract, which revests title to goods or land, for fraudulent misrepresentation). For these reasons, some may prefer to describe unjust enrichment as an event creating rights rather than as a cause of action. If one does describe unjust enrichment as a cause of action, it must be understood that one is talking about a cause of action in a very general sense.

Whichever description is preferred, whether event or cause of action (or principle or concept), the crucial point—which gives this subject its coherence and means that the excluded areas set out in this subsection are excluded for a principled reason—is that one is concerned with the creation of rights by an unjust enrichment of the defendant at the claimant's expense, rather than by another event/cause of action; and the right that is almost always created by unjust enrichment is the *right to restitution*.

1(3)(a)

The enforcement of a contractual or other legally binding promise to repay money (eg a promise to repay a loan) or to pay for services rendered is not restitution for unjust enrichment. The justification for the enforcement rests on the binding nature of the promise and nothing extra is added by the fact that the promise is to make restitution. Historically, most of the common law of restitution of an unjust enrichment was fictionally seen as resting on an implied contract (hence the historical label, quasi-contract). The implied contract theory was explicitly rejected in favour of unjust enrichment in *Westdeutsche Landesbank Girozentrale v Islington London Borough Council* [1996] AC 669, HL (see also, eg, *Haugesund Kommune v Depfa ACS Bank* [2010] EWCA Civ 579, [2012] 2 WLR 199), having been implicitly rejected in *Lipkin Gorman v Karpnale Ltd* [1991] 2 AC 548, HL.

1(3)(b)

This clarifies that restitution for unjust enrichment is to be differentiated from 'restitution for wrongs' (ie where there has been the breach by the defendant of a primary duty owed to the claimant). Where one is dealing with restitution for a wrong, the relevant event or cause of action is the wrong (and hence, eg, the limitation period runs from the commission of the wrong) and the enrichment adds nothing to that: it purely goes to the remedial question of whether the claimant is entitled to restitution, rather than the more usual compensation. So falling outside this Restatement, because not concerned with the event/cause of action of unjust enrichment, are the following:

(i) restitution for torts (see, eg, *United Australia v Barclays Bank Ltd* [1941] AC 1, HL (conversion); *Ministry of Defence v Ashman* (1993) 66 P & CR 195, CA (trespass to land); and *Siddell v Vickers* (1892) 9 RPC 152, CA (infringement of patent));

(ii) restitution for breach of contract (see, eg, *A-G v Blake* [2001] 1 AC 268, HL);

(iii) restitution for the equitable wrongs of breach of fiduciary duty (including breach of trust) or breach of confidence (see, eg, *Boardman v Phipps* [1964] 1 WLR 993, HL; *A-G v Guardian Newspapers Ltd (No 2)* [1990] 1 AC 109, HL).

The term 'civil wrong' is wide enough to cover, and therefore to exclude from this Restatement, restitution for a statutory wrong. A statutory wrong is normally actionable as a tort (or, less commonly, as a breach of fiduciary duty): but even where not (an example being unfair dismissal) a statutory wrong (unless purely criminal) is a civil wrong and any right to restitution created by it is excluded from this Restatement.

Commentary: Part 1

1(3)(c)

The right to restitution created by unjust enrichment and covered by this Restatement falls entirely within the civil law. Although a crime may, in one sense, be said to create a right to restitution under, eg, the Forfeiture Act 1982 or by means of confiscation under the Proceeds of Crime Act 2002, the aim of such a right is not to make restitution to the person at whose expense the criminal has been enriched. The proceeds of the crime are paid to the State and, under forfeiture, it is irrelevant whether the person benefited by the law's intervention is, or is not, the victim of the crime.

1(3)(d)

'That was and is my chattel or land and I want it back' (eg where the defendant has stolen the claimant's car and still has that car, or where the defendant is in possession of the claimant's land) is not an assertion of a new right created by the event/cause of action of unjust enrichment. It is simply the assertion of a pre-existing proprietary right. Indeed in respect of goods, common law, as opposed to equity, does not recognise the validity of such an assertion by itself and instead requires the claimant to establish the tort of conversion before specific restitution (by delivery up) of goods (eg a stolen car) can be ordered. (But note that nothing said here is intended to deny that the owner may have a claim in unjust enrichment against a thief *for the value* of a stolen car.)

In equity, the equivalent right of restitution under s 1(3)(d) (which in a loose sense we can also describe as founded on continuing 'ownership') is where an asset held on trust for C by X comes into the hands of D, who is not a bona fide purchaser for value without notice. C's assertion that D holds the asset on trust for C (and should transfer the asset to C or to X for C) is founded on C's pre-existing beneficial interest. It is not founded on D's unjust enrichment. For an example, see the claim in *Macmillan Inc v Bishopsgate Investment Trust plc (No 3)* [1996] 1 WLR 387, CA (where the assets in question were Berlitz shares). For a clear explanation of this point, see Birks, *Unjust Enrichment* (2nd edn, 2005) 64–5.

1(4)

Concurrent liability as between breach of contract and tort was accepted in *Henderson v Merrett Syndicates Ltd* [1995] 2 AC 145, HL, and there is no reason why it should not be equally applicable as between other events/causes of action and unjust enrichment. This is supported by observations in *Deutsche Morgan Grenfell Group plc v IRC* [2006] UKHL 49, [2007] 1 AC 558, albeit that that was dealing with the concurrence of different unjust factors *within* the law of unjust enrichment (see s 5(3) below). However, claimants cannot satisfy more than one claim to the extent that this would produce (unacceptable) double recovery (hence the need, ultimately, to make an election between claims: see *United Australia Ltd v Barclays Bank Ltd* [1941] 1 AC 1, HL).

Example

C is induced by a fraudulent misrepresentation by D to pay D £20,000. C is entitled to compensatory damages of £20,000 for the tort of deceit by D. C is alternatively entitled (and in this sense concurrent liability is being accepted) to restitution of £20,000 for restitution of the unjust enrichment based on mistake. But C cannot be awarded £20,000 twice over because this would constitute double recovery. C must therefore elect between the claim in tort and the claim in unjust enrichment. Applying the law on election laid down in the *United Australia* case, C does not need to make that election until judgment (and even then, it can be changed if D fails to comply with the judgment although, in practice, that is only likely to be useful where, as in *United Australia*, the claimant wishes to pursue a different defendant under the different claim).

1(5)

The Restatement sets out the English law on the law of unjust enrichment both at common law and under statute. The law on 'unjustified enrichment' in Scotland is significantly different and adopts a civilian approach.

The vast bulk of the law of unjust enrichment in England and Wales is common law (including equity) rather than statutory. The Restatement is therefore principally a Restatement of the common law. Indeed, if that were not the case, and most of the law was contained in statutes, one might regard a Restatement as an inappropriate instrument. However, there are references to statutes generally or to specific statutes at various points in the Restatement (see ss 3(6), 15(6), 21(5), 23(3), 30–32). Those references embrace the statutory provisions that are most relevant to the general law of unjust enrichment but it is acknowledged that there may be statutes, or provisions of EU law, which, in a specific context, modify the law set out in the Restatement. In other words, *the law as set out in the Restatement is subject to any statute, or provision of EU law, to the contrary*. If there were many examples of statutes, or provisions of EU law, falling outside the Restatement, the reliability, comprehensivity, and usefulness of the Restatement would be undermined. However, it is believed that there are very few such instances.

This is the most appropriate point to explain that, perhaps partly because of governing statutory provisions (see, eg, the Wills Act 1837 and, as regards rectification of wills, the Administration of Justice Act 1982, s 20), the law of unjust enrichment has, with limited exceptions (see, most obviously, *Ministry of Health v Simpson (Re Diplock)* [1951] AC 251, HL), not been regarded by the courts or by commentators on English law as having any role to play in relation to wills.

Commentary: Part 1

It is also appropriate to clarify here that the English private international law of unjust enrichment has been excluded from this Restatement. This is for two main reasons: first, the law is now largely governed by statute, in particular the 'Rome II' EU Regulation (Regulation 864/2007); and, secondly, it would be hard to improve on the treatment in Dicey, Morris and Collins, *The Conflict of Laws* (15th edn, 2012). See also Burrows, *The Law of Restitution* (3rd edn, 2011) ch 28.

> **2 Enrichment at the claimant's expense**
> Part 2 contains provisions about the meaning of—
> (a) enrichment (see section 7), and
> (b) at the claimant's expense (see sections 8 and 9).

2

This simply flags up that two of the central concepts in the law of unjust enrichment, 'enrichment' and 'at the claimant's expense', are to be dealt with in Part 2.

> **3 When the enrichment is unjust**
> (1) Part 3 is about when the defendant's enrichment is unjust.
> (2) It deals with two classes of case—
>   (a) the first is where the claimant's consent to the defendant's enrichment was impaired, qualified or absent;
>   (b) the second is where, even though the claimant consented to the defendant's enrichment, there is a valid reason why the enrichment is unjust.
> (3) In the first class are—
>   (a) mistake (see section 10);
>   (b) duress (see section 11);
>   (c) undue influence (see section 12);
>   (d) exploitation of weakness (see section 13);
>   (e) incapacity of the individual (see section 14);
>   (f) failure of consideration (see section 15);
>   (g) ignorance or powerlessness (see section 16);
>   (h) fiduciary's lack of authority (see section 17).
> (4) In the second class are—
>   (a) legal compulsion (see section 18);
>   (b) necessity (see section 19);
>   (c) factors concerned with illegality (see section 20);
>   (d) unlawful obtaining, or conferral, of a benefit by a public authority (see section 21).

When the enrichment is unjust

> (5) In this Restatement "unjust factor" means any of the cases mentioned in subsections (3) and (4).
> (6) In general, an enrichment is not unjust if the benefit was owed to the defendant by the claimant under a valid contractual, statutory or other legal obligation (see sections 10(6), 11(6), 12(6), 13(4), 14(4) and 19(3)(c); but cf. section 15(5)).
> (7) In the case dealt with in section 36(3) the enrichment is unjust because, if not reversed or prevented, the defendant would be over-indemnified.

3(1)

This flags up that the details of what one can call the 'unjust question' are to be dealt with in Part 3.

3(2)–(5)

Before getting to the details on the 'unjust question', these subsections provide an overview of the approach taken in English law. In contrast to the approach in civil law systems, which determine the 'unjust question' by reference to whether there has been an 'absence of basis', the best interpretation of English law—although in his final writings Birks, *Unjust Enrichment* (2nd edn, 2005) famously disputed this—is that this question is approached by requiring the claimant to establish an 'unjust factor'. For judicial statements on the need for an unjust factor in English law, see, eg, *Kleinwort Benson Ltd v Lincoln CC* [1999] 2 AC 349, esp at 408–9 (per Lord Hope); *Chief Constable of the Greater Manchester Police v Wigan Athletic AFC Ltd* [2008] EWCA Civ 1449, [2009] 1 WLR 1580 at [50], [62], [67]; *Test Claimants in the FII Group Litigation v Revenue and Customs Commissioners* [2012] UKSC 19, [2012] 2 WLR 1149, at [81]. See also Mitchell, Mitchell, and Watterson (eds), *Goff and Jones on the Law of Unjust Enrichment* (8th edn, 2011) paras 1-18–1-22.

Although very clear and specific—and with the advantage that it directly refers to the unjust aspect of the enquiry—it has to be acknowledged that 'unjust factor' is an inelegant term. Nevertheless it is in common use and has become familiar to the judiciary and to commentators across the world. An alternative is to refer to the more elegant term, 'ground for restitution': but this does not isolate merely the unjust element of unjust enrichment at the claimant's expense and is also unsatisfactory where one is talking about preventing an anticipated unjust enrichment (so that restitution is not in issue). The Restatement uses the term 'unjust factor' (see s 3(5)).

The unjust factors are not fixed for all time. Rather the common law tradition is for development to be incremental. Modern incremental developments in relation to the type or scope of the unjust factors include the expansion of mistake to include mistakes of law as well as fact (see s 10(1)) and the recognition, beyond duress, of the 'Woolwich principle' (see s 21(1)). In *CTN Cash and Carry Ltd v Gallaher Ltd* [1994] 4 All ER 714 at 720, CA, Sir Donald Nicholls V-C said: '[T]he categories of unjust enrichment are not closed'. For the need for claimants to plead an established category or a justifiable extension from such a category, see *Uren v First National Home Finance Ltd* [2005] EWHC 2529 (Ch) at [16], [18]. See also *Gibb v Maidstone and Tunbridge Wells NHS Trust* [2010] EWCA Civ 678, [2010] IRLR 786 at [26]–[27] per Laws LJ.

The unjust factors may be helpfully divided into those (s 3(2)(a) and s 3(3)) that are concerned with the claimant's non-voluntariness (ie problems with the claimant's consent); and those (s 3(2)(b) and s 3(4)) concerned with specific reasons for restitution even though the claimant has consented. The latter have often been referred to as 'policy-motivated restitution' (see Birks, *An Introduction to the Law of Restitution* (rvsd edn, 1989) ch 9). However, the Restatement here avoids the term 'policy', which might incorrectly be thought to suggest that the relevant reasons cannot be reasons of principle or reasons concerned with justice between the parties. The details of the different unjust factors are the subject matter of Part 3 of the Restatement. (But note that an additional unjust factor may be needed to explain restitution where a judgment is reversed: see *Goff and Jones*, ch 26.)

3(6)

An often overlooked but crucial element of the 'unjust factors' scheme, which one may regard as narrowing the gap between the common law approach and the civilian 'absence of basis' approach, is that an unjust factor does not normally override a legal obligation of the claimant to confer the benefit on the defendant. The existence of the legal obligation means that the unjust factor is nullified so that the enrichment at the claimant's expense is not unjust. This may be illustrated by a series of examples:

Example 1

C enters into a contract with D mistakenly believing that the goods it is buying are made of top quality material. There is no term, express or implied, to that effect and D has made no representation to that effect. In fact the goods are made of much cheaper material and are worth far less than C has paid for them. Although C has made a causative mistake, whereby it would not have paid the agreed price had it known the truth, C cannot have restitution of the contract price (in return for counter-restitution of the goods) because the contract is valid. See, eg, *Portman Building Society v Hamlyn Taylor Neck* [1998] 4 All ER 202 at 208 (per Millett LJ); *Deutsche Morgan Grenfell plc v IRC* [2006] UKHL 49, [2007] 1 AC 558 at [84]–[85] (per Lord Scott).

Example 2

C owes £1,000 to each of X and D. C intends to pay off X but by mistake of identity pays D instead of X. C cannot recover from D because D is legally entitled to that sum in the sense that D is owed it by C. See, eg, *Kleinwort Benson Ltd v Lincoln CC* [1999] 2 AC 349 at 407–8 (per Lord Hope). It would appear that the same would apply even if, instead of a mistake by C, D induced C to pay D by duress.

Example 3

C has paid inheritance tax lawfully demanded by the Revenue and Customs Commissioners (D). C mistakenly failed to exercise an election in a deed of variation. Had C exercised that election, she would not have had to pay that tax. C cannot recover the tax paid to D. Although C made a causal mistake, D was legally entitled to the tax in the sense that, subject to a valid election having been made, C had a statutory obligation to pay D that tax. See, eg, *Test Claimants in the FII Group Litigation v Revenue and Customs Commissioners* [2008] EWHC 2893 (Ch) at [257] and [2010] EWCA Civ 103 at [175]–[184] (there was no discussion of this on the appeal to the Supreme Court).

Example 4

C pays D £5,000 as required to by a court judgment in D's favour. The court and C were mistaken as to the facts (or law). C cannot have restitution of the £5,000 unless and until C is able to reverse the judgment. Until then D is entitled to the £5,000 under the valid legal obligation owed by C to D under the judgment.

Example 5

C owes D £500. The debt becomes time-barred so that D can no longer enforce the debt in legal proceedings. C pays D, mistakenly believing that D could bring a legal action against him to enforce the debt. It would appear that C is not entitled to restitution of the £500 as paid by mistake of law because, although legally unenforceable, C still has a valid legal obligation to pay the debt (unless the operation of the Limitation Act 1980 is to extinguish the debt). A legal obligation that is time-barred is still a valid legal obligation.

However, there are some limited exceptions where the unjust factor overrides the claimant's legal obligation to the defendant so as to allow restitution. The explanation for these exceptions is not easy to pinpoint but one might say that they are situations where there is no underlying conflict between the reason for allowing restitution and the defendant's legal entitlement (for example, because allowing restitution does not conflict with the allocation of risk in the contract or does not conflict with the contract as there is a good reason for the contract not to be enforced because it is unenforceable or has been validly terminated). It might help to think of the legal entitlement as being easily outweighed by the unjust factor. For example:

Example 6

An identified part of the price of cigarettes being bought by a retailer, C, from a wholesaler, D, represents a tax that it is thought D has to pay over to the State. The tax is subsequently held to be invalid so that that part of the price does not have to be paid over. Although the contract was valid, C is entitled to restitution of that part of the payment that represented the tax as paid for a consideration that has failed or by mistake. (This fact-situation is exemplified by *Roxborough v Rothmans of Pall Mall Australia Ltd* (2001) 208 CLR 516, High Court of Australia.)

Example 7

C pays advance corporation tax under a statutory scheme that is ultra vires the Revenue (D) because, contrary to EU law, it does not give C an option to avoid paying the tax by making a group income election. C is entitled to restitution from D (for mistake or under the *Woolwich* principle) even though (in one technical sense) D was legally entitled to the tax because C had a statutory duty to pay it unless and until it validly exercised a group income election. (This fact-situation is exemplified by *Deutsche Morgan Grenfell plc v IRC* [2006] UKHL 49, [2007] 1 AC 558.)

Example 8

C pays money to D under a contractual obligation. The contract is then terminated for frustration or for D's breach. C is entitled to restitution if there has been a failure of consideration, even though the contractual obligation under which the money was paid remains valid because termination of a contract wipes away contractual obligations for the future but not for the past. (This fact-situation, which is the most general of the exceptions, is exemplified by *Giles v Edwards* (1797) 7 Term Rep 181 and by the frustration case of *Fibrosa Spolka Akcyjna v Fairbairn Lawson Combe Barbour Ltd* [1943] AC 32, HL: see also the Law Reform (Frustrated Contracts) Act 1943.)

Example 9

C performs services for D under a contract that is unenforceable for want of formality. D refuses to pay C anything. C is entitled to restitution for failure of consideration for the value of the services rendered. This is so even though the

Defences

obligations under an unenforceable contract are valid (albeit unenforceable). (This fact-situation is exemplified by the leading Canadian case of *Deglman v Guaranty Trust Co of Canada and Constantineau* [1954] 3 DLR 785, Supreme Court of Canada; and by the leading Australian case of *Pavey & Matthews Pty Ltd v Paul* (1986) 162 CLR 221, High Court of Australia.)

It should be noted that s 3(6) refers only to where the benefit was owed under a valid *legal* obligation. The question arises whether a moral obligation also overrides the unjust factor. Although there is no authority on this in English law, the better view is probably that it does not. The contrary view would give rise to uncertainty as to what constitutes a moral obligation and might be thought to contradict the law on void contracts (where one might sometimes say that there is a morally binding agreement). This can be illustrated as follows:

Example 10
C gratuitously promises D £100. The promise is not legally binding because D has provided no consideration. C no longer wishes to pay D but, mistakenly believing that she is legally bound to do so, C pays D the £100. It would appear that C would be entitled to restitution of £100 from D as paid by a mistake of law. The natural or moral obligation that one might say that C owes D is overridden by the mistake. (Contrast Example 5 above, where there is a valid legal obligation to pay but it is unenforceable.)

3(7)
Although it could be added to the list in s 3(4), the injustice involved (avoiding over-indemnification) in an indemnity insurer's subrogation is specific to that particular type of subrogation. It has therefore been considered best to treat it separately from the other unjust factors and it is therefore set out in s 36(3).

---

4 Defences
(1) Part 4 sets out defences that defeat, in whole or in part, a claim based on unjust enrichment.
(2) Subject to subsection (3), the burden of proving a defence is on the defendant.
(3) The burden of proving that a limitation period has not expired is on the claimant.

4(1)
The different defences to the event or cause of action of unjust enrichment are the subject matter of Part 4 of the Restatement. Those defences are change of position,

estoppel, agency, counter-restitution, bona fide purchase for value without notice, illegality, resolved disputes, limitation, the special statutory defences of passing on and prevailing practice, contractual or statutory exclusion, and affirmation.

It should be noted that incapacity (meaning, as regards individuals, infancy, mental incapacity, or drunkenness; or, as regards institutions, ultra vires) is not regarded in the Restatement as a defence to unjust enrichment. It is therefore not dealt with in Part 4. There are cases where the contrary view has been taken (eg as regards infancy: *Leslie v Sheill* [1914] 3 KB 607, CA) but the reasoning in those cases is flawed (not least because of the adherence to the implied contract fallacy) and the best view is that they cannot stand in the wake of the overruling of *Sinclair v Brougham* [1914] AC 398, HL (which dealt with the defence of a company acting ultra vires) by *Westdeutsche Landesbank Girozentrale v Islington London BC* [1996] AC 669, HL. One complication in respect of infancy is that under s 3(1) of the Minors' Contracts Act 1987, where a contract is unenforceable against the infant defendant, or he repudiates it, because he was a minor when it was made 'the court may, if it is just and equitable to do so, require the defendant to transfer to the plaintiff any property acquired by the defendant under the contract, or any property representing it'. The precise purpose of this provision is obscure but fortunately it leaves such a wide discretion to the courts that it would be open to them to adopt the principled position in the Restatement that infancy is not a defence to unjust enrichment.

It should also be noted that the Restatement does not include as a defence what is sometimes referred to as a defence of 'good consideration' or 'discharge for value'. There has been considerable confusion in English law and among commentators as to whether this is a defence or not. It is discussed at the end of the commentary on s 27(1).

4(2)–4(3)

This makes clear that the legal burden of proof of a defence is on the defendant. The exception is limitation (other than the doctrine of laches: see s 30(8)). The position on limitation whatever the cause of action (and the best known authorities concern claims in tort: see *Clerk and Lindsell on Torts* (20th edn, 2010) para 32–03) is that, although the defendant must plead limitation, once it has done so the burden of proof falls on the claimant to show that its claim falls within a limitation period. Although this appears to be anomalous—the legal burden of proof of a defence should surely be on the defendant—and is inconsistent with the doctrine of laches, the present law is well-entrenched. It is also noteworthy that the Law Commission in its Report *Limitation of Actions* (Law Com No 270, 2001) paras 5.29–5.32 did not recommend a reform, which would simply shift the legal burden of proving the expiry of a limitation period to the defendant: instead it proposed a more complex splitting of the burden according to the limitation period in issue.

5 Restitutionary rights

(1) Part 5 sets out the rights available to the claimant ("the restitutionary rights").
(2) The restitutionary rights are of two types—
  (a) a personal right to a monetary restitutionary award (see section 34), which is available whatever the unjust factor, and
  (b) depending on the unjust factor, one or more of the rights mentioned in section 35(1).
(3) A claim may be made for—
  (a) a restitutionary right based on more than one unjust factor (for example, mistake and duress), or
  (b) more than one of the restitutionary rights, or
  (c) subject to section 25, a restitutionary right against both a principal and an agent;
  but satisfaction of more than one claim is not permitted where it would produce double recovery.

5(1)

This flags up that the details of the restitutionary rights that reverse an unjust enrichment are set out in Part 5. Some might prefer to switch here to the language of 'remedies' instead of 'rights'. But there is controversy about what exactly is meant by a 'remedy': see, in particular, Zakrzewski, *Remedies Reclassified* (2005). Moreover, there is particular difficulty in describing at least some of the 'rights' referred to in s 5(2)(b) and s 35(1) as 'remedies' rather than being declaratory of the legal position prior to any court pronouncement; and this may link in to the well-known, but confusing, debate about whether a trust in the context of unjust enrichment (see s 35(1)(d)) is a remedy or a substantive institution (see Burrows, *The Law of Restitution* (2011) 193). For all these reasons, it has been thought preferable in this Restatement to avoid the language of 'remedies' and to rely entirely on the language of 'rights'. (This also explains the inverted commas round the word 'remedies' where used in the commentary.)

5(2)

Before getting to the details in Part 5, this subsection provides an overview of the two types of right that reverse an unjust enrichment.

5(2)(a)

The right to restitution for unjust enrichment may, most obviously, be a personal right to restitution of the value of the enrichment received by the defendant (irrespective of whether the defendant still has that value although, if not, this may go to the defence of change of position). As a personal right, this is enforceable only against a particular person or his representatives. See s 34(1).

'A monetary restitutionary award' is the single simplifying modern term that has been chosen in this Restatement to replace the long list of 'remedies' enforcing the personal right to restitution of the value of an unjust enrichment received. That list includes the award of money had and received to the claimant's use, money paid to the defendant's use, a *quantum meruit*, a *quantum valebat*, recoupment or contribution, a money award consequent on rescission, and an account of money (or the value of an asset) received. That long list reflects the scattered history of the subject by which different 'remedies' (both common law and equitable) have evolved for different situations of restitution. In addition to making the law easier to understand, the advantage of having a single modern term is that claimants may plead that they are seeking 'a monetary restitutionary award' (or even just 'monetary restitution') without having to use one of the old labels.

It should be emphasised that it is the personal right to a monetary restitutionary award for the value of the enrichment received that is at issue in the vast majority of unjust enrichment cases.

Nothing is specifically said in the Restatement about interest as constituting, or in addition to, a monetary restitutionary award. This is because one can regard the award of interest as itself a monetary restitutionary award so that, even where it is separated out from a principal restitutionary award, it can be analysed as awarding full restitution of the defendant's enrichment at the claimant's expense. That the use of money may itself be the principal unjust enrichment in issue was made clear in *Sempra Metals Ltd v IRC* [2007] UKHL 34, [2008] 1 AC 561; and all their Lordships agreed that, where this best reflected the defendant's enrichment, compound (rather than simple) interest should be awarded. Simple interest can be awarded on a 'debt or damages' under s 35A of the Senior Courts Act 1981. The relationship between *Sempra Metals* and s 35A is not entirely clear but it would appear that, without proof that the defendant has been enriched by compound interest rates, a claimant will need to rely on s 35A where simple interest only can be awarded.

5(2)(b)

Some would confine restitution for unjust enrichment to the personal right in s 5(2)(a). That would certainly simplify the law. But it would seriously limit the explanatory force of unjust enrichment. Beyond such a personal right to value received there are other rights to restitution which, on the best analysis, are created by unjust enrichment. In loose terms, they concern 'proprietary rights' (but note that that precise term has not been used in the Restatement because of the continuing controversy about what it means and whether it includes a beneficial interest under a trust: see, eg, McFarlane, *The Structure of Property Law* (2008) 29–30; McFarlane and Stevens, 'The Nature of Equitable Property' (2010) 4 Journal

Restitutionary rights

of Equity 1, esp 3–6). This area of 'proprietary restitution' is one of the most complex and controversial in the law of unjust enrichment. As set out in s 35(1), four kinds of right may be said to be involved: liens, subrogation to a discharged security, rescission/rectification revesting title, and a beneficiary's right under a trust imposed by law (namely a resulting or constructive trust). Those four are set out respectively in s 35(1)(a)–(d).

Such rights do not always arise where there has been an unjust enrichment. It is made clear, by the opening words of s 5(2)(b), that one must look at the particular unjust factor in Part 3 to know the precise circumstances in which (ie when it is that) these rights arise. This may simply be because factually, in the context of a particular unjust factor, there is no real scope for one or more of these types of right. But there may also be objections to recognising such rights in relation to particular unjust factors, the most obvious being where the unjust factor is failure of consideration. All this is set out in detail in s 35 (as is a general restriction on these rights, which is set out in s 35(3)).

At a high level of generality, it is helpful to see from the outset that, in contrast to the restitutionary right in s 5(2)(a), the restitutionary rights referred to in s 5(2)(b) and s 35(1) are dependent on the defendant *retaining* an asset or a right in property or on the defendant having had a secured liability discharged. This explains why for some commentators (see, especially, Lodder, *Enrichment in the Law of Unjust Enrichment and Restitution* (2012)) the distinction between s 5(2)(a) and (b) marks a fundamental division between personal restitution of value received and proprietary restitution of rights retained (or discharged).

Although there can be other advantages of 'proprietary restitution' (see Mitchell, Mitchell, and Watterson (eds), *Goff and Jones on the Law of Unjust Enrichment* (8th edn, 2011) para 37-02), the insolvency of the defendant (with the consequence that a personal right to a monetary restitutionary award is unlikely to be satisfied) is the main reason why a claimant is likely to take on the extra factual (and legal) difficulties involved in seeking to invoke one of the additional rights referred to in ss 5(2)(b) and 35(1).

5(3)

It was established in *Deutsche Morgan Grenfell v IRC* [2006] UKHL 49, [2007] 1 AC 558 that a claimant is free to choose its unjust factor within the law of unjust enrichment so that claims can be based on more than one unjust factor (s 5(3)(a)). In that case, the existence of a claim for restitution under the *Woolwich* principle (see s 21 below) did not preclude a claim for restitution based on mistake (with its attendant advantage of the postponement of the running of the limitation period). Similarly, as regards s 5(3)(b), there can be no objection to a claimant seeking a monetary restitutionary award to enforce a personal right to restitution plus 'proprietary restitution' (eg through revesting of a right in property or being a beneficiary of a right in property under a trust). However, the essential thrust of this subsection is to make the perhaps obvious point that one cannot combine, so as to have double recovery, satisfaction of more than one claim (eg one cannot have restitution of a mistaken payment of £100 by having both a monetary restitutionary award of £100 plus being a trust beneficiary of the right to £100).

It has been thought helpful to include here (as s 5(3)(c)) that, where an agent obtains a benefit on behalf of a principal, and subject to the avoidance of double recovery, any claim for unjust enrichment can be brought against both principal and agent (although the agent may be able to invoke the defence of agency: see s 25). See also s 7(4). This is explained further at the end of the commentary to s 25.

6 Prevention of anticipated unjust enrichment

(1) In limited circumstances, a claimant has a right to prevent an anticipated unjust enrichment of a defendant at the claimant's expense.

(2) In particular, subrogation under section 36(3) may prevent an anticipated unjust enrichment.

6

It is sometimes said that unjust enrichment is concerned with 'prevention' as well as 'reversal' of an unjust enrichment (see, eg, the use of the language of 'prevention' in *Banque Financière de la Cité v Parc (Battersea) Ltd* [1999] 1 AC 221, HL); and there do appear to be some limited pockets of law (most obviously, an indemnity insurer's non-contractual subrogation rights where the assured has not been paid by the third party: see commentary to s 36(3)) where an unjust enrichment explanation is helpful, and yet prevention and not reversal is in issue. See generally Mitchell, Mitchell, and Watterson (eds), *Goff and Jones on the Law of Unjust Enrichment* (8th edn, 2011) paras 36-28–36-37.

Moreover, although there have been no clear examples of this in the case law, it is conceivable in principle that an injunction could be obtained to prevent an unjust enrichment (eg C seeks an injunction to stop D exerting duress, or undue influence, over C under which C is making payments to D). One probable case law example is a surety's right (irrespective of contract) to a *quia timet* injunction to require the principal debtor to pay the creditor: on one interpretation this anticipates the surety's unjust enrichment contribution claim against the principal debtor so that the injunction prevents the principal debtor's unjust enrichment at the surety's expense. See *Re Richardson* [1911] 2 KB 705, CA; and the discussion in Mitchell, *The Law of Contribution and Reimbursement* (2003) at paras 3.11 and 14.38–14.45.

So, although not well established, the Restatement accepts that in certain (at present, very limited) circumstances the claimant may have the right to prevent an anticipated unjust enrichment rather than to reverse an accrued unjust enrichment.

PART 2
ENRICHMENT AT THE CLAIMANT'S EXPENSE

7 Enrichment
(1) "Enrichment" requires the obtaining of a benefit.
(2) The benefits which may constitute enrichment include: money, goods or land; the use of money, goods or land; services; the crediting of a bank account; the discharge of a debt or other liability; the forgoing of a claim; and intangible property (such as intellectual property, receivables or shares).
(3) But a defendant is not to be regarded as enriched unless the claimant shows that—
   (a) no reasonable person would deny that the defendant has been enriched (as is normally the case where, for example, the defendant has obtained money or has been saved necessary expense or has turned a non-monetary benefit into money), or
   (b) the defendant chose the benefit (by, for example, requesting it, or demanding or taking it or, after a request for its return, retaining it when it was readily returnable), or
   (c) the defendant, having had the opportunity to reject the benefit, freely accepted it knowing or believing that the claimant expected payment for it.
(4) Subject to section 25, where an agent is acting for a principal, the enrichment of the agent is to be treated as also being the enrichment of the principal.

7(1)–(2)

Section 7(1) clarifies that a defendant cannot be enriched unless a benefit has been obtained; and s 7(2) lists the main types of benefit that have been the subject matter of successful claims for restitution for unjust enrichment in past cases. As regards the discharge of a debt, there is a complex body of law on when an unrequested payment of another's debt discharges that debt (see the commentary to s 18(1) below). The forgoing of a claim was for the first time judicially recognised as a relevant benefit in *Gibb v Maidstone & Tunbridge Wells NHS Trust* [2010] EWCA Civ 678, [2010] IRLR 786. Although no doubt obvious, it should be noted that the reference to 'money, goods or land' should be taken as encompassing 'a right' in or to money, goods, or land.

There is a difficult on-going debate as to whether enrichment in the law of unjust enrichment can include obtaining benefits that have no value. So, for example, Chambers, 'Two Kinds of Enrichment' in Chambers, Mitchell, and Penner (eds), *Philosophical Foundations of The Law of Unjust Enrichment* (2009) 242 argues that there are two kinds of enrichment: 'value' and 'rights'. The revesting of title to goods or land by rescission is the reversal of an enrichment even if the goods or land are valueless. He suggests, as examples (at 255), a revesting of title to a child's painting, which has sentimental value to the claimant but no value to anyone else, or a revesting of land that is contaminated and therefore valueless to an owner. However, these are plainly 'fringe' cases that are very unlikely to give rise to practical disputes. In at least the vast majority of cases, title to property does have value. The fact that the law may effect restitution by revesting title without the need for a valuation exercise does not mean that the title has no value. In any event, one would have thought (although Chambers does not accept this) that, in the rare case where there has been the unjust acquisition of title to property that is of no value, one is outside the law of unjust enrichment (and dealing with an analogous miscellaneous event within the law of property). The Restatement does not take a view on whether Chambers is correct or not. In other words, nothing in the Restatement dictates that the benefit/enrichment must have value. But, as a matter of the ordinary understanding of words, it is natural to think that a benefit/enrichment has value. A valueless benefit/enrichment appears to be an oxymoron.

7(3)

That the law is concerned with the benefit to the particular defendant was made clear in *Sempra Metals Ltd v IRC* [2007] UKHL 34, [2008] 1 AC 561. This is often expressed by saying that the law recognises 'subjective devaluation' (see Birks, *An Introduction to the Law of Restitution* (rvsd edn, 1989) 109–110; *Cressman v Coys of Kensington (Sales) Ltd* [2004] EWCA Civ 47, [2004] 1 WLR 2775 at [28]; *Sempra Metals Ltd v IRC* [2007] UKHL 34, [2008] 1 AC 56 at [119]). The law looks for indicators that the particular defendant has been enriched: ie that override subjective devaluation. These are set out in s 7(3)(a), 7(3)(b) and 7(3)(c). (We shall see later, in s 34, that the notion of 'subjective devaluation' carries on through to the stage of valuing the enrichment.)

7(3)(a)

We are here concerned with what has been termed 'an incontrovertible benefit' (see Birks, *An Introduction to the Law of Restitution* (rvsd edn, 1989) 116–24). This is intended to capture the idea that, irrespective of choice or the opportunity to reject by the defendant, no reasonable person would deny that the defendant has been enriched. The concept has been referred to with approval in a number of cases: see, eg, *BP Exploration Co (Libya) Ltd v Hunt (No 2)* [1979] 1 WLR 783; *Rowe v Vale of White Horse DC* [2003] EWHC 388 (Admin), [2003] 1 Lloyd's Rep 418; and *Chief Constable of the Greater Manchester Police v Wigan Athletic AFC Ltd* [2008] EWCA Civ 1449, [2009] 1 WLR 1580. The receipt of money and the crediting of one's bank account are examples. So is the saving of a necessary expense (eg the cost of sewerage services in *Rowe*) or a non-money benefit that has been turned into money (eg improvements to a house that has been sold at an enhanced value).

Enrichment

However, one must bear in mind that, especially because of an opportunity foregone, it is possible that even the receipt of money is, overall, not beneficial to the defendant. An example of this is as follows:

Example

C pays D £100 by mistake. As a result, a third party does not pay D the £100 she would otherwise have paid him.

One approach to this type of example is to view the lost opportunity as an aspect of the defendant's change of position defence (see s 23 below). An alternative approach, which is reflected in the words 'as is normally the case', is to say that the underlying idea of no reasonable person denying that the defendant is enriched is better captured by the notion of there being a strong, but rebuttable, presumption that the defendant is enriched rather than by referring to an 'incontrovertible benefit'.

7(3)(b)

The defendant's choosing of the benefit indicates that it is a benefit *to the defendant*. Most of the cases have concerned *requested* services. Retaining readily returnable property after a request for its return was held to show that the defendant was enriched in *Cressman v Coys of Kensington (Sales) Ltd* [2004] EWCA Civ 47, [2004] 1 WLR 2775. A test of 'demanding or taking a benefit' explains why the defendant who takes or demands services (eg by stowing away on a ship or pointing a gun to force someone to perform services) cannot deny that he or she is enriched.

7(3)(c)

Although controversial (because there is no overt choice made) it now appears to have been accepted by the courts that one of the indicators of benefit to the defendant is 'free acceptance'. 'Free acceptance' was a term coined by Goff and Jones, *The Law of Restitution* (1st edn, 1966) and refers to where the defendant, having the opportunity to reject, allows services to be rendered (or retains goods) knowing that the claimant expects payment. Recent cases accepting this as showing enrichment include *Cressman v Coys of Kensington (Sales) Ltd* [2004] EWCA Civ 47, [2004] 1 WLR 2775, *Chief Constable of the Greater Manchester Police v Wigan Athletic AFC Ltd* [2008] EWCA Civ 1449, [2009] 1 WLR 1580, and *Benedetti v Sawiris* [2010] EWCA Civ 1427. See also Mitchell, Mitchell, and Watterson (eds), *Goff and Jones on the Law of Unjust Enrichment* (8th edn, 2011) paras 4-27–4-33.

7(4)

This is explained below under s 25 at the end of the commentary on agency as a defence.

8 At the claimant's expense: general

(1) The defendant's enrichment is at the claimant's expense if the benefit obtained by the defendant is—
   (a) from the claimant, and
   (b) directly from the claimant rather than by way of another person.

(2) In any of the following cases, it does not matter that the benefit obtained by the defendant (D) is from the claimant (C) by way of another person (X)—
   (a) where X transfers an asset to D but C has a better right to that asset than X;
   (b) where X transfers an asset to D but X was holding the asset on trust for C;
   (c) where X is acting as C's agent in respect of the benefit;
   (d) where X charges and receives from C an amount representing tax on X's supply of goods or services to C and pays or accounts for that amount to D (Her Majesty's Revenue and Customs) as tax due;
   (e) where C is subrogated to X's (or another's) present or former rights against D in a situation where the benefit was supplied to D by X;
   (f) where X was under a legal obligation to supply the benefit to C but instead supplied the benefit to D and—
      (i) the supply to D discharged X's obligation to C, or
      (ii) the supply to D was in breach of X's fiduciary duty to C but C's claim against X has been exhausted.

(3) In a contract for the benefit of a third party, the third party's benefit is to be treated as obtained directly from the contracting party who required the benefit to be supplied rather than from the contracting party who supplied it.

(4) Even if the benefit obtained by the defendant is directly from the claimant, the enrichment is generally not at the claimant's expense if the benefit is merely incidental to the furtherance by the claimant of an objective unconnected with the defendant's enrichment.

8(1)

'At the claimant's expense' is the concept that, in very general terms, describes the need for 'causation' between the claimant and the defendant's enrichment. It is best understood as requiring that the benefit is from the claimant and that it is directly from the claimant rather than from a third party. Those two elements are respectively covered by s 8(1)(a) and (b); and s 8(1)(b) is then amplified in s 8(2) and (3). A third element is that the benefit is not merely an incidental benefit: this is dealt with in s 8(4).

8(1)(a)

How best to explain the meaning of 'at the expense of' in the law of unjust enrichment is controversial. Birks focussed on the idea that the enrichment must be a 'subtraction from the claimant' (*An Introduction to the Law of Restitution* (rvsd edn, 1989) 23–4, 132–9). Another popular idea is that the enrichment must be a 'transfer of value' from the claimant (although this has been criticised as straining the meaning of 'transfer' by, eg, Penner, 'Value, Property, and Unjust Enrichment: Trusts of Traceable Proceeds' in Chambers, Mitchell, and Penner (eds), *Philosophical Foundations of The Law of Unjust Enrichment* (2009) 306–12). In general, it would seem that the ideas of 'subtraction' and 'transfer of value' are helpful. But it is probably correct that each is, at the margins, misleading. In particular, 'subtraction' may give the false impression that a loss to the claimant is essential and 'transfer of value' may be misleading in implying that there must be active conduct by the claimant. The Restatement seeks to avoid these difficulties by using the simple formulation that the benefit obtained by the defendant is *from the claimant*.

That there need be no active conduct by the claimant means that the defendant can be enriched 'at the claimant's expense' where the defendant picks up money that falls from the claimant's pocket, or where the defendant takes goods from the claimant without her knowledge. Furthermore, the defendant can be enriched at the claimant's expense even though there is no transfer of any right from the claimant to the defendant. This is most clearly shown by the services cases, or where the claimant discharges the defendant's debt to a third party. The same applies in many other cases. So if a claimant by a mistake of identity transfers goods to the defendant, there will be no transfer of title to the goods (because the mistake is fundamental) but the defendant obtains the benefit (of having possession of the goods) from the claimant.

In some jurisdictions (eg Canada) it has been said that the enrichment of the defendant must be equivalent to a loss to the claimant (so that the enrichment is capped by the loss). Enrichment and impoverishment must coincide. Certainly, the equivalence of a plus and a minus does have a strong normative appeal. Nevertheless, while that equivalence will commonly be present in the law of unjust enrichment, the best interpretation of English law is that such equivalence is not necessary (but note that, leaning towards the contrary view, are Mitchell, Mitchell, and Watterson (eds), *Goff and Jones on the Law of Unjust Enrichment* (8th edn, 2011) paras 6-63–6-74.) While the benefit must be obtained from the claimant, this need not involve a loss to the claimant, or a loss to the claimant equivalent to (or that acts as a cap on) the enrichment of the defendant (although, if one wishes to insist on a loss, one might say that the defendant's enrichment is capped by the claimant's *objective* loss). This may be illustrated as follows:

Commentary: Part 2

Example 1

C mistakenly carries out repairs to D's car believing that it is C's own car. Assuming that D is enriched, the restitutionary monetary award (*quantum meruit*) will be assessed by reference to the enrichment of the defendant (prima facie measured by the market value of the services: see s 34(2)) and it is irrelevant to consider whether C has suffered any loss or the extent of that loss.

Example 2

D takes C's bicycle without C's consent and uses it for a week and then returns it undamaged. The restitutionary monetary award (*quantum valebat*) will be assessed by reference to the enrichment of D (prima facie measured by the market use value of the bicycle) and it is irrelevant to consider whether C has suffered any loss or the extent of that loss.

Example 3

C gives her laptop to D to use for six months, mistakenly believing that D is X. D uses the laptop for six months and then returns it undamaged. Assuming that D is enriched by the use of the laptop (eg because she is thereby saved necessary expense) the restitutionary monetary award (*quantum valebat*) will be assessed by reference to the enrichment of D (prima facie measured by the market use value of the laptop) and it is irrelevant to consider whether C has suffered any loss or the extent of that loss.

That there is no need to look at whether the claimant has suffered any loss, or the extent of a loss suffered, is supported by *Sempra Metals Ltd v IRC* [2007] UKHL 34, [2008] 1 AC 561, esp at [30]–[31], [66] and [126]–[129]: in assessing restitution for the use value of tax mistakenly paid earlier than it needed to have been, it was thought irrelevant to consider the position of the claimant (eg whether the claimant might have made no use of the money or might have borrowed at a different rate of interest than the defendant). See also *Kleinwort Benson Ltd v Birmingham CC* [1997] QB 380, CA (in rejecting a passing on defence, the argument was rejected that in reversing an unjust enrichment one is to an extent compensating for loss); *Littlewoods Retail Ltd v Revenue and Customs Commissioners* [2010] EWHC 1071 (Ch), [2010] STC 2072, at [145]–[147]; and *Amin v Amin* [2010] EWHC 528 (Ch) at [4].

However, while there is no need for an equivalent loss to the claimant, it is also not sufficient that there is merely a 'but for' causal link between the enrichment of the defendant and the claimant's conduct or wealth. Rather the benefit must be obtained from the claimant and this is to be distinguished from a consequential gain resulting from that benefit. This may be illustrated as follows:

At the claimant's expense: general

Example 4

C mistakenly pays D £10. As a result of having that extra £10 (but using a different £10), D purchases ten lottery tickets. One of them is the winning ticket and D wins £1m. C does not have a claim against D in unjust enrichment for £1m. This is because the £1m has not been gained 'at the expense of' C. The benefit obtained from the claimant was the £10 plus interest and that is the limit of the restitutionary award. The £1m is a consequential gain resulting from that benefit.

Example 5

C repairs D's fence while D is away so as to save D's prize herd of cattle from straying over a cliff. It takes C one hour to do the work and the market value of such services is £100. The prize herd of cattle saved is worth £100,000. The benefit obtained from C was the rendering of the services (prima facie valued at £100) and the value of the services is the limit of the restitutionary award (we are here assuming that C has a claim in unjust enrichment for necessitous intervention). The £100,000 is a consequential gain (albeit by a loss avoided) resulting from that benefit.

Example 6

In anticipation of a contract for the sale of D's land to C, D requests C to seek planning permission for the erection of houses on D's land. C does so and obtains planning permission. D then withdraws from the contract negotiations with C so that no contract of sale is concluded between them. The market value of C's services is £150,000. By reason of the planning permission, the value of D's land is enhanced by £1m. The benefit obtained from C was the rendering of the services (prima facie valued at £150,000) and the value of the services is the limit of the restitutionary award. The £1m is a consequential gain resulting from that benefit. (This example is based on *Cobbe v Yeoman's Row Management Ltd* [2008] UKHL 55, [2008] 1 WLR 1752.)

Example 7

D requests C, a locksmith, under an invalid contract, to fashion a key to unlock an antique cabinet belonging to D. C does so and treasures belonging to D worth £10m are found inside the cabinet. The market value of C's services is £150. The benefit obtained from C was the rendering of the services (prima facie valued at £150) and the value of the services is the limit of the restitutionary award. The £10m is a consequential gain resulting from that benefit. (This example is based on the hypothetical example given by Lord Scott in *Cobbe v Yeoman's Row Management Ltd* [2008] UKHL 55, [2008] 1 WLR 1752 at [41].)

Example 8

C builds a house on D's land, mistakenly believing that it is C's own land. D sells the house for £1m. The market value of C's work and materials is £700,000. The benefits obtained from C were the rendering of the services and the provision of the materials and it is the value of those that is the limit of the restitutionary award (ie £700,000). The extra £300,000 is a consequential gain resulting from those benefits.

Example 9

D owes X £1,000. After negotiations with X, C obtains a total discharge of D's debt by C's payment to X of £800. Had C not paid, X would not have accepted discharge of D's debt for less than the full £1,000. The benefit obtained by D from C was the payment of the money (£800) plus the value of negotiating the discount (presumably between £1 and £200). That is the limit of the restitutionary award (we are here assuming that C has a claim in unjust enrichment for, eg, legal compulsion). The full amount of the debt discharged, over and above that value, is a consequential gain resulting from the benefit obtained from C.

It can be seen from the above examples that the requirement that the benefit obtained is from the claimant operates both to deny the need for a strict equivalence between loss and gain and to cut off (analogously to a 'remoteness' limitation) the chain of consequential gain.

8(1)(b)

The second element going to establish 'at the expense of' is that, subject to exceptions, the benefit obtained by the defendant is directly from the claimant rather than from a third party. In other words, there is a general rule that 'direct providers only' are entitled to restitution. After a careful review of the authorities and academic literature, this has recently been confirmed by Henderson J in *Investment Trust Companies v HMRC* [2012] EWHC 458 (Ch). (For a contrary view, see Mitchell, Mitchell and Watterson (eds), *Goff and Jones on the Law of Unjust Enrichment* (8th edn, 2011) paras 6-12–6-62.) In taking that general rule as its starting point, the law has rejected the alternative general starting point of allowing more than one claimant to have a claim, with subsequent proceedings then following to sort out the respective entitlement between them.

The general 'direct providers only' rule is illustrated by the following example:

Example 10

C mistakenly overpays X £100. As a consequence, X makes a gift of (the same or a different) £100 to D. As a general rule, C is not entitled to restitution from D. This is because D's benefit is obtained directly from X and not from C.

At the claimant's expense: general

A useful case illustration of this general restriction is provided by *Uren v First National Home Finance Ltd* [2005] EWHC 2529 (Ch) (money paid by purchaser of flats, C, to developers, X, and not to the bank, D, who took over the development: obiter dicta of Mann J that enrichment of D was not at C's expense). The restriction is sometimes referred to by saying that C cannot 'leapfrog' X to claim against D (see Birks, *Unjust Enrichment* (2nd edn, 2005) ch 4, although Birks himself doubted whether this is the general rule).

8(2)

Assuming that there is a starting point of a 'direct providers only' rule, there are numerous exceptions to this. What are here set out are the principal exceptions but it is open to the courts to develop further exceptions.

What is not here classed as an exception is where C discharges D's liability to X by payment to X. This is because it is perfectly plausible to say that, while the money may be paid directly by C to X, the benefit of the discharge is obtained by D directly from both C and X. C's payment is analogous to rendering services to D.

8(2)(a)

This might loosely be referred to as the 'title exception' to the general 'direct providers only' rule: the transfer by X to D was of an asset belonging to C rather than X. This may be illustrated as follows:

Example 11

X steals C's £50 banknote and bicycle and gives them to D. D's enrichment is at the expense of C even though there has been a direct transfer by X. One might say that it was also at the expense of X (so that X could also claim restitution from D if there were any unjust factor in relation to X) but, as between X and C, C plainly has the superior claim.

Although the facts were more complex, and were dependent on the difficult idea of tracing, the reasoning in *Lipkin Gorman v Karpnale Ltd* [1991] 2 AC 548, HL, especially of Lord Templeman, accepted that the owner of stolen money has a claim in unjust enrichment against a person to whom the thief has given the money by way of gift.

8(2)(b)

This is the 'trust' exception. Although X, as trustee, has legal title to the asset which is transferred to D, the fact that the right to the asset was held on trust for C (the beneficiary or beneficiaries) means that D's enrichment is at the expense of C (as well as being at the expense of X). It should be stressed, however, that the enrichment is at the expense of the beneficiaries as a whole. A claim by any single beneficiary (unless the sole beneficiary) would only be concerned to restore the trust fund and it would be misleading to regard the enrichment as being at the expense of any one beneficiary where there is more than one. Indeed, one might most helpfully describe the enrichment as being at the expense of 'the trust estate'. The benefit obtained by D is not from any individual beneficiary, just as no individual beneficiary suffers loss. (For the contrary approach, regarding the beneficiaries as suffering their own losses in the context of the recovery of economic loss in the tort of negligence, see the controversial decision in *Shell UK Ltd v Total UK Ltd* [2010] EWCA Civ 180, [2011] QB 86.)

8(2)(c)

If X is acting as C's agent in transferring a benefit to D, that benefit is at the expense of C, even though directly provided by X, as well as being at the expense of X. See, eg, *Stevenson v Mortimer* (1778) 2 Cowp 805; *Niru Battery Manufacturing Co v Milestone Trading Ltd* [2002] EWHC 1425 (Comm), [2002] 2 All ER (Comm) 705 at [145]. The principles of the law of agency will determine whether X is C's agent but, as one is not here concerned with upholding expectations created by the external appearance of agency, X must have C's actual (rather than apparent) authority to act in this way. Agency of course operates in many different contexts, most of which have nothing to do with restitution for unjust enrichment. By including agency here as an exception to the 'direct providers only' general rule, it is not being denied that the exception can be explained by the application of the general principle that an agent's conduct is attributable to its principal.

8(2)(d)

This is illustrated by *Investment Trust Companies v HMRC* [2012] EWHC 458 (Ch). Henderson J reasoned that customers, who had been incorrectly charged VAT that was not due by suppliers of fund management services—applying EU law, those services should have been exempt from VAT—were at common law entitled to restitution from Her Majesty's Revenue and Customs ('HMRC') (to whom the tax had been paid by the suppliers) in so far as they had not been repaid the tax by the suppliers. In so doing, he explicitly recognised that he was applying an exception to the general 'direct providers only' rule so as to hold HMRC enriched *at the expense of the customers*, albeit that the suppliers had directly paid the VAT over to HMRC. Henderson J said, at [50], that, while there were dangers in pressing this point too far (because the customer is not in the ordinary sense a taxpayer vis-à-vis HMRC), 'at a fairly high level of generality for the purposes of VAT the final consumer is properly to be regarded as the taxpayer and...the role of the intermediate taxable persons in the chain of supply is to collect the tax and account for it to the tax authorities'. Although Henderson J's decision was that the common law of unjust enrichment was excluded by statute (applying s 80(7) of the

Value Added Tax Act 1994) his reasoning on the common law is part of the ratio decidendi because it underpinned his further reasoning on EU law (ie it was essential to his reasoning on EU law that there was a common law right to restitution).

8(2)(e)

Some examples of subrogation are exceptions to the 'direct providers only' rule because they allow C to stand in the shoes of another so as to have restitution from D. So, if a loan has been provided by C to X, which X has used to pay off a secured debt to Y (a bank) owed by X's wife, D, C is entitled to be subrogated to Y's former secured rights against D in order to have restitution of the enrichment comprising the discharge of D's debt. Yet X, not C, is the direct provider of D's enrichment. See, eg, *Butler v Rice* [1910] 2 Ch 277. For subrogation generally, see s 36.

8(2)(f)

Although not involving leapfrogging, a further exception to the 'direct providers only' rule is where X was under a legal obligation to supply the benefit to C but has instead supplied the benefit to D. In some cases, C has a claim against D even though X was the direct provider. This is the area which Birks explained by reference to 'interceptive subtraction' (*Unjust Enrichment* (2nd edn, 2005) ch 4). According to his interceptive subtraction approach, C is entitled to restitution from D because D has intercepted that which, as a matter of law, should have been (in Birks' terminology, was 'legally certain' to have been) paid to C. Birks applied the same reasoning to what he termed factual, rather than legal, certainty: ie where as a matter of fact it was certain that C would have been benefited by X had D not intercepted.

Lionel Smith has rejected 'interceptive subtraction' in 'Three-Party Restitution: A Critique of Birks' Theory of Interceptive Subtraction' (1991) 11 OJLS 481. His narrower explanation of the 'legal certainty' cases turns on the important point that the relevant decisions are ones where either X's incorrect payment to D discharges X's obligation to C or, if not, the law insists that C has first exhausted its claim against X. So, for example:

Example 12

C, a landlord, is entitled to rent from its tenant, X. D, by 'usurpation of C's office', collects the rent for its own benefit. C is entitled to restitution from D of the rent paid even though it has been directly paid to D by X not C. This is because C was legally owed the rent by X and X's payment to D discharges X's obligation to pay C. For 'usurpation of office' see, eg, *Boyter v Dodsworth* (1796) 6 Term Rep 681.

Commentary: Part 2

Example 13

X, a personal representative administering an estate, mistakenly and in breach of fiduciary duty to C (the correct beneficiary), pays D. C is entitled to restitution from D (albeit that this is conditional on having exhausted its claim against X) even though the payment to D has been directly made by X not C. This is because C was legally owed the payment by X and, by reason of the condition, C has no worthwhile claim against X. See *Ministry of Health v Simpson* [1951] AC 251, HL.

The Restatement adopts Smith's narrower explanation of the 'legal certainty' cases. Section 8(2)(f)(i) reflects Example 12 and s 8(2)(f)(ii) reflects Example 13.

Clearly, however, this is a complex area of the law and there may be developments which would render Smith's explanation too narrow. So, eg, there are obiter dicta in some cases (see, eg, *Rusden v Pope* (1868) LR 3 Ex 269, 278–9) in which it is indicated that, if a payment is made by X to the wrong person (D) in order to discharge a debt owed by X to the correct person (C), C has a right to restitution from D even though X's payment to D does not discharge the debt owed by X to C.

As regards interceptive subtraction involving factual certainty, Smith correctly argues that there has been no case in which this has been accepted by the courts. It is therefore not included in the Restatement. The most discussed situation is where X has mistakenly drawn up and executed a deed of gift in favour of D rather than C and then dies before realising the mistake and rectifying the gift. In *Lister v Hodgson* (1867) LR 4 Eq 30 at 34, Lord Romilly MR indicated in obiter dicta that C would be entitled to have the deed of gift rectified in his favour. *If* that were correct, it could only be explained by Birks' 'interceptive subtraction' theory: the explanation of D's benefit being 'at the expense of C' would be that, but for X's mistake, C and not D would certainly *as a matter of fact* have been the donee.

8(3)

This seeks to clarify the operation of the 'at the expense of' requirement in the situation where a contract is for the benefit of a third party. Which of the two contracting parties is the direct provider of the benefit for the purposes of any claim against the third party in unjust enrichment? The answer is that the benefit should be treated as being obtained directly from the contracting party who has required the benefit to be supplied (ie the party who has requested that benefit).

Example 14

A, a garage, under a contract with B, an insurer, repairs the car of C, the insured. If B fails to pay A, so that there is a failure of consideration, A has no claim in unjust enrichment against C. B required the repair work to be done and C's enrichment is therefore at the expense of B not A. (This fact-situation is exemplified by *Brown and Davis Ltd v Galbraith* [1972] 1 WLR 997, CA.)

Example 15

A, a sub-contractor, under a contract with B, the head-contractor, carries out building work on C's land. If B fails to pay A, so that there is a failure of consideration, A has no claim in unjust enrichment against C. B required the building work to be done and C's enrichment is therefore at the expense of B not A. (This fact-situation is exemplified by *Lumbers v W Cook Builders Pty Ltd* [2008] HCA 27, (2008) 232 CLR 635, High Court of Australia.)

Example 16

A enters into a building contract with B, a company owned by C, for the construction of houses on the land of C. B fails to pay A the full sum owed under the contract for the work A has done. Although there is therefore a failure of consideration, A has no claim in unjust enrichment against C for the value of the work done. B required the building work to be done and C's enrichment is therefore at the expense of B not A. (This fact-situation is exemplified by *MacDonald Dickens & Macklin v Costello* [2011] EWCA Civ 930, [2011] 3 WLR 1341.)

Example 17

A, a bank, has a banking contract with its customer, B. B calls upon A to make a credit transfer to B's creditor, C. A does so in the mistaken belief that B's account is in credit, whereas it is in fact overdrawn. A has no claim in unjust enrichment against C for A's mistaken payment. B required the payment to be made and C's enrichment is therefore at the expense of B not A. (This fact-situation is exemplified by *Lloyds Bank plc v Independent Insurance Co Ltd* [2000] QB 110, CA.)

It is important to note that there may be no contract between B and C: so in Example 15 above, the building work might be a gift from B to C and, indeed on the facts of the *Costello* case (Example 16 above), there was no contract between B and C. The explanation for the denial of a claim in unjust enrichment does not therefore rest on the existence of a contract between B and C.

However, an alternative valid explanation for the denial of restitution—alternative to the 'at the expense of' version offered above—is that, even if one were to regard *both* B and A as direct providers of C's enrichment, one would still not wish to allow A restitution from C because this would undermine the contractual risks (especially the risk of B's insolvency) undertaken by A in its contract with B. This was the reason relied on by the Court of Appeal in denying restitution for building work done for the third party under a contract between the builders and another party in *MacDonald v Costello* [2011] EWCA Civ 930, [2011] 3 WLR 1341 (see Example 16 above). The

Commentary: Part 2

argument that, in any event, restitution should be denied because the benefit to the third party should be treated as coming indirectly, rather than directly, from the builders was also carefully referred to in the judgment of Etherton LJ in that case: but he put that to one side in reaching his decision because it had played no part in the submissions to the court.

Although this has not been spelt out in s 8(3), the same approach applies, by direct analogy, where the benefit of a contract has been assigned to a third party. This may be illustrated as follows:

Example 18

A time-charters a ship from B. B assigns its right to hire to C. A makes an advance payment of hire to C for a period when, as it transpires, the ship is off-hire. A subsequently terminates the contract with B for B's repudiatory breach in failing to repair the ship. Although A's advance payment of hire to C was made for a consideration that has failed, A has no right to restitution of that advance payment from C. Under the contract between A and B, B required the payment to be made and C's enrichment is therefore at the expense of B not A. (This fact-situation is exemplified by *Pan Ocean Shipping Co Ltd v Creditcorp Ltd, The Trident Beauty* [1994] 1 WLR 161, HL.)

8(4)

There are no clear authorities in English law establishing that, even if the benefit obtained by the defendant is directly from the claimant, the enrichment is not at the expense of the claimant if the benefit is merely incidental in the sense that the claimant has an objective unconnected with the defendant's enrichment. Moreover, the examples in mind are usually ones where there is, in any event, no injustice (ie no 'unjust factor'). Nevertheless the concept of an 'incidental benefit' does seem the best explanation for a range of situations where one would wish to deny restitution: for discussion, see, eg, Birks, *Unjust Enrichment* (2nd edn, 2005) 158–60, Edelman and Bant, *Unjust Enrichment in Australia* (2006) 160–1.

Example 19

C cuts down trees on his land. This improves the view from his neighbour's, D's, land. Assuming D is enriched (eg by selling his land at a higher price because of the enhanced view) C is not entitled to restitution from D. This may be because there is no unjust factor. Even if there is (say, for example, C cut down the trees mistakenly thinking that they had 'Dutch Elm disease') C has no right to restitution from D because the benefit is merely incidental to C cutting down the trees for his own reasons. (This is based on the hypothetical example given in *Ruabon Steamship Co v London Assurance* [1900] AC 6 at 10, HL.)

At the claimant's expense: general

Example 20

C drains her land. This has the effect of also draining and improving her neighbour, D's, land. Assuming D is enriched, C is not entitled to restitution from D. Even if there is an unjust factor (say, for example, C was induced by the duress of a third party to drain the land), C is still not entitled to restitution because the benefit is merely incidental to C draining her own land. (This is based on the US case of *Ulmer v Farnsworth* 15 A 65 (1888).)

Example 21

C heats her own flat. This has the effect of also heating the upstairs flat of D. Assuming that D is enriched, C is not entitled to restitution from D. Even if there is an unjust factor (say, for example, C mistakenly thought that the heating was free and would not otherwise have switched it on), C is still not entitled to restitution because the benefit is merely incidental to C heating her own flat. (This is the example discussed by Birks, *Unjust Enrichment* (2nd edn, 2005) 158–60.)

Example 22

C runs horse races on its land. Spectators pay C to watch. D's house overlooks the racecourse and he enjoys watching the races without paying C. C is not entitled to restitution from D even if D is enriched and even if there is an unjust factor. This is because the benefit is merely incidental to C organising the races for the paying spectators.

It would appear that an exception to an 'incidental benefit' not being at the expense of the claimant is in some situations where C discharges the defendant's legal liability by payment to X or, more rarely, by the doing of work for X. The discharge of another's liability may be the relevant benefit for the purposes of restitution for unjust enrichment. While in most circumstances one would not describe that benefit as incidental, because it is precisely what was intended by the claimant, it appears that it is not excluded even where it is an unintended incidental benefit. Discharge of another's legal liability is primarily dealt with in s 18, where the discharge is made under legal compulsion (although another unjust factor, such as mistake, might conceivably be in play).

Example 23

C, under legal compulsion, pays off a liability it owes to X (in tort). Unknown to C, D was also liable to X for the same damage. C is entitled to contribution from D (best rationalised as within the law of unjust enrichment), even though D's benefit (in having its liability discharged) is incidental to C paying off its own liability to X.

9 At the claimant's expense: tracing

(1) The defendant's enrichment is at the claimant's expense if—
　(a) the benefit obtained by the defendant is an asset ("the substitute asset") which under the tracing rules is treated as being the substitute for another asset ("the original asset"), and
　(b) immediately before the first transaction to which the tracing rules are being applied—
　　(i) the claimant had a better right to the original asset than any person (whether or not the defendant) who was a party to that transaction, or
　　(ii) the original asset was held on trust for the claimant.
(2) For the purposes of subsection (1), "the tracing rules" means the rules set out below.
(3) One asset is treated as the substitute for another asset if—
　(a) it is not a mixed asset, and
　(b) under any transaction it was substituted for that other asset.
(4) An asset is a mixed asset if assets from more than one person have contributed to it.
(5) Subject to subsections (6) and (7), in the case of a mixed asset the proportionate share of the mixed asset is treated as the substitute for the contributing asset of the contributor.
(6) If—
　(a) the contribution was made by a person in breach of a fiduciary or other duty, and
　(b) part of the mixed asset has been dissipated by that person so that the mixed asset has declined in value,
　that decline in value is treated as borne first by that person.
(7) If there has been an additional contribution to a mixed asset, the substitute asset in respect of contributions prior to that additional contribution cannot be treated as exceeding the value of the mixed asset prior to the additional contribution.

9(1)

The difficult idea of 'tracing' is best understood as the legal process by which one asset is identified as being a *substitute* for another asset. Lord Millett in *Foskett v McKeown* [2001] 1 AC 102 at 127–8 accepted the persuasive arguments of Lionel Smith, *The Law of Tracing* (1997) that, contrary to how it has often been perceived, tracing should be distinguished from 'following' and 'claiming'. In Lord Millett's words, at 127, 'Following is the process of following the same asset as it moves from hand to hand. Tracing is the process of identifying a new asset as the substitute for the old.... Tracing is also distinct from claiming.... It enables the claimant to substitute the traceable proceeds for the original asset as the subject matter of his claim. But it does not affect or establish his claim.' Those two distinctions can be illustrated as follows:

Example 1

B steals A's bicycle and gives it to C and C gives it to D. If A asserts his rights to the bicycle in D's hands, that is by a process of 'following'. It does not involve tracing.

Example 2

A gives B £250 as a birthday gift, which B uses to buy a painting which she hangs on her wall. In principle, A can trace the £250 to the painting, but that tracing does not establish a claim against B. On the contrary, A plainly has no right to the painting or its value.

Does tracing have anything to do with unjust enrichment? Many commentators have argued that, where the substitution is unauthorised, it does; and there is strong support for this in the reasoning of the House of Lords in *Lipkin Gorman v Karpnale Ltd* [1991] 2 AC 548, which involved common law tracing leading to a monetary restitutionary award in favour of the claimant solicitors for value received by the defendant club (subject to the club's partial defence of change of position). The reasoning was that that restitution was based on the unjust enrichment of the club at the expense of the solicitors. The solicitors' chose in action comprising their in-credit client account was traced to the cash drawn out by one of the partners (Cass) and paid to the club. Unfortunately, this appears to clash with the reasoning of the House of Lords in *Foskett v McKeown* [2001] 1 AC 102. Trust money was there used, in breach of trust, to pay off some life-insurance premiums. The beneficiaries were held to be entitled to a proportionate beneficial interest in a trust of the £1m insurance proceeds that was imposed after equitable tracing. Their Lordships said that the claim was based on 'vindicating property rights' not reversing unjust enrichment. With respect, this is a false dichotomy in this context, and 'vindicating property rights' provides no explanation in itself for why a new right in property was created after the tracing. It should be noted, in particular, that it is unsatisfactory to say that the same right to the original asset carries on through to the substitute asset as if 'hoovering up' all substitutes. This is what Birks criticised as the 'fiction of persistence': see Birks, *Unjust Enrichment* (2nd edn, 2005) 35. A new right is created in respect of the traced asset and one needs an explanation for that: where the substitution is unauthorised, unjust enrichment can provide that explanation.

Commentary: Part 2

In the light of the apparent clash of reasoning between *Lipkin Gorman* and *Foskett*, and given the persuasive criticisms by Birks and others of their Lordships' reasoning in *Foskett*, the approach taken in the Restatement is that one acceptable analysis of restitution after unauthorised substitution is that it is based on unjust enrichment. (See also Mitchell, Mitchell, and Watterson (eds), *Goff and Jones on the Law of Unjust Enrichment* (8th edn, 2011) para 7-06 and ch 8.) While it should be stressed that, in the light of the reasoning in *Foskett*, that analysis is plainly controversial (and it was rejected as not representing the present law in *Armstrong DLW GmbH v Winnington Networks Ltd* [2012] EWHC 10 (Ch), [2012] 3 All ER 425, esp at [62]–[98]), it would stunt the explanatory force of unjust enrichment (and hence of this Restatement) if one were not to deal with rights created after unauthorised substitution. Tracing shows that the defendant obtained an asset that is a *substitute* (s 9(1)(a)) for an asset that 'belonged' to the claimant immediately prior to the first substitution (see s 9(1)(b)). So at the start of the tracing exercise (albeit not at every interim stage) the relevant asset must 'belong' to the claimant. Applying an unjust enrichment analysis, tracing is concerned to establish that the defendant's enrichment, through the substitute asset, has been *at the claimant's expense*. This is because the substitute asset, rather than the original asset, can be treated as being obtained from, and directly from, the claimant (see s 8(1)). This may give the claimant a higher value claim against the defendant (as illustrated by Example 3 below) or may allow the claimant a claim against an indirect recipient (as illustrated by *Lipkin Gorman* and by Example 4 below).

Example 3

C mistakenly transfers a ring, as a gift, to D. The mistake is fundamental so that title in the ring does not pass to D. The ring is valued at £1,000. D sells the ring to X for twice its market value (ie £2,000 cash). Assuming C has a claim against D for restitution of an unjust enrichment (without relying on the tort of conversion), C is entitled to restitution of £2,000. The £2,000 is the substitute asset and, as C had title to the ring immediately prior to its being substituted by the £2,000 (see s 9(1)(b)), C has obtained the £2,000 at the expense of C. Without being able to rely on tracing, restitution would be limited to £1,000 as being the benefit obtained by D from C.

Example 4

C mistakenly transfers a ring, as a gift, to X. The mistake is fundamental so that title in the ring does not pass to X. X exchanges the ring with Y for a watch, which X then gives to D. Assuming C has a claim against D for restitution of an unjust enrichment, C is entitled to restitution of the value of (or the right to) the watch. The watch is the traced asset. Applying s 9(1)(b), C had title to the ring immediately prior to its being substituted by the watch. The watch has been obtained by D at the expense of C. Without tracing, C would be limited to a claim against X or Y.

Although it has been thought unnecessary to spell this out explicitly in the Restatement (although it is implicit in the reference to 'first' transaction in s 9(1)(b)), the same principles apply to a series of substitutions.

The Restatement has steered clear of elaborating what it is that is being traced in the context of unjust enrichment. The view put forward by Lionel Smith, *The Law of Tracing* (1997) at 119–20 is that one is tracing value. That is probably the best view; but there is another view (see, eg, McFarlane, *The Structure of Property Law* (2008) 324–25) that one is tracing rights.

9(2)

This explains that s 9(3)–(7) lay down the 'tracing rules'. These are the legal rules that determine evidentially whether an asset is a *substitute* for an asset that 'belonged' to the claimant. Once one sees that these are evidential rules, there can be no rational reason for having different tracing rules at common law and in equity. That there should be fused rules of tracing is widely accepted by commentators and was accepted in obiter dicta of Lords Steyn and Millett in *Foskett v McKeown* [2001] 1 AC 102 at 113, 128–9. While we cannot yet say that the historical differences between tracing at common law and equity have been authoritatively abolished, the courts seem very close to doing this. The Restatement therefore states the tracing rules without making reference to common law and equity, although that distinction is referred to in the commentary.

9(3)

This is the most straightforward rule. It deals with what Lionel Smith, *The Law of Tracing* (1997), has referred to as a 'clean substitution': ie one where no mixing is involved. Examples of clean substitutions are the exchange of a car for a boat; or a cow for a goat; or £1,000 in cash for a picture. This has traditionally been viewed as the limit of common law tracing. Such tracing has been applied in a number of leading cases including: *Taylor (a firm) v Plumer* (1815) 3 M & S 562; *Banque Belge pour l'Etranger v Hambrouck* [1921] 1 KB 321, CA; *Lipkin Gorman v Karpnale Ltd* [1991] 2 AC 548, HL; and *Trustee of the Property of FC Jones & Sons v Jones* [1997] Ch 159, CA.

9(4)

Section 9(4) defines what is meant by a mixed asset. This sets the scene for s 9(5)–(7), which contain what have traditionally been viewed as the equitable tracing rules (although equity also allows tracing where there is a clean substitution:

Commentary: Part 2

see *Re Hallett's Estate* (1880) 13 Ch D 696 at 709, CA). Traditionally (albeit that there is no justification for this in principle) the equitable tracing rules have been triggered only where the asset sought to be traced was held on trust (or in an analogous fiduciary capacity) for the claimant: *Re Diplock* [1948] Ch 465 at 540, CA; *Agip (Africa) Ltd v Jackson* [1991] Ch 547 at 566, CA; *Boscawen v Bawja* [1996] 1 WLR 328 at 335, CA. The important feature of these equitable tracing rules is that they allow tracing even though mixing is involved: ie there is no clean substitution.

9(5)

The general proportionate sharing rule in s 9(5) is illustrated by *Sinclair v Brougham* [1914] AC 398, HL; *Re Diplock* [1948] Ch 465, CA (as regards, eg, the funds of the Royal Sailors Orphan Girls' School and Home); *Barlow Clowes International v Vaughan* [1992] 4 All ER 22, CA; and *Foskett v McKeown* [2001] 1 AC 102, HL. That general rule can be illustrated as follows:

Example 5

If X has innocently mixed in a deposit account £2,000 of its own money with £1,000 of C's trust money, which has been transferred to X as a result of D's breach of fiduciary duty to C, C can trace to one-third of the mixed fund and X to two-thirds. So if half the mixed fund has been dissipated, and it has therefore declined in value to £1,500, C will be entitled to trace to £500 of the fund and X to £1,000. If the fund has doubled in value to £6,000 (eg by the purchase of shares that have been sold) C will be entitled to trace to £2,000 of the fund and X to £4,000.

A 'first-in first-out' rule (which is a rule of banking accounting laid down in *Clayton's Case* (1816) 1 Mer 572) used to be applied where the mixed fund was in a current bank account: see, eg, *Re Diplock* [1948] Ch 465, CA (as regards the funds of, eg, Dr Barnardo's Homes). But that rule of accounting is inappropriate for tracing and, in the modern cases, it is not applied (see, eg, *Barlow Clowes International Ltd v Vaughan* [1992] 4 All ER 22, CA; *Russell-Cooke Trust Co v Prentis* [2002] EWHC 2227 (Ch), [2003] 2 All ER 478; *Commerzbank Aktiengesellschaft v IMB Morgan plc* [2004] EWHC 2771 (Ch), [2005] 2 All ER (Comm) 564). Although those cases have not abolished the 'first-in, first-out' rule, the Restatement reflects the principled view, supported by the tenor of those cases, that the 'first-in, first-out' rule is no longer applicable as a tracing rule.

9(6)

The exception to proportionate sharing in s 9(6) is established by *Re Hallett's Estate* (1880) 13 Ch D 696, CA, and *Re Oatway* [1903] 2 Ch 356. It can be illustrated as follows:

Example 6

A mixed fund in a deposit account is made up of £1,000 of C's (an innocent party's) money and £2,000 of D's money which has been mixed by D in breach of fiduciary duty to C. D dissipates £900 so that the value of the fund falls to £2,100. C can trace to £1,000 (and has the right to an equitable lien over the fund to secure an award of £1,000), rather than being confined to a proportionate share (one-third) of the £2,100.

It has been pointed out above that the Restatement sets out the rules on tracing without reference to common law and equity. The major practical consequence of accepting fused rules of tracing is that they allow a common law 'owner' to trace through mixtures (and to have equitable rights in relation to the mixed 'fund'). Drawing on both s 9(5) and (6), this may be illustrated as follows:

Example 7

A thief steals £1,000 of C's money, mixes it with £2,000 of her own, and buys a car. If the car is worth £6,000, C can trace to one-third of the car and the thief to two-thirds (with the appropriate rights being a proportionate share of the car, in the proportions of one-third and two-thirds, under a trust). If the car is worth only £2,000, the loss is first borne by the thief, so that C can trace to £1,000 (and has the right to an equitable lien over the car to secure an award of £1,000).

9(7)

This sets out what is often referred to as the 'lowest intermediate balance' rule. See, eg, *Roscoe (James) (Bolton) Ltd v Winder* [1915] 1 Ch 62; *Re Goldcorp Exchange Ltd* [1995] 1 AC 74, PC; *Bishopsgate Investment Management Ltd v Homan* [1995] Ch 211, CA.

Example 8

D misappropriates £450 of C's money and pays it into his own account, where he mixes it with £100 of his own money. He then dissipates all but £25 of the mixed fund before mixing more of his own money so that the balance stands at £350. C can trace through to only £25. (This is based on *Roscoe v Winder*).

This rule also covers the situation where the mixed asset has ceased to exist altogether (ie the mixed fund has been 'exhausted') so that there is no asset that can be treated as the substitute asset in respect of contributions prior to the additional contribution.

Although unprincipled, and not reflected in the Restatement, it should be noted that where there have been many payments in and out of a mixed fund comprising the money of many innocent parties, the courts have occasionally side-stepped the lowest intermediate balance rule in favour of proportionate sharing of the surviving fund: see, eg, *Barlow Clowes International Ltd v Vaughan* [1992] 4 All ER 22, CA.

The Restatement implicitly assumes that the tracing exercise goes forward from one asset to its substitute. Although highly controversial, there is obiter dicta supporting the idea of 'backward tracing': see Dillon LJ in *Bishopsgate Investment Management Ltd v Homan* [1995] Ch 211 at 216–17 (but see the apparently contrary view of Leggatt LJ at 222); *Shalson v Russo* [2003] EWHC 1637 (Ch), [2005] Ch 281 at [141]. This occurs where there is a clear causal link between money paid into an exhausted fund and assets purchased from that fund, albeit prior to the money being paid in. The idea is supported by Lionel Smith 'Tracing into the Payment of a Debt' [1995] CLJ 290, who argues that it explains how one can trace into the discharge of a debt.

Example 9

A thief buys a car on credit for £10,000 and the next day steals £10,000, which he uses to pay off the debt. Backward tracing would allow the owner of the stolen money to trace to the car.

It should be stressed that backward tracing requires a clear connection between the discharged debt and a particular asset. It misses the point to fear backward tracing on the ground that it allows a claimant to trace back to any assets previously acquired by the defendant.

However, against backward tracing, one might argue that it is supported only by obiter dicta, that there is no compelling reason of justice or policy to allow it, and that, given that tracing forwards is itself not an easy concept to explain, one ought to be cautious about extending it still further. At this stage in the development of the law, it has therefore been thought better for the Restatement not to include the idea of backward tracing. See also rejecting backward tracing, Conaglen, 'Difficulties with Tracing Backwards' (2011) 127 LQR 432. (For the controversial view that *Foskett v McKeown* [2001] 1 AC 102 is itself authority for backward tracing, albeit that none of their Lordships adverted to this, see Penner, 'Value, Property, and Unjust Enrichment: Trusts of Traceable Proceeds' in Chambers, Mitchell, and Penner (eds), *Philosophical Foundations of the Law of Unjust Enrichment* (2009) 306, 321: with respect, the substitute asset in mind was surely the £1m insurance pay-out on death, which did not exist prior to the payment of the premiums so that the tracing can be seen as straightforwardly going forwards from the premiums paid to the pay-out.)

PART 3
WHEN THE ENRICHMENT IS UNJUST

10 Mistake
(1) Subject to subsections (4) to (7), the defendant's enrichment is unjust if it is caused by a mistake of fact or law made by the claimant.
(2) For the purposes of subsection (1)—
  (a) the standard test of causation is the "but for" test which requires that the defendant would not have been enriched but for the mistake, but
  (b) there are exceptions to the "but for" test where—
   (i) mistake and another unjust factor were each independently sufficient to bring about the enrichment;
   (ii) the mistake was induced by a fraudulent misrepresentation, in which case the mistaken belief need merely have been a reason or present in the claimant's mind.
(3) The defendant's enrichment may be unjust under subsection (1) even though the claimant's conduct was negligent.
(4) If the enrichment is a gift—
  (a) there may be a rule that for the enrichment to be unjust, the mistake, if not induced by a misrepresentation, must be serious (as well as causing the enrichment), and
  (b) a mistake of law as to the tax consequences of the gift does not in itself render the enrichment unjust.
(5) The enrichment is not unjust if the claimant takes the risk that a mistake is being made; and the claimant is to be treated as having taken that risk if—
  (a) the mistake consists of the claimant's false prediction as to the future, or
  (b) the claimant is aware that a mistake is probably being made or recklessly fails to establish the truth.
(6) In general, mistake does not render the enrichment unjust if the benefit was owed to the defendant by the claimant under a valid contractual, statutory or other legal obligation.
(7) In the case of a mistake induced by a misrepresentation, the misrepresentation may be made by a person other than the defendant; but, if the claimant has entered into a contract because of the misrepresentation, the enrichment is unjust only if—
  (a) that other person was acting as the defendant's agent, or
  (b) the defendant had actual notice of the misrepresentation, or
  (c) the defendant had constructive notice of the misrepresentation under section 22.

Commentary: Part 3

10(1)

A mistaken payment is the central example of an unjust enrichment. There have been many cases on the restitution of payments made by mistake. Leading examples include *Kelly v Solari* (1841) 9 M & W 54; *Barclays Bank Ltd v WJ Simms, Son and Cooke (Southern) Ltd* [1980] QB 677; *Kleinwort Benson Ltd v Lincoln CC* [1999] 2 AC 349, HL; and, as regards the mistaken payment of advance corporation tax (with the restitution comprising the award of interest because the advance corporation tax had subsequently been set off against mainstream corporation tax), *Deutsche Morgan Grenfell Group plc v IRC* [2006] UKHL 49, [2007] 1 AC 558 and *Sempra Metals Ltd v IRC* [2007] UKHL 34, [2008] 1 AC 561. The same principles also apply to the restitution of non-money benefits rendered by mistake as shown by, eg, *Greenwood v Bennett* [1973] QB 195, CA (mistaken improvement of a car) and *Cressman v Coys of Kensington (Sales) Ltd* [2004] EWCA Civ 47, [2004] 1 WLR 2775 (mistaken transfer of personalised number plate). See also Torts (Interference with Goods) Act 1977, s 6(1), recognising an allowance for a mistaken improver of goods who is liable in damages for the tort of conversion.

The old law that the mistake had to be one of fact not law was departed from in *Kleinwort Benson Ltd v Lincoln CC* [1999] 2 AC 349, HL.

It was also at one time thought that, at least as regards payments, the mistake had to be one as to 'supposed liability' (ie on the facts, as the claimant mistakenly thought them to be, the claimant would have been under a present legal liability to pay the defendant). That was departed from, in favour of causation alone, in *Barclays Bank Ltd v WJ Simms* [1980] QB 677. The causation approach in *Simms* was approved and applied in *Lloyds Bank plc v Independent Insurance Co Ltd* [2000] QB 110, CA, and *Deutsche Morgan Grenfell Group plc v Inland Revenue Commissioners* [2006] UKHL 49, [2007] 1 AC 558.

It should be noted that a mistake can be active or tacit (ie the incorrect facts may, or may not, be actively present in the claimant's mind). This may be illustrated as follows:

Example 1

C intends to pay X £1,000 but by a mistake of identity pays D £1,000. It never crosses C's mind that D is not in fact X. C has a right to restitution for mistake, albeit that, arguably, C's mistake was tacit, not active.

10(2)(a)

Several cases have applied a 'but for' causation test in respect of mistaken payments. See, eg, *Kleinwort Benson Ltd v Lincoln CC* [1999] 2 AC 349, HL; *Deutsche Morgan Grenfell Group plc v IRC* [2006] UKHL 49, [2007] 1 AC 558; and, as regards

Mistake

a mistaken gift, *Re Griffiths* [2008] EWHC 118 (Ch), [2009] Ch 162 at [26]–[27] (but on gifts, see s 10(4) below).

10(2)(b)(i)

Although there appears to have been no example of this in the case law, it must be correct that, where there is another sufficient unjust factor, the 'but for' test of causation is displaced. This is illustrated by the following:

Example 2

C pays D £1,000 in a situation where C mistakenly believes that it owes D that money and where D has (illegitimately) threatened to break another contract it has with C unless C pays it that money. The mistake and the illegitimate threat would each have been sufficient alone to induce C's payment. C will be entitled to restitution of the £1,000 on the ground of mistake (and/or on the ground of economic duress) even though the £1,000 would have been paid irrespective of the mistake (ie the 'but for' test cannot be satisfied) because of the duress.

10(2)(b)(ii)

It is well established in respect of fraudulent misrepresentation that, irrespective of whether the 'but for' test can be satisfied, there is a sufficient causal link if the misrepresentation was 'a reason' or 'present in the claimant's mind': see, eg, *Edgington v Fitzmaurice* (1885) 29 Ch D 459, CA (although note that that was not a claim for restitution but rather for damages for the tort of deceit). An analogy can here be drawn with the acceptance of that wider test for physical duress in *Barton v Armstrong* [1976] AC 104, PC (see s 11(5)(b)(ii) below). It may be that the burden of proof in respect of that wider test lies on the defendant: see, eg, *Barton v County Natwest Ltd* [1999] Lloyd's Rep Bank 408, CA (fraudulent misrepresentation).

10(3)

It was established in *Kelly v Solari* (1841) 9 M & W 54, and can be seen from many of the leading cases (eg *Barclays Bank Ltd v WJ Simms* [1980] QB 677; *Cressman v Coys of Kensington (Sales) Ltd* [2004] EWCA Civ 47, [2004] 1 WLR 2775), that carelessness/negligence in mistakenly paying the defendant or rendering a non-money benefit is not a bar to restitution for mistake. Note, however, that recklessness may mean that the claimant falls foul of the 'risk-taking' bar in s 10(5).

10(4)(a)

A controversial and much debated issue is whether the *Barclays Bank Ltd v WJ Simms* approach, of it being sufficient that the mistake is causative, applies to mistaken gifts (even ignoring, as outside the law of unjust enrichment, mistakes in making a will: see the commentary under s 1(5) above). The language of the equity cases on the rescission of gifts for mistake is that the mistake of fact must be serious or basic to the transaction: *Ogilvie v Littleboy* (1987) 13 TLR 399, CA; affd (1899) 15 TLR 294, HL; *Lady Hood of Avalon v Mackinnon* [1909] 1 Ch 476; *Pitt v Holt* [2011] EWCA Civ 197, [2012] Ch 132 (see also obiter dicta of Lord Scott in *Deutsche Morgan Grenfell Group plc v Inland Revenue Commissioners* [2006] UKHL 49, [2007] 1 AC 558 at [87] referring to an example (Example 4 below).

Consider the following examples:

Example 3

C makes a gift of £10,000 to D on the occasion of D's engagement to C's daughter, not realising that D is an evil and violent fraudster, intent on destroying the life of C's daughter.

Example 4

C makes a gift of £1,000 to D, mistakenly believing that D is impecunious, whereas D is in fact a person of substantial wealth.

Example 5

C, a charterer, to maintain the goodwill of D, the shipowner, when the currency of payment has depreciated, increases his monthly hire payments to D. C then finds out that D is an enemy of a close relative of his. C would not have paid the extra had he known this.

Example 6

C, a Lloyd's syndicate, makes payments to another syndicate, D, which is in financial difficulties, in order to maintain the reputation of Lloyd's. C then finds out that it has overestimated its own financial position. C would not have paid had it known the truth.

Example 7

C makes a donation to D, the Red Cross, in the mistaken belief that the mayor and vicar have made donations too.

Example 8

C gives money to D, the Friends of the Earth, not knowing that they are opposed to an additional runway at Heathrow, which C supports.

On one view, even if 'but for' causation is satisfied in all those examples, there should be no right to restitution. Rather one needs, in the context of gifts (not induced by misrepresentation), an extra element of seriousness, otherwise it would be too easy for donors to unwind gifts. But it is very difficult to articulate what that added element of seriousness is meant to be. It is also not clear why one should fear the unwinding of gifts given that the donor would need to satisfy a court that he or she has made a causative mistake and is not merely changing his or her mind and given that change of position protects the defendant against detrimental reliance on the gift. The alternative view, therefore, is that 'but for' causation should suffice. That latter view derives some support from *Re Griffiths* [2008] EWHC 118 (Ch), [2009] Ch 162 at [26]-[27], although the decision in that case was subsequently criticised in *Pitt v Holt* [2011] EWCA Civ 197, [2012] Ch 132. That the latter might be the better view is left open in the Restatement by phrasing the need for an added element of seriousness somewhat tentatively ('there may be a rule that...').

10(4)(b)

It has now been established in *Pitt v Holt* [2011] EWCA Civ 197, [2012] Ch 132, that a mistake of law as to the consequences, rather than the effect, of a gift does not count; and, although that distinction can be elusive, it was clearly laid down that a mistake as to the tax consequences of a gift does not in itself give a right to restitution. Although that was a decision in relation to the rescission of a voluntary settlement in equity, there is no reason why it should not apply to gifts generally.

10(5)

This bar to restitution where the claimant has taken the risk of being mistaken appears to be what Robert Goff J had in mind in *Barclays Bank Ltd v WJ Simms* [1980] QB 677 at 695 when, in reliance on a dictum in *Kelly v Solari* (1841) 9 M & W 54 at 59, he said that a mistaken payor's claim may fail 'if...the payor intends that the payee shall have the money at all events whether the fact be true or false, or is deemed in law so to intend...'.

As made clear in s 10(5)(a), a misprediction, which is a mistake as to the future and involves taking the risk of being incorrect, does not in itself trigger restitution for mistake (although it may be that there is a different unjust factor in play, eg, failure of consideration): see *Dextra Bank & Trust Co Ltd v Bank of Jamaica* [2002] 1 All ER (Comm) 193, PC. (As an alternative way to reach the same result, some might say that, by definition, a mistake operates only as regards the present or the past.) See also, although not using the language of misprediction, the denial of restitution for the first two gifts in *Re Griffiths* [2008] EWHC 118 (Ch), [2009] Ch 162 (the deceased mistakenly thought—mispredicted—that he would live for more than seven years). In *Pitt v Holt* [2011] EWCA Civ 197, [2012] Ch 132, Lloyd LJ thought that *Re Griffiths* was incorrectly decided as regards the third gift, when unknown to the donor he had cancer, because the donor had also made that gift having taken the risk that he might not survive seven years.

Example 9

C pays D £100 in the belief that D is about to win the Booker Prize. C is not entitled to restitution when D does not win that prize. This is because C made a misprediction.

As regards s 10(5)(b), it is not clear from the case law what degree of doubt or suspicion as to the true facts or law rules out restitution for mistake. That some degree of doubt is compatible with a mistake claim was clarified by Lord Hoffmann (with a quiz contestant example) and by Lord Hope in *Deutsche Morgan Grenfell Group plc v Inland Revenue Commissioners* [2006] UKHL 49, [2007] 1 AC 558 at [26] and [65]. The Restatement takes the line (which derives some support from Flaux J in *Marine Trade SA v Pioneer Freight Futures Co Ltd BVI* [2009] EWHC 2656 (Comm), [2010] 1 Lloyd's Rep 631 at [76]–[77]) that the claimant should not be entitled to restitution where aware that he or she is probably making a mistake.

Although there is no direct authority supporting this, it would seem appropriate for restitution to be denied in the closely linked situation of the claimant recklessly failing to check the facts or law. This is embodied in s 10(5)(b).

Example 10

C pays D £10,000 under an insurance policy because, although it has strong doubts about this, it believes that the goods insured have been lost at sea. It subsequently comes to light that they have in fact been lost prior to loading and are therefore not covered by the insurance. C will not be entitled to restitution for mistake if one takes the view that C paid, taking the risk that it was mistaken. To establish that C was disqualified by being a risk-taker in this example one would need to establish that C paid either when aware that it was probably making a mistake or because it recklessly chose not to investigate the true facts.

A degree of flexibility is maintained in the Restatement because s 10(5) gives examples of risk-taking leading to a denial of restitution rather than defining what risk-taking here means. Although there is a danger of the language of 'risk-taking' being elusive and conclusionary, it is believed that this approach of specifying the main examples (in s 10(5)(a) and (b)) avoids undesirable uncertainty. In so far as a court goes beyond those examples, it is incumbent on it to explain precisely why the claimant is regarded as taking a risk that rules out restitution for mistake.

Mistake

10(6)

This has been discussed generally in the commentary on s 3(6) above. The examples there given of where restitution would be denied (Examples 1–5) exemplify mistaken payments where the mistake does not override the existence of a valid contractual or statutory obligation entitling the defendant to the payment. That this is the *general* position, and that there can be exceptions in mistake cases, is exemplified by the first two examples (Examples 6–7) in the second set of examples.

10(7)

Restitution in three-party cases—typically involving a contract of suretyship between a wife and a bank under which the wife guarantees the debts of her husband or his company—usually rests on undue influence exerted by the third party (eg the husband) rather than misrepresentation. However, in principle the same law should apply to a misrepresentation by the third party and one of the leading cases, *Barclays Bank plc v O'Brien* [1994] 1 AC 180, HL, did concern misrepresentation by the husband to the wife. In addition to agency, the concept of notice was accepted in *O'Brien*. It was subsequently elaborated on in *Royal Bank of Scotland v Etridge (No 2)* [2001] UKHL 44, [2002] 2 AC 773, which is best interpreted as applying constructive, as opposed to actual, notice only to non-commercial guarantees: see ss 12(7) and 22 below. It should be noted, however, that the application of even actual notice in three-party misrepresentation cases appears to produce an unresolved conflict with the rules on non-induced mistake (see, eg, *Smith v Hughes* (1867) LR 6 QB 597), where knowledge of the other party's mistake is irrelevant in deciding whether the contract is valid despite the mistake: see Cartwright, *Misrepresentation, Mistake and Non-Disclosure* (3rd edn, 2011) paras 4.72–4.78.

Example 11

X induces C to enter into a contract for the purchase of goods from D by a misrepresentation as to the quality of the goods. C can rescind the contract with D, and recover the purchase price paid, if D has actual notice of X's misrepresentation to C.

The requirement of notice (or agency) applies only where there is a contract between C and D. If a third party by misrepresentation induces C to make a gift to D, C is straightforwardly entitled to restitution from D: ie D's restitutionary liability is, as usual, strict. The added requirement of notice is therefore designed to ensure that a contract is less easy to unwind for a third party's misrepresentation than a gift.

11 Duress

(1) The defendant's enrichment is unjust if the claimant has enriched the defendant because of an illegitimate threat ("duress").

(2) The illegitimate threat may be express or implied.

(3) For this purpose a threat—
   (a) is illegitimate if the conduct threatened is unlawful (as in the case of a threat to the person or to goods);
   (b) may in some circumstances be illegitimate even though the conduct threatened is lawful (as in the case of a threat to prosecute, or expose the truth about, the claimant or a member of the claimant's family).

(4) But if the illegitimate threat is a threat to break a contract, the defendant's enrichment is unjust only if the claimant had no reasonable alternative to giving in to the threat.

(5) For the purposes of subsection (1)—
   (a) the standard test of causation is the "but for" test which requires that the defendant would not have been enriched but for the illegitimate threat, but
   (b) there are exceptions to the "but for" test where—
       (i) duress and another unjust factor were each independently sufficient to bring about the enrichment;
       (ii) the threat was to the person in which case the threat must merely have been a reason or present in the claimant's mind.

(6) In general, duress does not render the enrichment unjust if the benefit was owed to the defendant by the claimant under a valid contractual, statutory or other legal obligation.

(7) The illegitimate threat may be made by a person other than the defendant; but if the claimant has entered into a contract because of the threat, the enrichment is unjust only if—
   (a) that other person was acting as the defendant's agent, or
   (b) the defendant had actual notice of the threat, or
   (c) the defendant had constructive notice of the threat under section 22.

11(1)

The enrichment in nearly all the reported English duress cases has been the payment of money. In principle the same approach should apply to benefits in kind rendered under duress (eg D holds a gun to the head of C and demands work) provided that the defendant's enrichment can be established.

That there are two essential elements of duress—first an illegitimate threat which, secondly, causes the payment (or the rendering of the benefit in kind)—was established in the two leading cases: *Universe Tankships Inc of Monrovia v International Transport Workers' Federation, The Universe Sentinel* [1983] 1 AC 366, HL; *Dimskal Shipping Co SA v International Transport Workers' Federation, The Evia Luck (No 2)* [1992] 2 AC 152, HL.

11(2)

The perhaps obvious point that the threat may be express or implied was made clear by Lord Goff in *Woolwich Equitable Building Society v IRC* [1993] AC 70 at 165: 'In cases of compulsion, a threat which constitutes the compulsion may be expressed or implied....' This is supported by other cases: see, eg, *B & S Contracts and Design Ltd v Victor Green Publications Ltd* [1984] ICR 419, CA ('veiled threat'); and *The Alev* [1989] 1 Lloyd's Rep 138 at 142, 145.

11(3)(a)

What is meant by an illegitimate threat? The main traditional categories were duress of the person, where the illegitimate threat was of violence to the claimant or the claimant's family, as in *Barton v Armstrong* [1976] AC 104, PC; and duress of goods, where the illegitimate threat was to seize, or to refuse to return, the claimant's goods, as in *Astley v Reynolds* (1731) 2 Stra 915 and *Maskell v Horner* [1915] 3 KB 106, CA. In these traditional categories the conduct that is threatened is a tort (eg trespass to the person or to goods). The same can be said of the two leading cases on economic duress, *The Universe Sentinel* and *The Evia Luck (No 2)*, in which the threatened tort was to induce another to break a contract by the unlawful 'blacking' of a ship. Most of the cases on the modern doctrine of economic duress have involved the threat to break a contract which is, again, a civil wrong. It would seem therefore that all threats to commit a civil wrong (whether a tort or equitable wrong or breach of contract) should be treated as illegitimate.

Also within the ambit of 'unlawful act' duress are demands *colore officii* ('under colour of office'). Here what is threatened is a breach of a public duty but not a civil wrong as such (ie the claimant could not sue for loss caused by the breach of duty). It occurs where a public authority demands money under the threat of denying to the claimant something to which he is entitled from the public authority either for nothing or for less than the sum demanded. In practice this category of duress has been entirely subsumed within the wider '*Woolwich* principle' set out in s 21 below. However, a directly analogous type of duress may still be of some practical relevance in the admittedly rare case where a *private body* demands more money than it is entitled to under a statute for providing a service: see *Great Western Rly Co v Sutton* (1869) LR 4 HL 226 (C entitled to restitution where D, a railway company, had refused to carry C's goods unless paid more than the statute permitted).

11(3)(b)

The very language chosen by the courts of the threat needing to be illegitimate (rather than unlawful) suggests that there may be 'lawful act' duress. This is borne out by the case law. A long-established area, although traditionally thought of as within the equitable doctrine of undue influence rather than the common law doctrine of duress (an historical difference that, in this area, we can cut through so as to unite all examples of illegitimate threats: see the commentary to s 12(1)–(2) below), comprised illegitimate threats by, for example, threatening to prosecute or expose the truth about the claimant or a relative of the claimant: see, eg, *Williams v Bayley* (1866) LR 1 HL 200; *Mutual Finance Ltd v John Wetton & Sons Ltd* [1937] 2 KB 389. Again, although rare, it has been accepted that economic duress can extend to threatened lawful acts: *CTN Cash and Carry Ltd v Gallaher Ltd* [1994] 4 All ER 714, CA; *Alf Vaughan & Co Ltd v Royscot Trust plc* [1999] 1 All ER (Comm) 856; *R v A-G for England and Wales* [2003] UKPC 22; *Progress Bulk Carriers Ltd v Tube City IMS LLC* [2012] EWHC 273 (Comm), [2012] 1 Lloyd's Rep 501.

11(4)

The most debated category of duress is the one that has featured in most of the recent cases, namely economic duress by threatened breach of contract. See, eg, *The Siboen and The Sibotre* [1976] 1 Lloyd's Rep 293; *North Ocean Shipping Co Ltd v Hyundai Construction Co Ltd* [1979] QB 705; *Pao On v Lau Yiu Long* [1980] AC 614, PC; *B & S Contracts and Design Ltd v Victor Green Publications Ltd* [1984] ICR 419, CA; *Atlas Express Ltd v Kafco Ltd* [1989] QB 833; *The Alev* [1989] 1 Lloyd's Rep 138; *Huyton SA v Peter Cremer GmbH & Co* [1999] 1 Lloyd's Rep 620; *DSND Subsea Ltd v Petroleum Geo-Services ASA* [2000] BLR 530; *Carillion Construction Ltd v Felix (UK) Ltd* [2001] BLR 1; *Adam Opel GmbH v Mitras Automotive (UK) Ltd* [2007] EWHC 3481 (QB); *Kolmar Group AG v Traxpo Enterprises Pvt Ltd* [2010] EWHC 113 (Comm), [2010] 2 Lloyd's Rep 653. It remains unclear precisely when a threat to break a contract will constitute duress. No single approach can reconcile all the cases. The approach adopted in the Restatement is to say that every threatened breach of contract is illegitimate and that the ambit of economic duress is controlled by causation and by insisting in this context on the additional requirement that the claimant had no reasonable alternative other than giving in to the threat.

That there is that third element for economic duress, in the context of a threatened breach of contract, has been accepted in a number of cases: see especially Dyson J in *DSND Subsea Ltd v Petroleum Geo-Services ASA* [2000] BLR 530 at 545–6. In contrast, it was rejected as irrelevant in the context of duress of goods in *Astley v Reynolds* (1731) 2 Stra 915. Although the Restatement accepts that third requirement in relation to a threatened breach of contract, it is unlikely that it will be of much practical significance because normally there is no reasonable alternative (given the cost and time of legal action). Certainly, there appears to be no reported case in which a claim for duress failed because the claimant was held to have had a reasonable alternative that was not taken.

It would appear that the effect of treating every threatened breach of contract as illegitimate is that one has a wide doctrine of economic duress, which tends to protect the original contract made. If genuine renegotiations are not to be curbed the courts will need to be astute to ensure that a party's genuine warnings as to the difficulties it has in performing are not too readily construed as constituting threats to breach. Under the old law the original contract was protected in a blunt way by the rule that performing, or a promise to perform, one's pre-existing contractual duty was not good consideration for a payment of extra money. That was departed from in *Williams v Roffey Bros & Nicholls (Contractors) Ltd* [1991] 1 QB 1, CA, in favour of an approach that relies on economic duress to draw the line between renegotiations that one wishes to protect and those that should not be upheld.

An alternative approach to that adopted in the Restatement, which does have some attractions, would be to reject the idea that every threatened breach of contract is illegitimate and to develop a narrower test for when a threatened breach of contract is illegitimate. One possible such test (see Birks, *An Introduction to the Law of Restitution* (rvsd edn, 1989) 183) would be whether the threat to break the contract was made in bad faith as being concerned to exploit the claimant's weak position rather than to solve genuine problems in performing of the party making the threat. For support for bad faith as a relevant factor in assessing the illegitimacy of a threatened breach of contract, see Dyson J in *DSND Subsea Ltd v Petroleum Geo-Services ASA* [2000] BLR 530 at 545–6. However, in general the English cases do not appear to have embraced that approach and reliance on 'bad faith' is alien to traditional English commercial law.

Example 1

D is bound by contract to supply potatoes to C's hotel at 30p per pound. At the time that that price was agreed, D could buy in the potatoes at 20p per pound. There has since been a potato blight so that D cannot buy in the potatoes for less than £5 per pound. D tells C that it will be unable to deliver unless C pays £5 per pound and agrees to waive any right to damages. C reluctantly does so as it cannot acquire the potatoes elsewhere but, when normal conditions return, seeks restitution of £4.70 for each pound of potatoes bought from D. C's claim should succeed. There has been economic duress because D threatened a breach of contract which caused C to pay the extra and C had no reasonable alternative. C did not want to renegotiate, as was its right. The original contract is therefore protected by the doctrine of economic duress (as indeed it would have been had C, instead of giving in to the threat, sought damages for breach by D). It is irrelevant that D was not acting in bad faith concerned to exploit C's weakness.

11(5)

To constitute duress, the illegitimate threat must have caused the enrichment: ie the claimant must have enriched the defendant (eg by paying money) because of the illegitimate threat. It would appear that the normal causation test is the 'but for' test (see *Huyton SA v Peter Cremer GmbH* [1999] 1 Lloyd's Rep 620 at 636; *Kolmar Group AG v Traxpo Enterprises Pvt Ltd* [2010] EWHC 113 (Comm), [2010] 2 Lloyd's Rep 653 at [92]) but exceptions to this are where there is more than one unjust factor (see the commentary to s 10(2)(b)(i) Example 2) or where physical duress is in issue, in which case the wider 'a reason' or 'present in the claimant's mind' test applies (*Barton v Armstrong* [1976] AC 104, PC, which also indicated that the burden of proof on this is on the defendant).

Although the language of the claimant's will being overborne has sometimes been used (see Lord Scarman in *Pao On v Lau Yiu Long* [1980] AC 614 at 635, PC) that approach was thought to be unhelpful by Lords Goff and Diplock in *The Evia Luck (No 2)* [1992] 2 AC 152, HL.

11(6)

This general principle has been explained in detail above: see s 3(6). It explains why, where the payment has been made under a contract induced by duress, that contract must first be rescinded before there can be restitution of the payments made by duress. It would appear that there is no difference between the scope of duress for contractual and non-contractual payments (or other benefits).

11(7)

Although there are no reported cases on this, in principle—and by analogy to undue influence—if a third party induces the claimant under duress to pay money to the defendant, the claimant is entitled to restitution from the defendant. This helps to clarify that duress is primarily concerned with the claimant's impaired consent and not with the reprehensible conduct of the defendant. Where a contract is induced by a third party's duress, the rules laid down in *O'Brien* and *Etridge* apply (see s 10 (7) above, and ss 12(7) and 22 below).

Example 2

X threatens C with violence unless C pays D £10,000. C does so. C is entitled to restitution from D for duress (subject to any defences).

12 Undue influence

(1) The defendant's enrichment is unjust if the claimant enriched the defendant while under undue influence.
(2) A claimant is under the undue influence of another person if the claimant's judgement is not free and independent of that person.
(3) There is a rebuttable presumption of undue influence if—
   (a) the claimant was in a relationship of influence with the defendant or another person, and
   (b) the transaction in question was disadvantageous to the claimant in the sense that it was not readily explicable on ordinary motives.
(4) A relationship of influence—
   (a) is to be treated as existing in certain cases (for example, parent and child, solicitor and client, doctor and patient, and spiritual adviser and follower), but
   (b) otherwise must be proved on the facts.
(5) It is for the defendant to rebut the presumption mentioned in subsection (3) by proving that the claimant exercised free and independent judgement.
The defendant may be able to rebut the presumption by showing that the claimant obtained the fully informed and competent independent advice of a qualified person, such as a solicitor.
(6) In general, undue influence does not render the enrichment unjust if the benefit was owed to the defendant by the claimant under a valid contractual, statutory or other legal obligation.
(7) The undue influence may be that of a person other than the defendant; but, if the claimant has entered into a contract under undue influence, the enrichment is unjust only if—
   (a) that other person was acting as the defendant's agent, or
   (b) the defendant had actual notice of the undue influence, or
   (c) the defendant had constructive notice of the undue influence under section 22.

12(1)–12(2)

The enrichment in undue influence cases has generally been the payment of money or the acquisition of a right in property. Almost invariably the enrichment has been conferred under a voidable transaction, whether a contract or gift, which the claimant will be seeking to rescind.

Undue influence in the past embraced illegitimate threats that fell outside the then narrow doctrine of duress. As recognised by many commentators and by some judges (see Lord Nicholls in *Royal Bank of Scotland v Etridge (No 2)* [2001] UKHL

44, [2002] 2 AC 773 at [8]), in the light of the acceptance of economic duress it is rational, in order to avoid an overlap of undue influence and duress, to treat cases on illegitimate threats as examples solely of duress. So if one takes out examples of duress, undue influence is concerned with where, as a result of the relationship between them, one party is in a position to, and does, exercise undue influence over the other. The objection is that, because of the undue influence, the claimant does not exercise a full and free judgement, independent of the other person, in relation to the transaction.

It should be noted that, in contrast to mistake and duress, it would appear that it is not a requirement for undue influence that 'but for' causation is satisfied (see *UCB Corporate Services Ltd v Williams* [2002] EWCA Civ 555, [2003] 1 P & CR 12) and indeed it would be odd to insist even on the influence being 'present in the claimant's mind' or 'a reason' given the likelihood that the claimant is precisely unaware of the influence. It appears to be sufficient that at the time of, and in relation to, the relevant transaction the claimant was under undue influence (not acting with free and independent judgement) and it does not matter that the claimant would have acted in the same way even if not under undue influence.

12(3)

Ever since *Allcard v Skinner* (1887) 36 Ch D 145, CA, undue influence has been divided into two categories: actual and presumed. In *Royal Bank of Scotland v Etridge (No 2)* [2001] UKHL 44, [2002] 2 AC 773, the House of Lords clarified, or redefined, the difference between the categories. Undue influence is a single concept. It does not have two different forms. The presumption of undue influence is an evidential (not a legal) presumption. It follows that the correct analysis of the categories is that they refer to two different ways of *proving* undue influence. Presumed undue influence refers to where the person alleging undue influence relies on an evidential presumption. Actual undue influence refers to where the person alleging undue influence relies on direct proof and does not raise an evidential presumption. Not surprisingly, cases in which a person has sought to establish undue influence (as distinct from duress) by direct proof rather than by relying on an evidential presumption are very rare. In other words, one is almost always concerned with presumed, rather than actual, undue influence.

As the Restatement makes clear, one can manage without the two categories although, not surprisingly, many courts subsequent to *Etridge* have continued to use them. It is for the claimant to prove that the transaction was entered into while he or she was under undue influence but, in some situations, the claimant is assisted by a rebuttable evidential presumption of undue influence which shifts the evidential burden of proof to the other party.

As *Etridge* made clear, there are two requirements for establishing the evidential rebuttable presumption of undue influence; first, as reflected in s 12(3)(a), a

Undue influence

relationship of influence; secondly, as reflected in s 12(3)(b), that the transaction is disadvantageous to the claimant in the sense of being 'not readily explicable on ordinary motives'.

12(4)

The relationship of influence in s 12(3)(a) is most easily made out by showing that the parties were within certain well-established categories of relationship which, by their very nature, involve influence by one over the other. These are relationships in which there is a legal rule (sometimes judicially referred to, in confusing and inappropriate language, as an 'irrebuttable legal presumption') that the relationship is one of influence (but note that this is not a legal rule that there is *undue* influence). Examples of such relationships include parent over child (*Lancashire Loans Ltd v Black* [1934] 1 KB 380, CA), spiritual adviser over follower (*Allcard v Skinner* (1887) 36 Ch D 145, CA), solicitor over client (*Wright v Carter* [1903] 1 Ch 27, CA), or doctor over patient (*Mitchell v Homfray* (1881) 8 QBD 587, CA). Although there has been some doubt over this (perhaps because a breach of fiduciary duty is an equitable wrong so that, irrespective of, and overlapping with, undue influence as a ground for restitution of unjust enrichment, there may be compensatory and restitutionary remedies for the breach of fiduciary duty), it also appears that trustee and beneficiary is such a relationship (*Plowright v Lambert* (1885) 52 LT 646; *Tito v Waddell (No 2)* [1977] Ch 106 at 241). However, a husband and wife relationship is not a relationship of this type (that is, it is not automatically a relationship of influence): *Barclays Bank plc v O'Brien* [1994] 1 AC 180, HL; *Royal Bank of Scotland v Etridge (No 2)* [2001] UKHL 44, [2002] 2 AC 773.

Example 1

C, after spending two years as a novice at a convent run by D, the Mother Superior, joins the convent as a nun. On so doing, she gives all her inherited wealth, worth some £750,000, to D for the sisterhood. C obtains no independent advice. C is entitled to restitution for undue influence. Applying s 12(3) and (4), there is a rebuttable presumption of undue influence by D over C constituted by, first, the relationship of influence as between a spiritual adviser and follower (s 12(4)(a)) and, secondly, the transaction being disadvantageous to C in the sense of not being readily explicable on ordinary motives (s 12(3)(b)). On the face of it, D will not be able to rebut that presumption (under s 12(5)) because C has not obtained any independent advice. (This example is based on *Allcard v Skinner* (1887) 36 Ch D 145.)

Although it is clear that there is the legal rule set out in s 12(4)(a), one may doubt the validity of such a rule. In some, admittedly rare, situations it seems odd to say that the relationship is one of influence (eg where a Supreme Court judge is advised by his solicitor). The Restatement reflects the present law but to regard the fixed relationship as setting up a rebuttable factual presumption of influence would perhaps be preferable to regarding it as a legal rule.

As an alternative to the fixed categories, s 12(4)(b) makes clear that the claimant may be able to establish that, on the facts, there was a relationship in which he or she was under the defendant's or another's influence: *Tate v Williamson* (1866) 2 Ch App 55, CA. In important modern cases a factual relationship of influence has been established between a husband and a wife (*Royal Bank of Scotland v Etridge (No 2)*), between a housekeeper and her elderly charge (*Re Craig* [1971] Ch 95), between a bank and its elderly customer (*Lloyds Bank Ltd v Bundy* [1975] QB 326, CA), between a manager and his pop-singer 'employer' (*O'Sullivan v Management Agency and Music Ltd* [1985] QB 428, CA), between a farm manager and an elderly farm owner (*Goldsworthy v Brickell* [1987] Ch 378, CA) and between an employer and a junior employee (*Crédit Lyonnais Bank Nederland v Burch* [1997] 1 All ER 144, CA).

12(5)

If the two requirements for the evidential rebuttable presumption of undue influence in s 12(3) are established by the claimant, the onus of proof switches to the defendant to rebut the presumption by proving that the claimant exercised free and independent judgement. Although neither necessary nor conclusive, the primary method of rebuttal is to show that the claimant obtained the fully informed and competent independent advice of a qualified person, most obviously a solicitor: *Inche Noriah v Shaik Allie Bin Omar* [1929] AC 127, PC; *Royal Bank of Scotland v Etridge (No 2)* [2001] UKHL 44, [2002] 2 AC 773.

12(6)

This general principle has been explained in detail above: see s 3(6). It explains why, where a payment has been made under a contract induced by undue influence, that contract must first be rescinded before there can be restitution of the payments made under undue influence.

12(7)

If the claimant under the undue influence of a third party is induced to pay money to the defendant, the claimant is entitled to restitution from the defendant. In relation to gifts, this is shown by *Bridgeman v Green* (1757) Wilm 58; and as regards contracts, where an added requirement is that the defendant has notice of the undue influence, this is shown by *Royal Bank of Scotland v Etridge (No 2)* [2001] UKHL 44, [2002] 2 AC 773. That the claim can be brought in this three-party situation helps to clarify that undue influence is primarily concerned with the

Exploitation of weakness

claimant's impaired consent and not with the reprehensible conduct of the defendant.

Although actually concerning misrepresentation by a third party, *Barclays Bank plc v O'Brien* [1994] 1 AC 180, HL, first established that, unless the third party was acting as the defendant's agent (which will be very rare), the relevant concept establishing the liability of the defendant is notice, which at least sometimes can include constructive as well as actual notice. Although the use of constructive notice in this context is controversial it was approved in *Etridge*. What remains unclear is whether *Etridge* is best interpreted as confining the concept of constructive, as opposed to actual, notice to non-commercial guarantees (ie non-commercial contracts of suretyship) only. On the one hand, it can be argued that there is no good reason why those contracts alone should trigger the concept of constructive, rather than actual, notice. On the other hand, one might say (and this is the interpretation favoured in O'Sullivan, Elliott, and Zakrzewski, *The Law of Rescission* (2008) ch 9) that the application of constructive notice, while approved by their Lordships, was being specially fashioned for, and confined to, a non-commercial guarantee, as was in issue in that case. At this stage in the development of the law, the Restatement adopts the latter view so that the general requirement is that there is actual notice. Section 22 below sets out what was laid down as regards constructive notice in *Etridge*.

The need for notice in this three-party situation does not apply to gifts, where strict liability applies: *Bridgeman v Green* (1757) Wilm 58. The added requirement of notice is therefore designed to ensure that a contract is less easy to unwind for a third party's undue influence than a gift.

Example 2

C, under the undue influence of X, pays D (a charity) £10,000. C is entitled to restitution of £10,000 from D (subject to any defences).

13   Exploitation of weakness
(1) The defendant's enrichment is unjust if it is the result of a weakness of the claimant having been exploited by the defendant.
(2) The weakness may be—
   (a) a mental weakness (such as inexperience, confusion because of old age, or emotional strain), or
   (b) the difficult position that the claimant is in.
(3) The claimant's weakness has been exploited by the defendant if—
   (a) the transaction in question was disadvantageous to the claimant in the sense that it was not readily explicable on ordinary motives, and

> (b) the defendant knew of the claimant's weakness and that the terms of the transaction were disadvantageous,
>
> unless the claimant obtained the fully informed and competent independent advice of a qualified person, such as a solicitor.
>
> (4) In general, exploitation of weakness does not render the enrichment unjust if the benefit was owed to the defendant by the claimant under a valid contractual, statutory or other legal obligation.

13(1)

'Exploitation of weakness' is the term that has been chosen as the best description of the principle underpinning both the equitable jurisdiction to set aside 'unconscionable bargains' and the common law jurisdiction to set aside extortionate salvage agreements. Although traditionally confined to contracts, there is no reason why the same principle should not extend to gifts or other transactions (and this derives support from *Louth v Diprose* (1992) 175 CLR 621, High Court of Australia). The enrichment in question has generally been the payment of money or the acquisition of a right in property.

The position on causation for exploitation of weakness is far from clear and no real help is gleaned from the cases. While a 'presence in the mind' or 'a reason' test cannot here be sensibly applied (not least because a mentally weak person may precisely be unaware of the exploitation), one could argue that a 'but for' test should be applied, ie that there is no relevant exploitation of weakness if the claimant would have enriched the defendant irrespective of the defendant's conduct. As against that, one might think that, analogously to undue influence (see s 12 above) and incapacity (see s 14 below), it should be sufficient that, at the time of, and in relation to, the enrichment at the claimant's expense, the claimant had the mental weakness, or was in the difficult position, that the defendant has exploited, ie that it should be sufficient that the claimant enriched the defendant while the claimant's weakness was being exploited by the defendant. This uncertainty on causation is left open in the Restatement by avoiding a reference to any test of causation and by using the general words 'the enrichment... is the result of...' a weakness having been exploited.

13(2)

The types of weakness in past cases can be divided into mental weakness (s 13(2)(a)) and circumstantial weakness (s 13(2)(b)). Examples of the former are: inexperience (as in the 'expectant heir' cases such as *Earl of Aylesford v Morris* (1873) 8 Ch App 484, CA, and the 'poor and ignorant' cases such as *Evans v Llewellin* (1787) 1

Exploitation of weakness

Cox Eq Cas 333; *Fry v Lane* (1888) 40 Ch D 312; and *Creswell v Potter* [1978] 1 WLR 255n); infirmity by reason of old age (as in *Boustany v Pigott* (1995) 69 P & CR 298, PC); and emotional strain (see obiter dicta in *Backhouse v Backhouse* [1978] 1 WLR 243 at 251). A main example of circumstantial weakness is where a person requires salvage, as in the extortionate salvage agreement cases of *The Medina* (1876) 1 PD 272 (affd (1876) 2 PD 5, CA) and *The Port Caledonia and Anna* [1903] P 184.

13(3)

It is not the weakness per se that is unacceptable but rather the exploitation of that weakness. The exploitation has three elements.

First, substantive unfairness (s 13(3)(a)). The need for the terms to be disadvantageous has been expressed in various ways. See, eg, 'an inadequate price' in *O'Rorke v Bolingbroke* (1877) 2 App Cas 814 at 835, HL (per Lord Blackburn); 'a considerable undervalue' in *Fry v Lane* (1888) 40 Ch D 312 at 322 per Kay J. The Restatement uses the reformulation of this idea ('not readily explicable on ordinary motives') that was established in *Royal Bank of Scotland v Etridge (No 2)* [2001] UKHL 44, [2002] 2 AC 773 for the analogous context of undue influence: see above s 12(3)(b).

Secondly, bad faith or reprehensible conduct (s 13(3)(b)). The Restatement has incorporated this idea by requiring that the exploiting party had a blameworthy state of mind in that he or she knew of the claimant's weakness and of the substantive unfairness. Although it is not absolutely clear that this is a requirement, the better view is that it is. Reasoning supporting such a requirement includes that in *O'Rorke v Bolingbroke* (1877) 2 App Cas 814, HL; *Alec Lobb Garages Ltd v Total Oil (GB) Ltd* [1985] 1 WLR 173, CA; and *Portman Building Soc v Dusangh* [2000] 2 All ER (Comm) 221, CA.

Thirdly, no independent advice (the proviso). The importance of independent advice was mentioned in *Fry v Lane* (1888) 40 Ch D 312 at 322 and is consistent with the reasoning and decisions in all the relevant cases. According to the reasoning in several cases, and by analogy to undue influence, it is best to see the evidential burden of proving this to be on the defendant; and the wording here adopted is again taken from *Etridge* (the leading modern case on undue influence).

Assuming that the second of these elements is correct, it marks a significant difference between exploitation of weakness, on the one hand, and duress and undue influence, on the other. Duress and undue influence do not *require* a blameworthy state of mind (although this will often be present) and this leads naturally on to the fact that a defendant can be liable for restitution even though the duress or undue influence has been exerted by a third party. In contrast, once one insists on a blameworthy state of mind, it would make no sense to grant restitution for exploitation of weakness other than against that blameworthy party. Strict liability imposed on a defendant would clash with the requirement of a blameworthy state of mind; and one could not sensibly apply a requirement of notice which would require the defendant to have notice of another's state of mind. So restitution for exploitation of weakness is only applicable against the exploiting party.

It may be thought to follow from this that exploitation of weakness is best conceptualised as always being an equitable wrong and that restitution is being given as an alternative to compensation for a wrong and not for an unjust enrichment and therefore falls outside this Restatement (see s 1(3)(b) above). For this debate, see Edelman and Bant, *Unjust Enrichment in Australia* (2006) 32–3 (not part of the law of unjust enrichment) and Bryan, 'Unconscionable Conduct as an Unjust Factor' in Degeling and Edelman, *Unjust Enrichment in Commercial Law* (2008) 295 (part of the law of unjust enrichment). In English law, it is far from clear that the claimant is entitled to compensation for exploitation of weakness (certainly there is no case in England in which compensation has been awarded). There is also historically a close link between this area of the law and undue influence so that, unless conceptually indisputable that the two should be seen as fundamentally different, there is good reason for seeing them alongside each other. At least for the present, it therefore seems preferable to treat this area as effecting restitution for unjust enrichment and as falling within this Restatement (albeit that the unjust factor is, to use Birks' terminology, partly 'defendant-sided' rather than 'claimant-sided': see Birks and Chin, 'On the Nature of Undue Influence' in Beatson and Friedmann (eds), *Good Faith and Fault in Contract Law* (1995) 57).

Example

An elderly man, C, who is often confused but has mental capacity, unexpectedly sells his car to his neighbour, D, for a twentieth of what it is worth. D realises that the elderly man is confused and also knows that C's family members would not approve of the sale. C may be entitled to rescind the contract for exploitation of weakness so as to revest title to the car. But, without a wrong, such as the tort of deceit, C will not be entitled to compensation for any consequential loss (eg taxi fares that he has to incur because he no longer has a car).

13(4)

This general principle has been explained in detail above: see s 3(6). It explains why, where a payment has been made under a contract induced by exploitation of weakness, that contract must first be rescinded before there can be restitution of the payment made under it.

14 Incapacity of the individual

(1) The defendant's enrichment is unjust if the claimant is an individual who enriched the defendant while under an incapacity.

(2) A claimant enriches the defendant while under an incapacity if the enrichment is a result of a contract, gift or other transaction which is invalid because the claimant was under 18 when the transaction was entered into.

(3) A claimant enriches the defendant while under an incapacity if the enrichment is the result of a contract, gift or other transaction which is invalid because the claimant lacked mental capacity, or was intoxicated, when the transaction was entered into.

(4) In general, the incapacity of the claimant does not render the enrichment unjust if the benefit was owed to the defendant by the claimant under a valid contractual, statutory or other legal obligation.

14(1)

We are here dealing only with human and not institutional incapacity (for the latter, see s 21(3) below). As appears to be the position with undue influence, there is no 'but for' causation requirement. This means that if the claimant was under 18 or lacked mental capacity at the time the contract (or gift) was made, it is irrelevant that he or she would have conferred the benefit even if over 18 or even if having full mental capacity.

14(2)

By referring to the concept of invalidity, the wording in s 14(2) relies on, without spelling it out, the complex law on when incapacity by reason of infancy (ie being under 18) invalidates a contract or gift (or other transaction) as against the minor. The history of the law on minors' *contracts* has been a tangled one, although less so since the repeal of the Infant Reliefs Act 1874 by the Minors' Contracts Act 1987. The present law is that there are two categories of contract invalidated by infancy. First, and most commonly, there are those that are 'unenforceable' against the minor unless he or she ratifies them on reaching adulthood. Secondly, there are those that can be rescinded (sometimes referred to as 'repudiated') by the minor before, or within a short time after, reaching adulthood (eg contracts for shares in companies or partnership agreements). A third category of contracts concluded by a minor do not concern us as they are valid (eg contracts for necessaries or beneficial contracts of service). In neither of the two invalidating categories is it relevant whether or not the adult knew that the other party was under 18. What we are therefore here addressing is the law on restitution of an unjust enrichment for

Commentary: Part 3

infancy where the contract is unenforceable against the minor (the first category) or has been validly rescinded by the minor (the second category).

The unsatisfactory but predominant view in the authorities (and note that the Minors' Contracts Act 1987 does not deal with restitution *to* the minor) is that a minor is only entitled to a personal right to the restitution of money, or a revesting of title to goods, where he or she can establish a total failure of consideration: *Steinberg v Scala (Leeds) Ltd* [1923] 2 Ch 452, CA; *Pearce v Brain* [1929] 2 KB 310. There are other cases that even suggest that rights in property cannot be revested: *Chaplin v Leslie Frewin Publishers Ltd* [1966] Ch 71, CA. Although this may reflect an underlying judicial view that infancy often does not justify restitution (and certainly it is hard to find cases where minors have been awarded restitution), the present state of the law, as traditionally understood, is unsatisfactory for two main reasons. First, as we discuss generally below in relation to failure of consideration (see s 15), the insistence on a failure of consideration being total for the restitution of payments is unnecessary. Secondly, if one accepts infancy as a ground of contractual invalidity, there is good reason for infancy to carry through to allow restitution of rights in property, and it is muddled thinking (without any precedent in analogous areas) to require a total failure of consideration for this. A better interpretation of the law is possible without legislative intervention. The Restatement therefore rejects the need for a total failure of consideration so that incapacity by reason of infancy itself gives rise both to a personal right to restitution and, for example, to a right to revest a right in property retained by the defendant (although the adult may be entitled to counter-restitution).

Example 1

C, aged 17, buys a sculpture for £2,000 from D. One month later, C seeks restitution of the £2,000. C should be entitled to restitution of £2,000 (subject to giving counter-restitution to D).

The law in relation to infancy *and gifts* is obscure. On one view, infancy does not invalidate gifts: see, for example, *Taylor v Johnston* (1882) 19 Ch D 603; and the *Report of the Committee on the Age of Majority* (the Latey Committee) (Cmnd 3342, 1967) which, at 98, said: 'There is no legal restriction upon the power of infants to make a gift of property that they can lawfully hold....' (note that a minor cannot hold a legal estate in land: Law of Property Act 1925, s 1(6)). However, there are other cases in which infants have been protected from giving away their property by treating the gift as voidable: see, eg, *Austin v Gervas* (1614) Hobart 77; *Zouch d Abbot v Parsons* (1765) 3 Burr 1794 (which also indicated that a gift not taking effect 'by delivery of his hand' was void). The latter view—that the law does sometimes protect infants against making gifts—seems preferable: it would be most odd, for example, if an infant were protected from contracting to sell her bicycle, but not protected from giving away her bicycle (and it is noteworthy that, although the law of unjust enrichment has not been regarded as applying where a will is made without capacity—see the commentary under s 1(5) above—under the Wills Act 1837, s 7, no person under 18, subject to a few exceptions, can make a valid will). While the wording in s 14(2) assumes that a gift will sometimes be invalid for infancy, its reliance on the concept of invalidity leaves open the details of when this will be so.

14(3)

The wording here relies, without spelling it out, on the law on when mental incapacity invalidates a contract or gift or other transaction. The meaning of mental incapacity is given in s 2(1) of the Mental Capacity Act 2005: 'a person lacks capacity in relation to a matter if at the material time he is unable to make a decision for himself in relation to the matter because of an impairment of, or a disturbance in the functioning of, the mind or brain'. Presumably the equivalent inability to make a decision for himself is required if intoxication (whether by drink or drug-taking) is involved (there are no helpful cases on those forms of incapacity). While there is some difference if the person is under the control of the Court of Protection, where this is not so, and the person retains control of his or her own affairs, a contract is only invalid if the other party knew of his or her mental incapacity: *Imperial Loan Co v Stone* [1892] 1 QB 599, CA; *Hart v O'Connor* [1985] AC 1000, PC. As regards a gift (putting to one side gifts by will: see commentary under s 1(5) above), the gift is void or voidable (the latter seems preferable, although the authorities do not make this clear) where the donor lacked mental capacity irrespective of the donee's knowledge of that mental incapacity: *Daily Telegraph Newspaper Co Ltd v McLoughlin* [1904] AC 776, PC; *Re Beaney* [1978] 1 WLR 770; *Simpson v Simpson* [1992] 1 FLR 601.

Example 2

C, who suffers from senile dementia and therefore lacks mental capacity, makes a gift of a car and £500 to D. C can rescind the gift, thereby revesting title to the car and becoming entitled to restitution of the £500.

14(4)

Although to ensure consistency, and out of an abundance of caution, this usual section has been included (and the general position is set out in s 3(6)), one might regard it as somewhat superfluous in the context of s 14 because s 14(2)–(3) have been drafted by relying on there being contractual invalidity; and if the claimant is under 18 or lacks mental capacity it is hard to envisage relevant circumstances in which he or she would have other valid legal obligations.

15 Failure of consideration

(1) The defendant's enrichment is unjust if the claimant has enriched the defendant on the basis of a consideration that fails.

(2) The consideration that fails may have been—

    (a) a promised counter-performance, whether under a valid contract or not, or

    (b) an event or a state of affairs that was not promised.

(3) It is a question of construction whether the consideration fails; and, in deciding this question, if the consideration was a promised counter-performance—

    (a) failure of consideration does not require that none of the promised counter-performance has been rendered;

    (b) the consideration is not normally regarded as failing if the promisor has been, and is, ready, able and willing to perform the promise.

(4) If the consideration was a promised counter-performance under a valid contract and the contract has been terminated (for example, by acceptance of a breach or by frustration)—

    (a) restitution for failure of consideration may enable a party to escape from a bad bargain;

    (b) normally, a person who breaks a contract may not rely on failure of consideration as an unjust factor.

(5) Where a contract has been terminated (for example, by acceptance of a breach or by frustration), failure of consideration may render the enrichment unjust even though the benefit was owed to the defendant by the claimant under a contractual obligation that remains valid because termination invalidates obligations prospectively and not retrospectively.

(6) Where a contract has been terminated by frustration, the right to restitution for failure of consideration is governed by the Law Reform (Frustrated Contracts) Act 1943, unless section 2(5) of that Act prevents that Act from applying to the contract.

15(1)

We are here concerned with where the claimant's consent in conferring the enrichment was qualified by a 'condition' that has failed. The terminology of 'failure of consideration' is long established and, although not ideal, to depart from it now (by referring instead, for example, to 'failure of condition' or 'failure of basis') may be more confusing than helpful. However, one must be careful to avoid the trap of incorrectly assuming that one is concerned only with where there is a valid contractual promise (see s 15(2) below).

Failure of consideration

Failure of consideration has traditionally been confined to where the benefit in question has been a payment. But on the best analysis, the line of cases (eg *William Lacey (Hounslow) Ltd v Davis* [1957] 1 WLR 932; *British Steel Corpn v Cleveland Bridge and Engineering Co Ltd* [1984] 1 All ER 504) concerned with restitution for the value of non-money benefits conferred in relation to an incomplete or anticipated contract also rests on failure of consideration as the unjust factor; and this derives support from the reference to failure of consideration in the context of restitution for services by the House of Lords in *Cobbe v Yeoman's Row Management Ltd* [2008] UKHL 55, [2008] 1 WLR 1752. Symmetry dictates that, unless there is good reason to the contrary, an unjust factor is applicable to all types of benefit.

15(2)

The usual consideration that fails is a promised counter-performance (s 15(2)(a)): see the classic formulation by Viscount Simon LC in *Fibrosa Spolka Akcyjna v Fairbairn Lawson Combe Barbour Ltd* [1943] AC 32, 48. Failure of consideration, used in that sense, has therefore been applied to where there was once a valid contract but that contract has been terminated for breach (*Giles v Edwards* (1797) 7 Term Rep 181; *Stocznia Gdanska SA v Latvia Shipping Co* [1998] 1 WLR 574, HL) or for frustration (the *Fibrosa* case). It has been used in the same sense where the contract was void (*Rover International Ltd v Cannon Film Sales Ltd (No 3)* [1989] 1 WLR 912, CA; *Westdeutsche Landesbank Girozentrale v Islington London BC* [1996] AC 669, HL) or unenforceable (*Thomas v Brown* (1876) 1 QBD 714) or anticipated (*Cobbe v Yeoman's Row Management Ltd* [2008] UKHL 55, [2008] 1 WLR 1752).

In the context of void contracts, the courts have sometimes instead used the term 'absence of consideration' (see Hobhouse J at first instance in *Westdeutsche Landesbank Girozentrale v Islington London BC* [1994] 4 All ER 890). This terminology rests on the false premise that failure of consideration is applicable only where there was once a valid contract. The term 'absence of consideration' is therefore best avoided.

For an example of restitution for failure of consideration, meaning the failure of a non-promissory event or state of affairs (see s 15(2)(b)), see the important High Court of Australia case of *Roxborough v Rothmans of Pall Mall Australia Ltd* (2001) 208 CLR 516 (referred to above under s 3(6)). That involved a non-promissory condition as to the future. But it is conceivable that a failure of consideration could comprise a non-promissory condition as to the present. This may be illustrated as follows:

Example 1

C pays D £1,000 on condition that D is unmarried. If at the time of payment D is already married, C is entitled to restitution for failure of consideration.

Usually an alternative ground for restitution would be C's mistake (C thinks D is unmarried) but the two grounds are different because C might not be mistaken and indeed might be insisting on the condition precisely because C believes that D is married.

15(3)

This makes clear that the question of whether a consideration fails cannot be answered in the abstract but depends on construing the relevant express or implied consideration that is the basis of the payment or other enrichment in question. See, e.g. *Sharma v Simposh Ltd* [2011] EWCA Civ 1383, [2012] 1 P & CR 12 esp at [26], [44]–[47], in which it was held that there was no failure of consideration where the claimants (under an oral, and hence void, contract giving an option to purchase land) had got what they paid the deposit for (namely, for the defendant to take the property off the market pending completion and to keep open its offer to sell to the claimants at a fixed price). An objective approach is taken to this construction exercise (see *Giedo Van der Garde BV v Force India Formula One Team Ltd* [2010] EWHC 2373, QB at [286] per Stadlen J). Furthermore, failure of consideration is an objective *concept* in the sense that the claimant's condition must be accepted by, or made clear to, the defendant. The explanation for this is that, in order to throw the relevant risk onto the defendant, it is insufficient that the condition is merely, subjectively, in the claimant's mind.

Where the consideration is a promised counter-performance, two points are helpful in determining, as a matter of construction, whether the consideration fails. As regards s 15(3)(a), it has traditionally been thought to be a requirement, in relation to payments, that the failure of consideration has been total. Total failure means that there has been none of the performance that the claimant was promised: *Stocznia Gdanska SA v Latvia Shipping Co* [1998] 1 WLR 574, HL. However, this insistence on total failure is not borne out by several cases which, while purporting to insist on a total failure, have often allowed restitution, even though there has been some of the promised performance: see, eg, *Rowland v Divall* [1923] 2 KB 500, CA; *Rover International Ltd v Cannon Film Sales Ltd (No 3)* [1989] 1 WLR 912, CA; *D O Ferguson & Associates (a firm) v Sohl* (1992) 62 BLR 95, CA. This is also consistent with the law on restitution where a contract has been terminated for frustration. As set out in the Law Reform (Frustrated Contracts) Act 1943 (which lays down the law on restitution for all frustrated contracts other than for the contracts excluded under s 2(5) of the 1943 Act: see s 15(6) below) restitution is to be awarded without any requirement that the failure of consideration be total. Furthermore, as many commentators have argued, there is no good reason in principle to confine failure of consideration to where the failure is total. The Restatement therefore takes the view, contrary to what the present law is thought to be, that, as regards a promised

Failure of consideration

counter-performance, there can be a failure of consideration even though some of the promised performance has been rendered. The question will always be whether, on its correct construction, the consideration fails or not. That it is unhelpful to talk of a total or partial failure of consideration is made especially clear when one thinks of a non-promissory condition: the condition (eg that D is unmarried) either fails or it does not fail.

Subsection 15(3)(b) embodies what has been referred to as the '*Thomas v Brown* (1876) 1 QBD 714 requirement'. That case concerned an oral contract for the sale of land which was unenforceable under the Statute of Frauds 1677. The purchaser was refused restitution of the purchase money paid because the vendor had been and remained ready, able, and willing to complete. There was therefore no failure of consideration. That is the default position. It is possible that, on particular facts, the consideration properly construed contradicts this as, for example, where the payment is made on the condition that the recipient performs within a reasonable time.

15(4)(a)

Where there has been a breach of contract, the primary reason why an innocent party may seek restitution for failure of consideration, rather than damages for breach of contract, is that restitution may allow the innocent party to escape from a bad bargain. This is shown as regards restitution of money paid under a contract discharged for breach by *Wilkinson v Lloyd* (1845) 7 QB 27 and by obiter dicta in *Ebrahim Dawood Ltd v Heath Ltd* [1961] 2 Lloyd's Rep 512 at 518–20; and as regards restitution for work done under a contract discharged for breach by *Lodder v Slowey* [1904] AC 442, PC (but cf *Taylor v Motability Finance Ltd* [2004] EWHC 2619). Although there is no case on this, the same should in principle apply as regards a contract that is terminated by frustration or under a clause expressly allowing termination.

The clash with contract reinforces the point that restitution of an unjust enrichment for failure of consideration is independent of a claim for breach of contract. It must be distinguished not only from a claim for expectation or reliance damages for breach of contract (which do not allow escape from a bad bargain) but also from a claim for an account of profits/restitutionary damages for breach of contract as in *A-G v Blake* [2001] 1 AC 268, HL (and see commentary on s 1(3)(b) above).

This is a convenient point at which to consider whether termination (sometimes referred to as 'discharge') of the contract is essential if an innocent party is to succeed in a claim for restitution for failure of consideration. Certainly, it is almost always the case that a contract will be terminated prior to an innocent party claiming restitution; and some cases may be thought to support the proposition that termination is a necessary pre-requisite to restitution for failure of consideration (see, eg, *Goodman v Pocock* (1850) 15 QB 576; *Kwei Tek Chao (Ha Zung Fu Co) v British Traders and Shippers Ltd* [1954] 2 QB 459; *The Olanda (1917)* [1919] 2 KB 728n, HL; *Re Richmond Gate Property Co Ltd* [1965] 1 WLR 335). However, provided the claimant can establish failure of consideration, it would appear that termination is not a necessary pre-requisite to restitution.

Example 2

D contracts to guard C's factory for five years for £100,000 payable for each year, at the beginning of that year, at a rate of £20,000. After two years, C discovers that D performed almost no guard work in the first year but has done an excellent job in the second year. Without terminating the five-year contract, it would seem that C is entitled to restitution of £20,000 for failure of consideration as that first-year payment was paid on condition that the first year's work would be carried out, which it was not.

In *Roxborough v Rothmans of Pall Mall Australia Ltd* (2001) 208 CLR 516, High Court of Australia, (see Example 6 under the commentary to s 3(6) above) it was also irrelevant to the availability of restitution for failure of consideration whether or not the contract had been terminated.

It should be noted that if, as seems correct, neither termination nor total failure is required for restitution, the requirement that, as a matter of (objective) construction, there has been a failure of consideration will need to be rigorously applied so as to ensure that spurious claims for restitution do not succeed. The argument that the consideration has failed (that is, that the claimant has paid on the basis of a condition that has failed) should not be lightly accepted. So in Example 2 above, it is highly likely that a court would not be satisfied that the consideration for the £20,000 payment in the first year had failed unless the claimant established that the contract was a severable contract requiring guard work to be done each year for £20,000.

15(4)(b)

A contract-breaker does not normally have a right to restitution for failure of consideration where a contract has been terminated (by the innocent party) for breach. This can be seen in the context of forfeiture and 'non-refundable' clauses in, eg, *Mayson v Clouet* [1924] AC 980, PC and *Stockloser v Johnson* [1954] 1 QB 476, CA; and, in the context of 'entire obligation' clauses where restitution is denied for work that is only partly completed, in, eg, *Sumpter v Hedges* [1898] 1 QB 673, CA. There are several possible explanations for this general denial. One is that it exemplifies the contractual exclusion of restitution for unjust enrichment under the general 'defence' of contractual exclusion (see s 32 below).That is, while there is a failure of consideration prima facie justifying restitution, the parties, by the terms

Failure of consideration

of their contract, have overridden, as they are free to do, what would otherwise be the law on restitution for unjust enrichment. On an alternative analysis, there is no failure of consideration in those situations because, where those clauses apply, one does not even reach the stage of there being a cause of action in unjust enrichment which is then overridden (ie as a matter of construction, there is no failure of consideration).

Whichever analysis is preferred, none denies that a contract-breaker may sometimes be entitled to restitution for failure of consideration. This may be said to be supported by the decision, although not the reasoning, in *Dies v British and International Mining and Finance Corpn* [1939] 1 KB 724; by the decision in *Rover International Ltd v Cannon Film Sales Ltd (No 3)* [1989] 1 WLR 912, CA; and by obiter dicta of Lord Wright in *Hain Steamship Co Ltd v Tate and Lyle Ltd* [1936] 2 All ER 579, 612.

Where a seller delivers a lesser quantity of goods than he contracted to sell, the buyer who accepts those goods must pay a proportionate part of the contract price under the Sale of Goods Act 1979, s 30(1). This may be regarded as an example of a contract-breaker being entitled to restitution for unjust enrichment, but it is probably more straightforwardly viewed as a contractual remedy. See also the Apportionment Act 1870, which is also best viewed as dealing with contractual remedies and, in any event, may not assist a contract-breaker (on which see the discussion at first instance, but not considered on appeal, in *Moriarty v Regent's Garage Co Ltd* [1921] 1 KB 423 at 43–5, 449).

15(5)

We have seen in s 3(6) above that, in general, an unjust factor does not render an enrichment at the claimant's expense unjust where the enrichment was owed to the defendant by the claimant under a valid contractual obligation. A major exception to that is where a contract has been terminated for breach or frustration or under a clause expressly allowing termination. The termination discharges future obligations but it does not invalidate past obligations, which remain binding. Nevertheless the claimant is entitled to restitution, for failure of consideration, of money paid or for work done in respect of those past valid obligations. See, eg, *Giles v Edwards* (1797) 7 Term Rep 181 (restitution of money paid where contract discharged for breach); *Fibrosa Spolka Akcyjna v Fairbairn Lawson Combe Barbour Ltd* [1943] AC 32, HL (restitution of money paid where contract discharged for frustration; and see Example 8 in the commentary on s 3(6) above); *Chandler Bros Ltd v Boswell* [1936] 3 All ER 179, CA (restitution for value of work done under contract discharged for breach).

Example 3

D contracts to guard C's factory for one year for £50,000, £10,000 to be paid by C in advance. D carries out the work for one week and then, in breach of contract, stops. Leaving aside any right to damages for breach, C has a right to restitution of the £10,000 for failure of consideration (subject to any counter-restitution for the value of the services performed): ie the money was paid on the condition that D would guard the factory for the year, which it has not done. It is not a bar to restitution that there was a valid contractual obligation to pay the £10,000 which has not been wiped away by C's termination of the contract. The same result should be reached—applying the Law Reform (Frustrated Contracts) Act 1943—if the factory is destroyed by a fire after the week so that the contract is frustrated.

We have already seen (see Example 6 in the commentary to s 3(6) above) that another 'failure of consideration' exception to the general rule in s 3(6) (but not involving termination) is provided by the Australian case of *Roxborough v Rothmans of Pall Mall Australia Ltd* (2001) 208 CLR 516, High Court of Australia. Here restitution was awarded for (a non-promissory) failure of consideration even though the contract was valid.

15(6)

Where a contract has been terminated for frustration, the Law Reform (Frustrated Contracts) Act 1943 governs restitution in respect of money and non-money benefits for most contracts. The contracts that are excluded from the 1943 Act by s 2(5) are contracts for the carriage of goods by sea and charterparties (other than time charterparties and charterparties by demise); contracts of insurance; and contracts for the sale of goods where the goods have perished. Although the 1943 Act displaces the common law for contracts to which it applies, the law as set out in this Restatement is essentially consistent with that under the 1943 Act (see the commentary on s 15(3) above) although the common law change of position defence appears to operate differently to the equivalent defence under the statute (see s 23(3) below).

16   Ignorance or powerlessness
(1) The defendant's enrichment is unjust if the claimant—
    (a) had no knowledge of the conduct which enriched the defendant at the claimant's expense, or
    (b) was powerless to prevent that conduct.
(2) Subsection (1) does not apply if, in the circumstances, the defendant—
    (a) is entitled to cause loss to the claimant, and
    (b) is therefore entitled to be enriched without the claimant's consent.
(3) Subsection (1) does not apply if section 17 applies.

> **17 Fiduciary's lack of authority**
> (1) Subject to subsection (2), the defendant's enrichment is unjust if—
>   (a) the claimant's asset or an asset held on trust for the claimant has been dealt with by a fiduciary of the claimant without authority and without the consent of the claimant, and
>   (b) as a result of that dealing, the defendant has obtained the benefit at the claimant's expense.
> (2) In the case of an asset held on trust for the claimant, there may be a rule applicable to the claimant's personal right to a monetary restitutionary award that the enrichment is not unjust unless the defendant knew, or ought to have known, that the fiduciary was dealing with the asset without authority and without the consent of the claimant.

16 and 17

Although ignorance/powerlessness and a fiduciary's lack of authority are different unjust factors, they are very closely connected. It has therefore been considered appropriate for them to be considered alongside each other in this commentary. It should be stressed that none of the three has yet been *explicitly* recognised by the courts as an unjust factor, albeit that they have been strongly advocated by commentators as best explaining the law. See generally Mitchell, Mitchell, and Watterson (eds), *Goff and Jones on the Law of Unjust Enrichment* (8th edn, 2011) ch 8, which is headed 'Lack of Consent and Want of Authority'.

16(1)

We are here concerned with where the claimant's consent, to the enrichment at its expense, is absent. There is no consent at all. This may occur because the claimant has no knowledge of the enriching conduct ('ignorance') (s 16(1)(a)) or was powerless to prevent it ('powerlessness') (s 16(1)(b)). Although it is controversial whether these are unjust factors, several commentators have argued that they provide an explanation for a number of decisions and that there is a strong argument of logic for recognising them (they are a fortiori from mistake). The argument for recognising ignorance was first put forward by Birks, *An Introduction to the Law of Restitution* (rvsd edn, 1989) 140–6.

Example 1

£100 drops from C's pocket and is picked up by D. Irrespective of a claim for the tort of conversion, D has been unjustly enriched at C's expense (just as if C had paid D the £100 by mistake). C has a personal right to restitution of

£100 from D. The unjust factor is C's ignorance. (This example is based on *Holiday v Sigil* (1826) 2 C & P 176.)

Example 2

D takes £200 from C's pocket without C's consent. Irrespective of a claim for the tort of conversion, D has been unjustly enriched at C's expense (just as if C had paid D the £200 by mistake). C has a personal right to restitution of £200 from D. The unjust factor is C's ignorance or powerlessness. (This example is based on *Neate v Harding* (1851) 6 Exch 349.)

Example 3

Unknown to C, D trespasses under C's land by opening up a spectacular cave to tourists. Irrespective of a claim for the tort of trespass to land, D has been unjustly enriched at C's expense. C has a personal right to restitution of the use value of the cave. The unjust factor is C's ignorance. (This example is based on the famous US case of *Edwards v Lee's Administrators* 96 SW 2d 1028 (1936)).

It will be very rare indeed for there to be any *practical* advantage to the claimant in these types of situation in basing the claim on unjust enrichment rather than seeking damages (whether compensatory or restitutionary) for the tort. However, it is not only theoretically important to recognise unjust enrichment based on absence of consent, but in some very rare situations (discussed below under s 16(2)) there is no concurrent civil wrong in play. Even where there plainly is a concurrent liability for a tort or other civil wrong, it is conceivable (eg because the cause of action will not always accrue at the same time for the purposes of the running of limitation periods) that an unjust enrichment claim could succeed when a claim based on a tort or other civil wrong would fail.

It has sometimes been suggested that 'absence of consent' is over-inclusive because it includes non-consensual incidental consequences of voluntary conduct. We have seen above (s 8(4)) that an incidental benefit is not 'at the expense of the claimant' so that there would be no right to restitution even if there were an unjust factor. But, in any event, the idea of absence of consent does not extend to such incidental consequences of voluntary conduct and there is no injustice in the defendant's enrichment by such incidental consequences: hence s 16(1) makes clear that it is the absence of consent to the conduct enriching the defendant that one is concerned with.

Example 4

C drains her land, which has the incidental consequence, unknown to C, of also draining her neighbour's (D's) land, thereby enhancing the value of D's land. D sells his land for a higher price than he would have obtained had the land been undrained. C has no claim in unjust enrichment against D. Even if the enrichment could be said to be at the claimant's expense (contrary to s 8(4) above), there is no claim because, although ignorant of the benefit to D at C's expense, C obviously knew of her own conduct (draining her own land). The fact that she did not know of the incidental consequences is irrelevant. There is no unjust factor. (This example is based on the US case of *Ulmer v Farnsworth* 15 A 65 (1888).)

16(2)

In certain circumstances a defendant is entitled to cause loss to the claimant so that there is no liability in tort for so doing. In such circumstances, there can be no injustice in the defendant being enriched at the claimant's expense, despite the claimant's absence of consent.

Example 5

D takes percolating water with the inevitable consequence that C's land is parched and D's land is fertile. Even if one were to say that D's enrichment is at the expense of C (although it would seem difficult to establish that it is from C) and that there is an unjust factor because C has not consented to that, C has no right to restitution because, as established by *Bradford Corpn v Pickles* [1895] AC 587, HL, D is entitled to cause loss to C by taking percolating water.

Example 6

D opens a shop, which successfully attracts custom away from C's shop. Even if one could say that D's enrichment is at the expense of C (although it would seem difficult to establish that it is directly from C) and that there is an unjust factor because C has not consented to that, C has no right to restitution from D. This is because, as established by *Allen v Flood* [1898] AC 1, HL, D is entitled to inflict economic loss on C by fair competition.

It would be a mistake to assume from this that absence of consent only operates where the defendant has committed a civil wrong to the claimant. While it will nearly always be the case that, where the unjust factor is ignorance or powerlessness, the defendant does commit a civil wrong against the claimant in being unjustly enriched, there is no need for the claimant to base the claim on the wrong rather than, within the law of unjust enrichment, on the absence of consent: and in some very rare situations, there is an absence of consent but no wrong committed by the defendant against the claimant. So, for example, C has a right to restitution from D in the following situations:

Example 7

In her sleep C makes an internet bank transfer from her account to the account of D. C knew nothing of what she was doing.

Example 8

C's computer, unknown to C, is set so that it automatically makes a bank transfer from C's account to the account of D.

Example 9

D usurps C's office and receives rents or fees owed by X to C. (See, eg, *Boyter v Dodsworth* (1796) 6 Term Rep 681 and s 8(2)(f)(i) above; and note that 'usurpation of office' has not traditionally been regarded as a civil wrong.)

Example 10

A payment order is made out to X by C. The payment order is received at the offices of X but the name of the payee is fraudulently altered by a clerk employed by X so the payment is paid into the account of D not X. (This is based on the facts in *Agip (Africa) Ltd v Jackson* [1991] Ch 547, CA.)

16(3) and 17

It is tempting to regard a fiduciary's 'lack of authority' as merely an aspect of ignorance or powerlessness. So it may be thought that, where property is held for another, the claimant's consent is given in advance but only within certain limits and that ignorance or powerlessness is then indicated by the limits of the authority given. However, that the real underlying ground is better seen as lack of authority, rather than ignorance or powerlessness (hence s 16(3)), is shown in situations where the beneficiary is incapable of giving consent because unborn or a minor and yet there is still a right to restitution, based on the lack of authority, on behalf of the unborn or minor. In a trust, the relevant authority is in any event conferred by the settlor and not by the claimant beneficiaries. The case for recognising 'lack of authority' is powerfully put by Chambers and Penner, 'Ignorance' in Degeling and Edelman (eds), *Unjust Enrichment in Commercial Law* (2008) 253.

The major practical importance of recognising a fiduciary's lack of authority as an unjust factor comes in relation to three-party cases where funds have been 'misdirected' to the defendant. This includes at common law *Lipkin Gorman v Karpnale Ltd* [1991] 2 AC 548, HL, and, although insisting on the condition that a claim against the fiduciary was first exhausted, *Ministry of Health v Simpson (Re Diplock)* [1951] AC 251, HL. As we shall see below, one can also argue that, in the 'knowing receipt' cases in equity, the courts should have been recognising a strict liability claim in unjust enrichment. As with all three-party cases within unjust enrichment, one issue is whether the defendant's enrichment was *at the claimant's expense* given that the direct provider was the third party rather than the claimant. However, this is normally overcome because of tracing and the exceptions to the 'direct providers only' rule (set ss 8–9). Even more problematic is the unjust factor and it is here that 'lack of authority' can provide the solution. In principle, therefore, there is a strong case for recognising a claim in unjust enrichment against the defendant in the three-party misdirected fund situation.

If that is correct, there is then a puzzling question. Unjust enrichment usually imposes strict liability (subject to defences, such as change of position). *Lipkin Gorman v Karpnale Ltd* fits that model, as does *Ministry of Health v Simpson* in equity. Strict liability for a fiduciary's lack of authority is also imposed where the claimant is seeking 'proprietary restitution', as is well illustrated by many cases on unauthorised substitution: see the commentary to s 9(5)–(7) above. In contrast, the 'knowing receipt' cases have required dishonesty, or negligence, by the defendant under the now-favoured test of 'unconscionable retention': *BCCI (Overseas) Ltd v Akindele* [2001] Ch 437, CA (although it is important to note Lord Nicholls's view in *Criterion Properties plc v Stratford UK Properties plc* [2004] UKHL 28, [2004] 1 WLR 1846, at [4], that *Akindele* should have been seen as an invalid contract case where, indisputably, the liability is strict). Is that apparent inconsistency justified?

Without wishing to deny that there may be an alternative cause of action for the wrong of 'knowing receipt', there is a powerful argument that the law should here recognise a uniform strict liability claim in unjust enrichment whether at common law (as is already the case) or, as regards misdirected trust funds, in equity. That argument is favoured in the well-known article written extra-judicially by Lord Nicholls, 'Knowing Receipt: The Need for a New Landmark' in Cornish et al (eds), *Restitution: Past, Present and Future* (1998) 230–45. Lord Nicholls there argued that, while dishonest receipt should be seen as an equitable wrong like dishonest assistance, that should not obscure the separate cause of action for restitution of an unjust enrichment where the liability should be strict, subject to defences. See also Birks, 'Receipt' in Birks and Pretto (eds), *Breach of Trust* (2002) 213–40. Cf Nourse LJ in the *Akindele* case at 456.

The Restatement pushes towards that uniform strict liability position while recognising that, on the present law, as regards misdirected trust funds, that position cannot yet be said to have been accepted as regards a personal right to restitution. Rather the defendant needs to have been either dishonest or at fault under the *Akindele* unconscionable retention test. Hence the wording in s 17(2): 'there may be a rule ... that ... the defendant knew, or ought to have known. ...' The strict liability position favoured by Lord Nicholls can be illustrated by the following example:

Commentary: Part 3

Example 11

X, a trustee of a fund of £80,000, in breach of trust to C, the beneficiaries under the trust, transfers trust assets to the value of £6,000 to D. D does not know, nor could reasonably know, that the assets are held on trust (although D is not a purchaser for value of those assets). D has been unjustly enriched at C's expense. Applying Lord Nicholls's argument, C (the beneficiaries) would have a personal right to restitution, to restore the trust fund, of £6,000 from D. The unjust factor, lying behind the breach of trust, is the fiduciary's lack of authority. (This example is based on the facts of *Baker* (GL) *Ltd v Medway Building and Supplies Ltd* [1958] 2 All ER 532 (Danckwerts J), [1958] 1 WLR 1216, CA).

It is worth stressing that, applying Lord Nicholls' argument, the defendant would be liable even though not a wrongdoer. Similarly, the defendant club in *Lipkin Gorman v Karpnale Ltd* was not itself a wrongdoer. The restitution envisaged is for unjust enrichment, based on the lack of authority, and not for a wrong. Indeed, albeit rare, one can imagine misdirected fund situations that involve a lack of authority and yet there is no wrong even by the trustee (eg where express or resulting trustees deal with trust assets contrary to the terms of the trust before they are aware of its existence).

18 Legal compulsion

(1) The defendant's enrichment is unjust if the claimant has enriched the defendant by discharging a liability of the defendant to another person (X) under legal compulsion exercised, or exercisable, by X.

The reason for this rule is the avoidance of the defendant's undeserved escape from liability.

(2) The following are examples of when the defendant's enrichment is unjust under subsection (1)—

(a) X is in lawful possession of an asset of the claimant, or there is an encumbrance over an asset of the claimant in favour of X, and the claimant discharges the defendant's liability to X to recover the asset or to remove the encumbrance;

(b) the claimant and defendant are under a common liability to X, which the claimant discharges, but the claimant's liability is secondary to the defendant's;

(c) the claimant and defendant are under a common liability to X, or are each liable to pay compensation for the same damage to X, and the claimant discharges the liability in circumstances in which the defendant should bear part of that liability.

Legal compulsion

18(1)

Where legal compulsion (ie legitimate legal process) exercised, or exercisable, by a third party, X, has led to the claimant, C, discharging a liability of the defendant, D, to X which, as between C and D, should have been borne, wholly or partly, by D not C, C has a claim in unjust enrichment against D for having discharged D's liability to X. The injustice in play is that, as between C and D, the legal process has compelled the 'wrong party' to pay or one party has been required to pay too much. Restitution is seeking to ensure that the appropriate party pays in the appropriate amount thereby avoiding an undeserved escape from liability.

It is important to emphasise that the undeserved escape from liability involves two elements. The first is that, as between C and D, the liability is one that, wholly or partly, should have been borne by D; and the second is that C was not acting officiously because C was under legal compulsion. A claimant who discharges another's legal liability under another unjust factor, such as mistake, has a right to restitution but that is best explained on the basis of the particular unjust factor in question rather than on the basis of this more general unjust factor.

That the injustice resulting from legal compulsion can lie only between C and the party whose liability is discharged (D) explains why legal compulsion is automatically linked to the particular form of enrichment in the standard phrase 'compulsory discharge of another's liability'.

Where the defendant (or a third party) makes *illegitimate* threats to detain the claimant or to seize goods or to prosecute the claimant unless the claimant pays money to the defendant, the relevant unjust factor is duress. In contrast, the situation with which we are here concerned involves legitimate application of the legal process so that, even if threats are involved (eg a threat to sue), those threats are legitimate and hence there is no duress.

Although it is tempting to regard the legal compulsion in play as showing that one is concerned with impaired consent, so that this area lines up alongside duress and undue influence, the fact that the relevant pressure is legitimate makes that approach misleading. Instead the injustice lies in there being an undeserved escape from liability and the legal compulsion is important, within that justification, in showing that the intervention was not officious. There is therefore a valid reason for restitution even though the claimant has consented to the defendant's enrichment (ie we are dealing with 'policy-motivated restitution': see ss 3(2)(b) and 3(4) above). As shorthand, Mitchell has labelled the unjust factor as 'secondary liability' (see Burrows (ed), *English Private Law* (2nd edn, 2007) ch 18 and see also Mitchell, Mitchell, and Watterson (eds), *Goff and Jones on the Law of Unjust Enrichment* (8th edn, 2011) chs 19–21). While having the merit of removing any link to impaired consent, the main difficulty with 'secondary liability' is that it only naturally covers part of the field (ie it naturally covers s 18(2)(b) but not (a) or (c)).

Turning to the enrichment, the discharge of another's legal liability, at least in most situations, is an 'incontrovertible benefit' (ie no reasonable person would deny that the defendant has been enriched): see s 7(3)(a). In some well-known cases, restitution has been denied precisely because no liability of the defendant has been discharged by the claimant: see, eg, *Bonner v Tottenham and Edmonton Permanent Investment Building Soc* [1899] 1 QB 161, CA; *Re Nott and Cardiff Corpn* [1918] 2 KB 146, CA; *Metropolitan Police District Receiver v Croydon Corpn* [1957] 2 QB 154, CA; *Fortis Bank SA v Indian Overseas Bank* [2011] EWHC 538 (Comm), [2011] 2 Lloyd's Rep 190. One might argue that, while having the merit of certainty, in the middle two cases an over-technical approach was taken to the question of whether the liability was discharged (in the former, it was held that D had no liability because, incorrectly, D was not entered in the rate book; and in the latter, it was held that D was only legally liable to pay what the court would award as damages and, in assessing damages, a court would deduct the benefit paid by C).

There is a difficult body of law on when an unrequested (by the debtor) payment of another's debt discharges that debt. Although in principle the creditor's acceptance should mean that the debt is automatically discharged (ie without the debtor's acceptance), the conventional interpretation of the cases is that the debt is only automatically discharged where paid under legal compulsion or necessity: see, eg, *Crantrave Ltd v Lloyds Bank plc* [2000] QB 917, CA; *Ibrahim v Barclays Bank plc* [2012] EWCA Civ 640; Burrows, *The Law of Restitution* (3rd edn, 2011) 460–8; Mitchell, Mitchell, and Watterson (eds), *Goff and Jones on the Law of Unjust Enrichment* (8th edn, 2011) paras 5-44–5-57. Note that the potential problem (raised by the US case of *Norton v Haggett* 85 A 2d 571 (1952)) of there being a claim for restitution by C, who is maliciously motivated towards D and discharges D's liability to X in order to have a hold over D, can be adequately dealt with by recognising that the defence to restitution of illegality (which includes conduct contrary to public policy: see s 28(2)(b)) should apply to rule out a claim by C against D in that situation. The possible hostility of the intervener is not a good reason for treating the debt as not being automatically discharged.

In nearly all cases the defendant's liability will have been discharged by the claimant paying money to the third party. For a rare example of restitution where the liability was discharged by the carrying out of work, see *Gebhardt v Saunders* [1892] 2 QB 452 (abating a nuisance).

18(2)

This sets out the three classic examples of restitution for 'compulsory discharge of another's liability'. Restitution to avoid an undeserved escape from liability (where money has been paid) is commonly divided into 'recoupment' (sometimes called 'reimbursement'), where the restitution is of the whole sum paid to discharge D's

Legal compulsion

liability (as in the first two examples); and 'contribution' where the restitution is of part of the sum paid to discharge D's liability (as in the third example). The same principles do, and ought to, apply to both recoupment and contribution (and indeed that division is not always clearly, drawn as is shown most starkly by the courts' occasional reference to '100 per cent contribution'). The Restatement avoids referring to 'recoupment' or 'contribution' in favour of the general term 'monetary restitutionary award' (see s 5(2)(a)).

Mitchell, *The Law of Contribution and Reimbursement* (2003) at 1.11 argues that there are the following four features of all the relevant cases: (i) that C and D must both have been legally liable to X; (ii) that X must have been forbidden from accumulating recoveries from both of them; (iii) that X must have been able to choose to recover in full from either of them; and (iv) that some or all of the burden of paying should ultimately be borne by D. But assuming that one confines this list to the situations covered in s 18(2)(b) and (c) (because requirement (i) seems inapplicable to s 18(2)(a)), there seems no need separately to recognise (ii) and (iii). This is because (ii) inevitably follows from the requirement that C's payment must discharge D's liability to X; and (iii) follows inevitably because both C and D have a common liability to X.

18(2)(a)

This is exemplified by *Exall v Partridge* (1799) 8 Term Rep 308 (in order to recover his carriage, C paid off D's rent, where C's carriage on D's premises had been lawfully seized by the landlord as distress for payment of D's rent) and *Johnson v Royal Mail Steam Packet Co* (1867) LR 3 CP 38 (in order to recover two ships from the crew, who were lawfully exercising their lien, the claimant mortgagees of the ships paid off the wages of the crew owed by the defendants). See also, analogously, *Kleinwort Benson Ltd v Vaughan* [1996] CLC 620, CA.

Example 1

D has hire-purchased a car from C. The car is damaged in an accident and D takes it for repair to X. D refuses to pay X for the repairs and X exercises its lawful right to retain the car by reason of its repairer's lien. D has also failed to pay instalments to C under the hire-purchase agreement. C, having lawfully terminated the hire-purchase agreement, pays off D's liability to X for the repairs in order to recover the car. C has a right to restitution from D for the payment made to X which has discharged D's liability to X.

18(2)(b)

This is exemplified by *Moule v Garrett* (1872) LR 7 Exch 101, *Brook's Wharf and Bull Wharf Ltd v Goodman Bros* [1937] 1 KB 534, CA, and *Niru Battery*

Manufacturing v Milestone Trading Ltd (No 2) [2004] EWCA Civ 487, [2004] 2 Lloyd's Rep 319.

Example 2

D, a firm of furriers, imports squirrel skins and stores them in C's bonded warehouse. Without any negligence by C, the skins are stolen from the warehouse. D is liable to pay import duties on the skins but the customs authority (X), as it is statutorily entitled to do as regards goods removed from the warehouse, demands payment of the import duties on the skins from C. C pays X. C has a right to restitution from D for the money paid because, while both C and D were under a common liability to X, C's liability was secondary to D's. C's liability was secondary because D had imported, and owned, the skins. (These were the facts in the *Brook's Wharf* case.)

The *Niru Battery (No 2)* case in effect decided that a defendant liable to make restitution of an unjust enrichment is primarily liable as against a defendant liable to make compensation for a tort. Apportioned contribution was therefore thought inapplicable, while all-or-nothing recoupment and '100 per cent contribution' were thought applicable. However, in *Charter plc v City Index Ltd* [2007] EWCA Civ 1382, [2008] Ch 313, *Niru Battery (No 2)* was controversially distinguished in a situation where the enrichment had not been retained but had been paid away in bad faith.

In *Owen v Tate* [1976] QB 402, CA, it was held that a voluntary surety (ie one who has not been requested to act as surety by the debtor) is not entitled to restitution for having discharged the debtor's liability to his creditor. This seems incorrect and has been widely criticised (not least because it is inconsistent with, and yet did not mention, s 5 of the Mercantile Law Amendment Act 1856, which entitles a surety, whether voluntary or not, to be subrogated to the creditor's rights: see also commentary to s 36(2) below).

18(2)(c)

This is exemplified both by the *common law* (including equity) on contribution, which is primarily applicable where there is a common liability to pay the same debt (as in, eg, *Deering v Earl of Winchelsea* (1787) 2 Bos & P 270 dealing with contribution between co-sureties of the same debt); and by contribution under the Civil Liability (Contribution) Act 1978, which applies where more than one person is liable to pay compensation in respect of the same damage to the same person. In *Dubai Aluminium Co Ltd v Salaam* [2002] UKHL 48, [2003] 2 AC 366 at [76], Lord Hobhouse said: 'The 1978 Act is an application of the principle that there should be restitutionary remedies for unjust enrichment at the expense of another'. Cases on common law contribution have determined how much contribution should be awarded (so that, eg, where co-sureties are equally bound, the aim of the contribution will be to achieve equality between C and D); and under the 1978 Act, where the relevant wording requires that the amount of the contribution shall be such as may be found to be 'just and equitable', the courts have clarified that, in exercising their discretion, both the relative culpability and the causative potency of the co-obligor's conduct are relevant (see, eg, *Dubai Aluminium Co Ltd v Salaam* [2002] UKHL 48, [2003] 2 AC 366 at [51] per Lord Nicholls).

Although the wording of the 1978 Act confers a wide-ranging discretion on the courts in deciding on the appropriate apportionment, once the courts have decided the appropriate apportionment (eg that D1 and D2 are equally responsible) contribution applies in the same way as recoupment (ie where D1 and D2 are equally responsible, D1 should not ultimately pay more than 50 per cent of the damages).

There has been controversy as to whether the wording of the 1978 Act, which is restricted to a liability to pay compensation in respect of the same damage, extends to a liability to make restitution for unjust enrichment. The Court of Appeal in *Friends' Provident Life Office v Hillier Parker May & Rowden (a firm)* [1997] QB 85 and *Charter plc v City Index Ltd* [2007] EWCA Civ 1382, [2008] Ch 313 have given the 1978 Act a wide meaning that includes a liability to make restitution for unjust enrichment. For the contrary view, see obiter dicta in *Royal Brompton Hospital NHS Trust v Hammond* [2002] UKHL 14, [2002] 1 WLR 1397. It is worth emphasising that, given the existence of the common law of contribution, there ought to be no need to distort the wording of the 1978 Act to produce the desired result that contribution is applicable. Rather the common law of contribution can be developed, applying the principles of the law of unjust enrichment, so as to cover the situation.

Although s 18(2)(a)–(c) are the classic examples of restitution to avoid an undeserved escape from liability, there is no reason to think that the existing categories of restitution for this unjust factor are closed. So, although there has been no case on this, consider the following example, based on *Exall v Partridge*.

Example 3

A painting on D's premises that is jointly owned by C1 and C2 is lawfully seized by the landlord, X, as distress for payment of D's rent. C1 pays off D's liability to X in order to recover the painting. Apart from having a claim for the full payment from D, C1 surely ought to have a claim for contribution from C2.

19 Necessity

(1) Subject to subsections (3) and (4), the defendant's enrichment is unjust if the claimant, in responding to a necessity, enriches the defendant by—
   (a) supplying or paying for goods or services, or
   (b) discharging a liability of the defendant.
(2) There is a necessity for the purposes of subsection (1) if intervention is needed to preserve another's health or assets, especially against imminent harm.
(3) The claimant—
   (a) must be a suitable person to intervene, and
   (b) if possible, must make reasonable attempts to communicate with the defendant before intervening, and
   (c) must not be under a contractual or statutory duty to intervene.
(4) The defendant's enrichment is not unjust if the claimant's intention at the time of intervention was that no payment would be sought for the intervention.

19(1)

It has traditionally been thought that, in contrast to the position in the civil law, necessitous interveners have bleak prospects of recovery under English law. Nevertheless there are several areas where such recovery has been granted and, adopting the typical common law methodology, the approach taken in the Restatement is to treat these as underpinned by a general principle that allows recovery for necessitous intervention. Cases that may be interpreted as supporting this approach include *Jenkins v Tucker* (1788) 1 Hy Bl 90; *Rogers v Price* (1829) 3 Y & J 28 (both burial cases); *Great Northern Rly Co v Swaffield* (1874) LR 9 Exch 132; *China-Pacific SA v Food Corpn of India, The Winson* [1982] AC 939, HL (both 'agency of necessity' cases although, in the latter, Lord Diplock preferred to reason in terms of 'bailment', which was also the approach taken—contrasting unjust enrichment—in *ENE Kos 1 Ltd v Petroleo Brasileiro SA (No 2)* [2012] UKSC 17, [2012] 2 WLR 976); and *Re Berkeley Applegate (Investment Consultants) Ltd* [1989] Ch 32 (necessitous services rendered by a liquidator). See also the Sale of Goods Act 1979, s 3(2), and the Mental Capacity Act 2005, s 7, imposing an obligation to pay a reasonable price for necessary goods supplied to an individual who lacks capacity or, where the *incapax* lacks mental capacity, for necessary services supplied. There is also the voluminous and specialised law on maritime salvage (see Kennedy and Rose, *Law of Salvage* (7th edn, 2009)). The best-known example of judicial hostility to recovery by a necessitous intervener is *Falcke v Scottish Imperial Insurance Co* (1886) 34 Ch D 234, CA (refusing a claim for a lien by a mortgagor of a life insurance policy who had paid premiums to keep the

Necessity

policy alive). See also *The Goring* [1988] AC 832, HL, in which it was held that the law on maritime salvage does not extend to saving a boat on non-tidal inland waters.

Perhaps more problematic is whether this area is best seen as awarding restitution for unjust enrichment. In civil law, *negotiorum gestio* ('management of the affairs of another') is treated as an independent area of the law outside the law of unjust enrichment and, in line with this, Birks, *Unjust Enrichment* (2nd edn, 2005) 22–4 argued that the English cases are concerned to compensate for loss incurred, irrespective of the defendant's enrichment. Ultimately this debate turns on whether one interprets past cases as having awarded restitution, rather than compensation, and on whether this is thought justified. The view underpinning the Restatement is that, at least at this stage of development, the cases (including those on maritime salvage) are best interpreted as awarding restitution rather than compensation; and that, while an argument can be made for going beyond restitution, to include compensation, it is a good reason for at least granting restitution that this may encourage (or, at least, may remove a disincentive to) necessitous intervention.

Example 1

C is D's neighbour. While D is away on holiday, there is a storm that damages the roof of D's house. D cannot be contacted. C repairs the damage so as to prevent further damage to D's property. C is entitled to restitution from D for the value of the services rendered.

Example 2

C has contracted to carry D's goods to be collected by D on arrival. There is noone to collect the goods on arrival. C pays for them to be warehoused. C is entitled to restitution from D for the cost of the warehousing.

That the intervention is necessitous will normally mean that the defendant is enriched: see s 7(3)(a). In some situations, where intervention is thought particularly important, even intervention contrary to the known wishes of the assisted person will merit restitution: see, eg, *Matheson v Smiley* [1932] 2 DLR 787, Supreme Court of Canada, where a surgeon was held entitled to remuneration in attempting to save the life of a suicide victim who wanted to die. But, in general, the defendant's refusal to consent at the time of the intervention means that there is no enrichment. Hence in *F v West Berkshire Health Authority* [1990] 2 AC 1 at 76, HL, Lord Goff thought that necessitous intervention was not justified 'when it is contrary to the known wishes of the assisted person to the extent that he is capable of rationally forming such a wish'; and, although there is some doubt about this, the owner's refusal of consent to a salvage probably debars an award: see Mitchell, Mitchell, and Watterson (eds), *Goff and Jones on the Law of Unjust Enrichment* (8th edn, 2011) para 18-25.

In general, it should not matter whether the necessitous services are successful. In principle, it is the services (and therefore the saving of expense) that constitute the enrichment, irrespective of their success. So in *Matheson v Smiley* [1932] 2 DLR 787 the surgeon was held entitled to remuneration even though he failed to save the life of the suicide victim. In contrast, it is clear law that success is essential for a salvage award but this is tied in with the particularly generous measure (which includes a reward) that is granted in that area (see the commentary below to s 34(1): necessity).

19(2)

The essential element underpinning a necessity for intervention is that there is a need to protect the health or assets of the defendant (or, as in the old burial cases, the health of the public for which the defendant is responsible). It may be helpful to think of a core concept of an emergency (hence the emphasis in s 19(2) on 'imminent harm') although, as Lord Goff stressed in *F v West Berkshire Health Authority* [1990] 2 AC 1, 75, this idea may be inapt for necessitous services rendered over a period of time (eg supplying necessaries to an *incapax*).

19(3)

The requirements in this paragraph focus on the appropriateness of the claimant's intervention or of awarding restitution for that intervention. One can argue that at least some of these requirements are also bound up with whether in s 19(1) there is a necessity.

19(3)(a)

One of the arguments put by some judges against allowing restitution for necessitous interveners is that this might encourage officious intervention by busy-bodies: see, eg, *Nicholson v Chapman* (1793) 2 Hy Bl 254, 259 (per Eyre CJ). Consistently with the decisions in past cases, this fear can be met by a requirement that the claimant is a suitable person to intervene. Eyre CJ's example of people setting boats adrift in order to rescue them and then claiming reimbursement would in any event surely be ruled out by the 'illegality' defence (see s 28 below).

19(3)(b)

This requirement derives support from the cases on agency of necessity: see, eg, *Prager v Blatspiel, Stamp and Heacock Ltd* [1924] 1 KB 566 at 569.

19(3)(c)

It would be inappropriate if those who are already being paid or funded to provide emergency services had a right to restitution for rendering those necessitous services. Apart from the need to avoid double recovery, the justification for restitution—to encourage, or to remove a disincentive to, intervention—is absent where there is already a contractual or statutory duty to intervene.

Example 3

The fire service is called and puts out a fire at D's house. The fire-fighters involved, and their employers, are not entitled to restitution from D because they were under a legal duty to intervene.

In contrast, the fact that the law of tort may, for example, impose a duty of care to look after goods should not rule out a claim for restitution for preserving those goods. Indeed in *China-Pacific SA v Food Corp of India, The Winson* [1982] AC 939, HL, the House of Lords precisely viewed reimbursement for the necessitous intervener as correlative to the duty of care owed by a bailee of goods.

19(4)

In *Re Rhodes* (1890) 44 Ch D 94, CA, relatives of a woman with mental incapacity had paid some of the cost of her care over a 25-year-period. It was held that there should be no right to restitution from her estate because the relatives had not established that they intended to be repaid. This puts too much of an onus on the claimant and would rule out restitution in many cases where it would be wanted. On the other hand, restitution should not be granted where the claimant had intended a gift and has since changed his or her mind, and it would appear that this is what the Court of Appeal in *Re Rhodes* was concerned about. The preferable way of achieving this is to apply the negative formulation ('intention...that no payment would be sought') set out in the Restatement.

---

20 Factors concerned with illegality

The defendant's enrichment is unjust if the claimant has enriched the defendant under an illegal contract and either—
  (a) the claimant withdraws from the contract before the illegal purpose is achieved and when it remains likely that it will be achieved, or
  (b) the reason the contract is illegal is to protect the claimant as a member of a class.

20

Illegality usually operates as a defence to restitution for unjust enrichment (see s 28 below). Indeed some commentators take the view that that is the *only* role of illegality in the law of unjust enrichment. Although that approach would make the law simpler to state, it is inaccurate, as was first explained by Birks, *An Introduction to the Law of Restitution* (rvsd edn, 1989) 299-303, 424-32. In two main situations the illegality leads to an unjust factor. The first, dealt with in s 20(a), is where the law encourages the claimant to abandon an illegal purpose by giving a right to restitution by withdrawal during the *locus poenitentiae* ('opportunity for repentance'). (This cannot be explained as restitution for failure of consideration because the claimant is able to withdraw even though the defendant is ready, able, and willing to perform the contract so that there is no failure of consideration.) The second, dealt with in s 20(b), is that, where the reason for the contract being illegal is to protect the class to which the claimant belongs, that itself provides a good reason for restitution.

This section is confined to unjust enrichment arising out of illegal *contracts*. Illegality in relation to trusts and gifts raises different issues turning on the law on resulting/constructive trusts and the presumption of advancement (although the latter will be abolished if, and when, s 199 of the Equality Act 2010 comes into force), which appear to lie outside the law of unjust enrichment.

20(a)

Although there has been some inconsistency in the case law, the approach favoured in obiter dicta of Millett LJ in *Tribe v Tribe* [1996] Ch 107, CA (which was a trusts not a contract case) is that there is a right to restitution by withdrawal (provided the illegal purpose has not been carried out) *irrespective of whether the claimant genuinely repents*: see also the earlier case of *Taylor v Bowers* (1876) 1 QBD 291, CA. But while genuine repentance seems unnecessary, it is extremely difficult to work out what the case law lays down as to the precise point at which withdrawal should no longer be possible. Moreover, one also needs to explain why one cannot have restitution by withdrawal where the purpose has been frustrated (eg *Alexander v Rayson* [1936] 1 KB 169, CA; *Bigos v Bousted* [1951] 1 All ER 92). Several academic articles have tried to rationalise the law on these issues: see, eg, Grodecki, 'In Pari Delicto Potior Est Conditio Defendentis' (1955) LQR 254; Beatson, 'Repudiation of Illegal Purpose as a Ground for Restitution' (1975) 91 LQR 313. See also the discussion by the Law Commission in its Consultation Paper CP No 154, *Illegal Transactions: The Effect of Illegality on Contracts and Trusts* (1999) paras 2.49-2.56, 7.58-7.69. Developing Beatson's approach, the interpretation taken in the Restatement is that there is a right to restitution by withdrawal at a time before the illegal purpose has been carried out and when it is still likely that it will be carried out. Although this tends to allow withdrawal at a relatively late stage, it is important to stress that withdrawal will not be permitted once the other party has made clear that he or she is not going to perform: once the equivalent of 'repudiatory breach' has occurred, the purpose is unlikely to be carried out irrespective of withdrawal.

Example 1

To prevent his creditors seizing his goods, C contracts with his nephew (X) that C will temporarily transfer his goods to X until settlement is reached with his creditors and then X will transfer the goods back to C. This is an illegal contract as it is designed to defraud C's creditors. X, in breach of the agreement, sells the goods to D (who is aware of the scheme to defraud C's creditors). C seeks to withdraw from the contract and to have title to his goods revested, and therefore to recover them (or their value) from D, prior to any settlement with his creditors. C is able to do so because he is seeking to withdraw before the illegal purpose has been achieved and when, without withdrawal, it is still likely that the creditors will be defrauded. (This example is based on *Taylor v Bowers* (1876) 1 QBD 291, CA.)

Example 2

C and D enter into a contract whereby C pays D for him to ensure that C is given a knighthood. D fails to bring this about and indeed does not have the power to do so. C seeks to withdraw from the contract and to recover the money paid. He cannot do so. Although the illegal purpose has not been achieved, there is no reason to allow restitution by withdrawal because the illegal purpose will not, and cannot, be achieved in any event. It does not remain likely that the illegal purpose will be carried out. (This example is based on the facts but not the reasoning—which relied on the now discredited idea that C had not genuinely repented—in *Parkinson v College of Ambulance Ltd and Harrison* [1925] 2 KB 1.)

It has sometimes been suggested in obiter dicta (see, eg, *Tappenden v Randall* (1801) 2 B & P 467 at 471) that withdrawal will not be granted in cases involving gross turpitude by the claimant (although, for obvious reasons, such cases are in practice unlikely to come to court). However, to deny the application of the *locus poenitentiae* doctrine in the most serious cases would produce the perverse result that the law is encouraging withdrawal only in cases where the illegality is less serious. The better view, therefore, is that there is no such 'gross turpitude' restriction on withdrawal.

Example 3

C and D enter into a contract whereby D is hired by C to murder C's wife. C pays D £10,000. C changes his mind and, before his wife has been murdered, seeks to withdraw and claims restitution from D. C is entitled to restitution.

20(b)

Where class protection is the very reason why a contract is illegal, that provides a good reason for restitution of an enrichment conferred under the contract. So while it is true that in most situations there will in any event be a standard unjust factor (whether, eg, failure of consideration or mistake or duress), there will be some situations where the class protection in play is itself a good reason for restitution. See, eg, the classic obiter dicta of Lord Mansfield in *Browning v Morris* (1778) 2 Cowp 790 at 792; and the decision in *Lodge v National Union Investment Co Ltd* [1907] 1 Ch 300. (Note that the right to restitution in this type of case is not explicable by the exploitation of weakness unjust factor (see s 13 above) because that requires substantive unfairness and bad faith, whereas the class protection here in mind does not insist on those two requirements.) One might also include here (taking the wide view that illegality embraces contracts contrary to public policy) ss 140A–140B of the Consumer Credit Act 1974, which seek to protect consumers who need credit by giving them a wide range of 'remedies', including restitutionary 'remedies', to undo credit agreements where the relationship between the creditor and the debtor is unfair. Further examples are where one can regard the protected class as comprising those who might otherwise unjustifiably lose out as a result of transactions to which they are not parties: see, eg, ss 238–9 and 423 of the Insolvency Act 1986 (transactions at an undervalue, preferences, and transactions defrauding creditors).

Example 4

Let us assume that, by legislation, it is a criminal offence for landlords to accept a higher rent than the standard rent laid down. C, a tenant, pays D, a landlord, an extra amount referred to as 'key money' for renting a flat. The contract is illegal as being contrary to the legislation. C is entitled to restitution of the key money paid whether or not he was making a mistake of law in paying it. That is because the reason for the illegality—the need to protect a vulnerable class—extends through to give the tenant a right to restitution of the extra money paid. (These were the facts in *Kiriri Cotton Co Ltd v Dewani* [1960] AC 192, PC, which was dealing with rent restriction legislation in Uganda.)

21 Unlawful obtaining or conferral of a benefit by a public authority

(1) The defendant's enrichment is unjust if the defendant is a public authority which unlawfully obtained the benefit from the claimant.
(2) The obtaining of the benefit need not be preceded by a demand.
(3) The defendant's enrichment is unjust if the claimant is a public authority which unlawfully conferred the benefit on the defendant.
(4) The question whether the obtaining or conferral of the benefit was unlawful is to be decided by applying the principles of public law; but there is no requirement that the claimant must proceed by first seeking judicial review.
(5) There are statutory provisions, especially in the context of tax and social security, that govern the right to restitution from or for a public authority.

21(1)

In *Woolwich Equitable Building Soc v Inland Revenue Commissioners* [1993] AC 70, HL, it was decided that, where a public authority has obtained money ultra vires, the payor has a right to restitution irrespective of mistake or duress. This is the core '*Woolwich* principle'. Protection against State unlawfulness, epitomised in the idea that there shall be 'no taxation without Parliament', is the underlying reason for restitution.

Example 1

The Revenue charges C tax under a regulation that is ultra vires. While arguing that the tax is invalid, C pays it but then seeks restitution. C has a right to restitution from the Revenue, including (compound) interest, under the *Woolwich* principle. It does not matter that C was not mistaken or that there was no duress (as there would not be if any threat was merely one to sue and was therefore legitimate).

The controlling concept, which determines the types of situations, bodies, and payments (or, in principle, other enrichments) to which the *Woolwich* principle applies, is public law unlawfulness. As developed in cases subsequent to the *Woolwich* case, this can cover the misconstruction or misapplication of a relevant statute or regulation as well as where the relevant regulation is ultra vires and invalid (as in *Woolwich* itself). Several recent cases (see, eg, *Test Claimants in the FII Group Litigation v Revenue and Customs Commissioners* [2012] UKSC 19, [2012] 2 WLR 1149) have dealt with the *Woolwich* principle in the context of charges being exacted by the State that are unlawful because contrary to the payor's directly effective EU rights. EU law requires (under the '*San Giorgio* principle' named after *Amministrazione delle Finanze dello Stato v SpA San Giorgio* Case 199/82 [1983] ECR 3595) that, subject to defences, the payor is entitled to repayment of such charges. The requirement of a right to repayment is satisfied in English domestic law by restitution under the *Woolwich* principle.

The recognition of the *Woolwich* principle does not mean that a more traditional claim for mistake (or duress) against the public authority is precluded. So, eg, in cases for restitution of tax levied ultra vires, claimants have been allowed to base their claims on mistake of law so as to take advantage of the postponement of the limitation period in mistake claims under s 32(1)(c) of the Limitation Act 1980: *Deutsche Morgan Grenfell Group plc v Inland Revenue Commissioners* [2006] UKHL 49, [2007] 1 AC 558.

Although the *Woolwich* principle is wide-ranging, it is theoretically important to recognise that it belongs within the unjust factors scheme and requires that the benefit was unlawfully obtained. It is insufficient to show that the money (or other benefit) was not due. So, as Lord Sumption clarified in *Test Claimants in the FII Group Litigation v Revenue and Customs Commissioners* [2012] UKSC 19, [2012] 2 WLR 1149 at [186], mistakenly miscalculated self-assessed tax and tax mistakenly paid twice to the Revenue probably do not fall within the *Woolwich* principle, although there would be recovery on the ground of mistake.

It is worth emphasising here that, while it appears that change of position is not a defence to a public authority under the *Woolwich* principle (see s 23(2)(b)), the 'prevailing practice' and 'passing on' defences are sometimes made available to a public authority by statute whereas they are not available defences at common law: see s 31 below.

21(2)

Although an unlawful obtaining of a benefit will often involve a demand by the public authority, a formal or official demand is not necessary: *Test Claimants in the FII Group Litigation v Revenue and Customs Commissioners* [2012] UKSC 19, [2012] 2 WLR 1149. There is, therefore, a right to restitution of ultra vires tax even though it was paid under self-assessment or in anticipation of a demand. In the Restatement, therefore, it has been thought preferable to use the language of an unlawful 'obtaining' by the public authority.

21(3)

A public authority that makes a payment to (or, in principle, confers any other enrichment on) the defendant unlawfully has a right to restitution. The reason for the restitution lies in the desire to protect the public generally from the spending of funds by a public authority unlawfully. Put shortly, like the *Woolwich* principle, one is concerned with protecting against State unlawfulness, although here the unlawfulness is the mirror image of that in *Woolwich* (ie one is concerned with payment out, not payment in). This can be explained by saying that the public authority does not have the institutional capacity to make the payment. However, as there is no real link to human incapacity (dealt with in s 14 above), where the reason for restitution is to protect the *incapax* whose consent is impaired, one can focus directly on the unlawful conduct without viewing it through the prism of incapacity. Restitution for a public authority was recognised to be 'well-established' in the speech of Lord Goff in the *Woolwich* case [1993] AC 70 at 177, with his Lordship there relying on the Privy Council decision, given by Lord Haldane, granting restitution in *Auckland Harbour Board v R* [1924] AC 318, PC. Although both Lord Goff and Lord Haldane confined the principle to the recovery of moneys paid out of *the consolidated fund*, in principle the unjust factor extends to all payments made ultra vires or otherwise unlawfully by public authorities. This is now borne out by *Charles Terence Estates Ltd v The Cornwall Council* [2011] EWHC 2542 (QB), [2012] 1 P & CR 2, in which it was held that a local authority was entitled to restitution by reason of its own ultra vires conduct (albeit, on the facts, restitution was refused in respect of the rents paid by the public authority because the defendant had a change of position defence).

Example 2

Under a void interest-rate swap transaction, a local authority, C, pays £237,000 more to a bank, D, than D pays to C. C was acting ultra vires in entering into the swap transaction. C is entitled to restitution from D with the unjust factor being the ultra vires conferral of the benefit, irrespective of establishing mistake. (In most of the well-known swap cases, restitution was being sought by a bank from a public authority. But this example is based on *South Tyneside Metropolitan BC v Svenska International plc* [1995] 1 All ER 545, where the claim was *by* the public authority, albeit that the *Auckland Harbour Board* case was not mentioned.)

21(4)

We have already explained in the commentary on s 21(1) above that the *Woolwich* principle rests on the public law principle of unlawfulness. Nevertheless, the claim for restitution is a private law claim. The determination of whether the receipt was, or was not, unlawful or ultra vires does not, therefore, require initial judicial review proceedings: see, eg, *British Steel plc v Customs and Excise Comrs* [1997] 2 All ER 366, CA, where the *Woolwich* claim succeeded even though there had been no judicial review proceedings.

The same applies to claims *by* public authorities. While the controlling concept is public law unlawfulness, the claim for restitution is a private law claim; and, as shown in *Charles Terence Estates Ltd v The Cornwall Council* [2011] EWHC 2542 (QB), [2012] 1 P & CR 2, there is plainly no requirement that the public authority first goes through judicial review proceedings.

21(5)

It cannot be overstated that the common law of restitution in this area—and hence the law laid down in the Restatement—is residual. Normally the right to restitution from a public authority, especially of tax from HMRC, is embodied in a statute. As Lord Goff said in *Woolwich* [1993] AC 70 at 176: 'most cases will continue for the time being to be regulated by the various statutory regimes now in force'. In conformity with that, the picture in respect of restitution from public authorities appears to be as follows (and it should be noted that, while it is convenient to refer to these provisions here under s 21, the provisions—depending on their wording—may govern claims for restitution against public authorities whether based on the *Woolwich* principle or mistake or any other unjust factor): some provisions expressly replace the common law (eg s 80(7) of the Value Added Tax Act 1994 dealing with overpaid VAT; and s 137A(5) of the Customs and Excise Management Act 1979 concerning overpaid excise duty). Others (eg s 33 of, and Sch 1AB to, the Taxes Management Act 1970 dealing with overpaid income tax and capital gains tax; and s 241 of the Inheritance Tax Act 1984 dealing with overpaid inheritance tax) may do so by necessary implication. So in *Monro v Revenue and Customs Commissioners* [2008] EWCA Civ 306, [2009] Ch 69 it was held that the common law right to restitution of overpaid capital gains tax (which is a tax payable after assessment) on the ground of mistake or under the *Woolwich* principle was impliedly replaced by s 33 of the Taxes Management Act 1970: the statutory remedy was inconsistent with common law restitution.

In contrast, s 33 was held inapplicable in *Woolwich* itself because the regulation under which the tax was charged was ultra vires; and in *Deutsche Morgan Grenfell Group plc v Inland Revenue Commissioners* [2006] UKHL 49, [2007] 1 AC 558, s 33 was held inapplicable because advance corporation tax was payable and paid without any assessment being raised and s 33 was not to be interpreted as impliedly ruling out all other claims (falling outside the express wording of s 33) for mistaken payment of tax. Similarly, in the context of tax levied contrary to EU law, s 33 was held to be non-exclusive—and *Monro* was distinguished—in *Test Claimants in the FII Group Litigation v Revenue and Customs Commissioners* [2012] UKSC 19, [2012] 2 WLR 1149.

Whatever their impact on the common law, it should be noted that the present statutory restrictions are unsatisfactorily inconsistent with one another. For example, the Taxes Management Act 1970, s 33 and Sch 1AB, dealing with overpaid income tax and capital gains tax, gives HMRC a discretionary power whether to make restitution of mistakenly paid tax; there is no passing on defence; but there is a defence where the tax was paid in accordance with prevailing practice. In contrast, the Value Added Tax Act 1994, s 80, gives the taxpayer a right to restitution of VAT that was not due; there is a passing on defence; but there is no prevailing practice

Financial institutions and constructive notice

defence. For the statutory defences of passing on and prevailing practice, see s 31 below.

As with claims against public authorities, so with claims by public authorities, it would appear correct to say that the common law of restitution—and hence the law laid down in the Restatement—is residual. So, for example, claims for restitution of overpaid social security benefits are governed by s 71 of the Social Security Administration Act 1992; and in *R v Secretary of State for Work and Pensions* [2010] UKSC 54, [2011] 2 AC 15, it was decided that s 71 of the 1992 Act was exclusive of any right to restitution at common law. It should be noted that, while it is convenient to refer to that provision here under s 21, s 71 of the 1992 Act (and any other analogous provisions, depending on their wording) displace claims for restitution by public authorities, whether based on the *Auckland Harbour Board* case, or mistake, or any other unjust factor.

22 Financial institutions and constructive notice
(1) Unless subsection (2) applies, the defendant is treated as having constructive notice of a misrepresentation, illegitimate threat or undue influence if—
   (a) the defendant is a financial institution with whom the claimant entered into a contract of suretyship guaranteeing a debt owed to the defendant, and
   (b) the claimant has a non-commercial relationship with the debtor and entered into the contract because the misrepresentation or illegitimate threat was made by the debtor or while under the undue influence of the debtor.
(2) The defendant is not treated as having constructive notice if, before the contract was entered into, it—
   (a) informed the claimant, by direct communication, that it required written confirmation from the claimant's adviser that the claimant understood what the claimant was doing, and
   (b) forwarded to the claimant, or the claimant's adviser, the financial circumstances regarding the debtor's loan application to it, and
   (c) received confirmation from the claimant's adviser that the adviser had provided the claimant with fully informed and competent advice.
(3) In this section "adviser" means a solicitor or other legal adviser.

22(1)

In relation to contracts induced by a third party's misrepresentation, illegitimate threat, or undue influence, we have seen (see ss 10(7), 11(7) and 12(7) and especially the commentary to s 12(7)) that the concept of constructive notice has been accepted by the House of Lords (in *Barclays Bank plc v O'Brien* [1994] 1 AC 180, HL and *Royal Bank of Scotland v Etridge (No 2)* [2001] UKHL 44, [2002] 2 AC 773) as regards non-commercial guarantees typically given by a wife as surety for her husband's, or her husband's company's, debts. In line with that, s 22(1) summarises when the concept of constructive notice is applicable.

22(2)–(3)

In the *Etridge* case the House of Lords clarified the steps a bank needs to take in order to avoid being fixed with constructive notice. Section 22(2) sets out those steps.

PART 4
DEFENCES

23 Change of position
(1) The defendant has a defence to the extent that—
   (a) the defendant's position has changed as a consequence of, or in anticipatory reliance on, obtaining the benefit, and
   (b) the change is such that the defendant would be worse off by making restitution than if the defendant had not obtained, or relied in anticipation on obtaining, the benefit.
(2) But the defendant does not have this defence if—
   (a) the change of position—
      (i) was made in bad faith, or
      (ii) involved significant criminal illegality, or
      (iii) consisted of taking a risk with loaned money, or
   (b) the weight to be attached to the unjust factor is greater than that to be attached to the change of position (as, for example, where the unjust factor is the unlawful obtaining of a benefit by a public authority).
(3) In the case of a contract to which the Law Reform (Frustrated Contracts) Act 1943 applies, the defence of change of position is governed by section 1(2) and (3) of that Act.

23(1)

(i) General points

This defence—which in theory and in practice is the most important in the law of unjust enrichment—was authoritatively accepted as part of English law in *Lipkin Gorman v Karpnale Ltd* [1991] 2 AC 548, HL. Although most commonly applied in relation to mistaken payments, it is a general defence to unjust enrichment that can apply to almost all unjust factors (*Haugesund Kommune v Depfa ACS Bank* [2010] EWCA Civ 579, [2012] 2 WLR 199 at [122]; and note that *Lipkin Gorman* itself did not involve a mistake) and to all types of benefit (see, eg, *Cressman v Coys of Kensington (Sales) Ltd* [2004] EWCA Civ 47, [2004] 1 WLR 2775 at [41]) and to all types of defendant, including a public authority (see, eg, *Test Claimants in the FII Group Litigation v Revenue and Customs Commissioners* [2008] EWHC 2893 (Ch) at [302]–[352], [445] (per Henderson J) but not where the unjust factor is the '*Woolwich* principle').

In principle, change of position ought to be a defence to proprietary restitution, as well as to a personal right to restitution, triggered by the cause of action of unjust enrichment. Although there has, as yet, been no case directly confirming this, it may be illustrated as follows:

Example 1

C mistakenly pays D £10,000. D buys shares with that money and, because of her new financial security, bets and loses £4,000. C brings a claim asserting a right in property in the shares (based on unjust enrichment). There would clearly be a change of position defence to a personal claim to £10,000 and the same should apply to the claim for proprietary restitution. This would mean that if C's personal right to restitution were being secured by an equitable lien over the shares, that lien would secure the sum of £6,000 rather than £10,000; and, although this may be more controversial, if C's right to restitution was the right to be a beneficiary under a trust of the shares, C's right should be conditional on C compensating D for her loss of £4,000.

For change of position as a defence to rescission of an executed contract or gift for undue influence see, eg, *Cheese v Thomas* [1994] 1 WLR 129, CA (helpfully analysed by Chen-Wishart, 'Loss Sharing, Undue Influence and Manifest Disadvantage' (1994) 110 LQR 173 at 178).

Many of the precise elements of the defence have been established by cases subsequent to *Lipkin Gorman*. The best underlying justification of the defence—which, as *Lipkin Gorman* shows, is a proportionate not an all-or-nothing defence (hence the wording in the Restatement 'to the extent that')—is that it is essentially concerned with 'disenrichment': ie while prima facie enriched, the defendant is overall not enriched because the enrichment has been cancelled out, wholly or partly, by a causally relevant loss to the defendant. However, 'disenrichment' alone cannot be the full explanation for the defence because, as set out in s 23(2), there are situations where the defence cannot be invoked despite the defendant's disenrichment.

(ii) Establishing loss (ie the change is such that the defendant would be 'worse off')

To constitute a change of position, it is insufficient for the defendant to show merely that it has spent the money obtained because it might have had to spend the same amount of money in any event (most obviously, where the spending has been on discharging pre-existing debts) so that the spending does not constitute a loss (ie the defendant's position is no worse than it was before the obtaining of the money). In principle, non-pecuniary, as well as pecuniary, loss should count in determining whether the defendant is worse off and this is supported by obiter dicta in *Commerzbank AG v Gareth Price-Jones* [2003] EWCA Civ 1663. But one must be

Change of position

careful not to elide non-pecuniary loss with disappointed expectations (every defendant asked to make restitution may be regarded as suffering the latter).

As we have seen in s 4(2) above, the burden of proving (on the usual balance of probabilities) that the defendant has changed its position is on the defendant. A broad-brush approach has been taken to the evidence required, which recognises the difficulties defendants face where required, after the event, to prove what they have done with money: see *Philip Collins Ltd v Davis* [2000] 3 All ER 808; *Scottish Equitable plc v Derby* [2001] EWCA Civ 369, [2001] 3 All ER 818 at [33]. Where there are many payments, a global approach (looking at all the payments in and out together rather than separately) was taken in *Lipkin Gorman v Karpnale Ltd* [1991] 2 AC 548, HL. If the defendant buys property that it still retains, it appears that the change of position will take into account the resale value of the property (see *Lipkin Gorman v Karpnale Ltd* per Lord Templeman). This may be illustrated as follows:

Example 2

D is mistakenly paid £500 by C. As a result of having that extra money, D buys a new television costing £500. C discovers the mistake six months later. The television can be sold for £300. D's change of position is £200 not £500.

In principle, although not yet discussed judicially, rights that the defendant has to recoup the loss from a third party, and the ease of exercising those rights, ought to be relevant in determining the defendant's loss. So in Example 5 below, one ought to take into account that D itself has a right to restitution from the charity.

(iii) Causally relevant loss or loss incurred in 'anticipatory reliance'

That the loss must be 'a consequence of...obtaining the benefit' (ie causally relevant) explains why general hardship to the defendant, subsequent to the enrichment, does not count: see *Scottish Equitable plc v Derby* [2001] EWCA Civ 369, [2001] 3 All ER 818 at [31].

Example 3

C pays D £1,000 by mistake and, subsequent to the receipt, D is made redundant or is injured in a car crash. Those misfortunes, which may make it more difficult for D to make restitution to C, do not constitute the defence of change of position.

On the other hand, it would not seem necessary for there to have been detrimental *reliance* by the defendant in any meaningful sense provided there has been a causally relevant loss: see *Scottish Equitable plc v Derby* [2001] EWCA Civ 369, [2001] 3 All ER 818 at [30]–[31].

Example 4

C pays D £1,000 by mistake. That money is then immediately stolen from D or destroyed when D's house is burnt down by an arsonist. Those subsequent losses should count—assuming D would not have suffered the loss of £1,000 had he not obtained the money in the first place—even though D cannot be said to have relied in any meaningful sense on the money being his.

The relevant test for 'causally relevant loss' has not been laid down in the cases, although the 'but for' test, provable by the defendant, is the appropriate starting point: see *Scottish Equitable plc v Derby* [2001] EWCA Civ 369, [2001] 3 All ER 818 at [31].

However, it has been accepted that loss incurred in anticipation of, as well as subsequent to, an enrichment should count: *Dextra Bank and Trust Co Ltd v Bank of Jamaica* [2002] 1 All ER (Comm) 193, PC; *Commerzbank AG v Gareth Price-Jones* [2003] EWCA Civ 1663. In that anticipatory context, it is hard to see how there can be relevant loss unless there has been detrimental reliance on obtaining the benefit.

Example 5

D is mistakenly told that she has won £5,000 in an essay competition. In reliance on obtaining that £5,000, D pays £5,000 to a charity. D is then mistakenly paid the £5,000 by C. When C finds out its mistake, it seeks restitution from D. D in that situation has a change of position defence, even though her loss in paying the charity has been incurred prior to obtaining the £5,000, because that loss was incurred in anticipatory reliance on obtaining the £5,000.

23(2)

It would be unfair to a claimant if all causally relevant or detrimental reliance losses counted so s 23(2) lays down the four situations in which a defendant is disqualified from the change of position defence.

23(2)(a)(i)

That the change of position must be in good faith was made clear in *Lipkin Gorman v Karpnale Ltd* [1991] 2 AC 548, HL: see also *Cressman v Coys of Kensington (Sales) Ltd* [2004] EWCA Civ 47, [2004] 1 WLR 2775 at [41]. It would appear that bad faith extends beyond dishonesty to include 'failure to act in a commercially acceptable way and sharp practice': *Niru Battery Manufacturing Co v Milestone Trading Ltd* [2002] EWHC 1425 (Comm), [2002] 2 All ER (Comm) 705 at [135] (per

Change of position

Moore-Bick J, approved by the CA in that case [2003] EWCA Civ 1446, [2004] 1 All ER (Comm) 193); *Abou-Rahmah v Abacha* [2006] EWCA Civ 1492, [2007] 1 All ER (Comm) 827; *Jones v Churcher* [2009] EWHC 722 (QB), [2009] 2 Lloyd's Rep 94. The cases make clear that bad faith includes where one pays money away knowing that the claimant was mistaken or otherwise had a right to restitution.

Fault short of bad faith does not disqualify the defendant: *Dextra Bank and Trust Ltd v Bank of Jamaica* [2002] 1 All ER (Comm) 193, PC; *Haugesund Kommune v Depfa ACS Bank* [2010] EWCA Civ 579, [2012] 2 WLR 199 at [152] (cf *Commerzbank AG v Gareth Price-Jones* [2003] EWCA Civ 1663 where, although not clearly analysed, the defendant's fault appeared to be an alternative reason for refusing the defence).

23(2)(a)(ii)

In *Barros Mattos Jnr v MacDaniels* [2004] EWHC 1188 (Ch), [2005] 1 WLR 247 it was thought that criminal illegality in incurring the change of position was an absolute bar to the defence, subject to the possibility that minor illegality might be ignored under the *de minimis* principle. That seems too rigid a view and has been criticised by, eg, the Law Commission CP No 189, *The Illegality Defence, A Consultative Report* (2009) paras 4.60–4.62. The criminality may be relatively trivial (and yet more than *de minimis*) so that denying the defence may impose too harsh a sanction. The better view therefore is that the defendant should only be disqualified from the defence by illegality where the criminality is significant and not trivial. The word 'significant' allows some flexibility; and it may be that the courts will in due course move to the preferable position of applying illegality as a bar to change of position only where that is a 'proportionate' response to the illegality taking into account the various policies in play (see analogously s 28(3)(c) below).

The reference by Lord Goff in *Lipkin Gorman* to the defence not being available to a wrongdoer is best interpreted as making the point—irrelevant to restitution for unjust enrichment—that change of position is not a defence to restitution for a tort or other civil wrong: see *Test Claimants in the FII Group Litigation v Revenue and Customs Commissioners* [2008] EWHC 2893 (Ch) at [320], [337]–[342] (per Henderson J).

23(2)(a)(iii)

The defendant's change of position in taking a risk with loaned money—for example, using money under a void loan agreement to make a losing investment—will not afford a defence because the defendant will have known throughout that it would have to repay the loaned sum: *Goss v Chilcott* [1996] AC 788,

PC; *Haugesund Kommune v Depfa ACS Bank* [2010] EWCA Civ 579, [2012] 2 WLR 199.

23(2)(b)

It appears that, applying domestic or EU law (in particular, the *San Giorgio* principle), the change of position defence cannot be invoked by a public authority that is liable to make restitution under the *Woolwich* principle: *Test Claimants in the FII Group Litigation v Revenue and Customs Commissioners* [2008] EWHC 2893 (Ch) at [302]–[352], [445] (per Henderson J). The best explanation for this is that the justification for the *Woolwich* principle outweighs concern for the position of the defendant. Conceivably another example of this is where a bank has constructive notice of another's undue influence over a surety who has given the bank a non-commercial guarantee: certainly the bank's good faith change of position was not mentioned in *Royal Bank of Scotland v Etridge (No 2)* [2001] UKHL 44, [2002] 2 AC 773.

23(3)

Where a contract has been terminated for frustration, restitution of an unjust enrichment is governed by the Law Reform (Frustrated Contracts) Act 1943 (subject to s 2(5) of the Act, which excludes some types of contract, such as contracts of insurance). While, as we have seen under s 15(6), the Act is consistent with the approach to restitution for failure of consideration set out in the Restatement, there is more difficulty in saying that the change of position defence that would apply at common law (and under the Restatement) can be applied under the Act. The starting point is that the wording of the proviso to s 1(2) dealing with expenses, and the references to expenses in s 1(3)(a) and to the effect on the benefit of the frustrating event in s 1(3)(b), can all be interpreted as allowing the courts to apply *a form of* the change of position defence. Indeed, although this has been regarded as unhelpful by other judges, Robert Goff J in obiter dicta in *BP Exploration Co (Libya) Ltd v Hunt (No 2)* [1979] 1 WLR 783 at 800, precisely said that the proviso to s 1(2) was 'probably best rationalised as a statutory recognition of the defence of change of position'. However, while ideally the courts should strive to achieve consistency between the Act and the common law on change of position, some of the wording in the Act makes that extremely difficult. One must also recognise that the Act is best interpreted as permitting the courts to go beyond restitution for unjust enrichment so as to effect a limited form of loss apportionment (as appears to have been Garland J's approach in *Gamerco SA v ICM/Fair Warning (Agency) Ltd* [1995] 1 WLR 1226, which is the only reported case on the proviso to s 1(2)).

Estoppel

24 Estoppel
The defendant has a defence to the extent that the defendant has detrimentally relied on a representation by the claimant that the defendant is entitled to the enrichment.

24

That estoppel is a defence to restitution of an unjust enrichment is shown by, eg, *Deutsche Bank (London Agency) v Beriro & Co* (1895) 73 LT 669, CA; *Holt v Markham* [1923] 1 KB 504, CA; and *Scottish Equitable plc v Derby* [2001] EWCA Civ 369, [2001] 3 All ER 818. The relevant representation need not be express and can be implied from the circumstances (see, eg, *Holt v Markham*). In *United Overseas Bank v Jiwani* [1976] 1 WLR 964 Mocatta J indicated that it is a requirement of estoppel that the defendant's detrimental reliance has been in good faith. But it would appear that this adds nothing to the requirement of reliance because if D knows that C's representation is false, D is not relying on it.

Although estoppel has been said to be an 'all-or-nothing' rule of evidence (*Avon CC v Howlett* [1983] 1 WLR 605, CA), in practice the courts have applied it in a proportionate way. This has been achieved (see *Scottish Equitable plc v Derby* [2001] EWCA Civ 369, [2001] 3 All ER 818; *National Westminster Bank plc v Somer International (UK) Ltd* [2001] EWCA Civ 970, [2002] QB 1286) by insisting that estoppel defeats restitution only to the extent that it is not unconscionable for the defendant to retain the balance of the enrichment; and where unconscionable (as it surely always will be), it is a condition of the estoppel that the defendant makes restitution of the balance. Given, therefore, that the defence *operates* in a proportionate way—and this is directly reflected in the words of the Restatement 'to the extent that'—it offers no advantage to a defendant over the change of position defence and is, of course, more onerous in requiring a representation. One can expect, therefore, that in this context, estoppel will wither away, although defendants may continue to use it if for no other reason than that proof of a representation may assist the merits of their defence.

Example

C mistakenly overpays D £1,000 under C's annual bonus scheme. D asks C for confirmation that the bonus paid is correct and is assured by C that it is correct. As a consequence, D spends £750 on a holiday that she would not otherwise have spent. C later discovers its mistake and claims restitution of £1,000 as paid by mistake. If estoppel is an all-or-nothing defence, D would have a complete defence to C's claim. However, applying the better view that estoppel is a proportionate defence, the defence of estoppel would offer D no advantage over the change of position defence and D would have a defence as to £750 but would be bound to make restitution of £250.

> **25 Agency as a defence**
> (1) The defendant may have a defence simply by reason of obtaining the benefit as an agent.
> (2) In any event, if the defendant has obtained the benefit as an agent the defendant has a defence to the extent that the defendant—
>   (a) has transferred the benefit (by payment over or otherwise) to the principal, and
>   (b) has done so without actual notice of the claimant's right to restitution.

25

It is very difficult to state what the present law is on agency as a defence to restitution for unjust enrichment (sometimes referred to as the defence of 'ministerial receipt'). Two different versions of the defence can be detected in the cases (that only the principal can be sued; or, as favoured in most cases, that the agent can also be sued subject to 'payment over') and, indeed, it has sometimes been suggested that this is a distinction between the defence at common law and the defence in equity. The formulation in the Restatement ('may have a defence' in s 25(1) and 'in any event' in s 25(2)) holds open both versions while rejecting any distinction between the defence at common law and in equity.

It should be stressed at the outset that we are, of course, purely concerned here with the law of unjust enrichment. Plainly an agent liable in unjust enrichment can be concurrently liable for the commission of a civil wrong (including, eg, the tort of deceit or the equitable wrongs of breach of fiduciary duty and dishonest assistance).

The uncontroversial starting point is that the agent must obtain the payment (or other benefit) as agent and not as principal. The defence therefore failed in, eg, *Baylis v Bishop of London* [1913] 1 Ch 127, CA, where the defendant obtained mistaken payments as principal and not as agent. Whether a person obtains a payment (or other benefit) as agent or principal turns on the general principles of the law of agency and an agent's authority. However, it should be noted that in this context, where one is essentially focussing on the internal relationship between the agent and the principal, rather than upholding expectations created by the external appearance of agency, one is concerned with actual (not apparent) authority: and the defence applies to undisclosed, as well as disclosed, agents (*Transvaal and Delagoa Bay Investment Co Ltd v Atkinson* [1944] 1 All ER 579; for the contrary view, see obiter dicta of Millett LJ in *Portman Building Society v Hamlyn Taylor Neck* [1998] 4 All ER 202 at 207).

Agency as a defence

Assuming obtaining as agent, one version of the agency defence (which we can label the 'strong version' and is set out at s 25(1)) is that only the principal can be sued. The agent drops out of the picture. This strong version may be said to be supported by the following cases: *Sadler v Evans* (1766) 4 Burr 1984; *Duke of Norfolk v Worthy* (1808) 1 Camp 337; *Ellis v Goulton* [1893] 1 QB 350, CA; and *Agip (Africa) Ltd v Jackson* [1990] Ch 265 (aff'd [1991] Ch 547, CA) (equitable claim). There is a powerful argument that this strong version of the defence is justified because agents should not be caught up in disputes between their principals and third parties. It can further be elaborated on, albeit controversially, by saying that the principal is immediately enriched because the agent has a duty to account to the principal. The principal is, in other words, enriched by the right it has against the agent to the benefit obtained by the agent; and the agent is not enriched because of its duty to account to the principal. However, this elaboration is controversial because, if it were correct, one ought to consider the value of the principal's right against the agent (discounting, for example, for the risk of non-payment or late payment) and there is no hint in the cases that the principal is regarded as enriched only by that value (which will often be less than the value of what the agent has received).

The alternative version of the agency defence (which we can label the 'weak version' and is set out in s 25(2)) has tended to be favoured in the cases. According to this weak version, the agent has a defence provided (a) it has transferred the benefit to the principal by payment over or something equivalent (such as settling an account with the principal); and (b) it has done so without (actual) notice of the claimant's right to restitution. Both these requirements were satisfied so that the defence succeeded in, eg, *Holland v Russell* (1861) 1 B & S 424 (affd (1863) 4 B & S 14); *Gowers v Lloyds and National Provincial Foreign Bank Ltd* [1938] 1 All ER 766, CA; *Transvaal and Delagoa Bay Investment Co Ltd v Atkinson* [1944] 1 All ER 579; and *Agip (Africa) Ltd v Jackson* [1990] Ch 265 (affd [1991] Ch 547, CA) (common law claim). The defence failed because the first requirement was not made out in, eg, *Kleinwort Sons & Co v Dunlop Rubber Co* (1907) 97 LT 263, HL; and it failed because the second requirement was not made out in *Jones v Churcher* [2009] EWHC 722 (QB), [2009] 2 Lloyd's Rep 94 (bank had paid money over to customer after it had notice that the payment had been made by mistake). The words 'to the extent that' clarify that this is a proportionate defence so that there will only be a partial defence if, for example, only part of the money has been paid over.

Example 1

C mistakenly believes that it owes P £5,000 on a contract between them. C pays the £5,000 to A bank for the account of P. A credits that sum to P and P withdraws all the money from that account. A has an agent's payment over defence to C's claim for restitution of the £5,000.

Commentary: Part 4

One matter left unclear in the case law on the weak version is what is regarded as being equivalent to a payment over to the principal (this is captured by the words 'or otherwise' in s 25(2)(a)). It would appear that what is in mind is the agent doing something that cannot easily, or unilaterally, be reversed by the agent. Very important in practice is how this applies to collecting banks. While not all cases are consistent with this, it would seem that a crediting by a bank of its customer's bank account is equivalent to a payment over to that customer by the bank. After that crediting, a bank would be in breach of contract with its customer if it altered that account unless the terms of the contract governing the account permitted that alteration (as they standardly would, for example, where the bank has made an accounting error). Certainly whether a bank is permitted to debit a customer's account is unlikely to turn on whether the customer has, or has not, subsequently withdrawn funds from the account and yet the courts have consistently held that an agent, without notice, is protected after there has been withdrawal of funds by the principal.

Example 2

C mistakenly believes that it owes P £10,000 on a contract between them. C pays the £10,000 to A bank for the account of P. It would appear that A has an agent's payment over defence as soon as A credits P's account with the £10,000 provided A did not know of C's mistake before it credited P's account.

It is strongly arguable that this weak version of the defence of agency is swallowed up by the change of position defence. This is so if the two requirements for the defence (payment over, without notice) are seen as merely specific manifestations of the need for establishing, respectively, that the defendant's position has changed for the worse because of the enrichment and that the defendant has changed its position in good faith. Nevertheless the agent's 'payment over' has continued to be treated as a defence separate from change of position (see, eg, *Portman Building Society v Hamlyn Taylor Neck* [1998] 4 All ER 202, 207; *Jones v Churcher* [2009] EWHC 722 (QB), [2009] 2 Lloyd's Rep 94). The view taken in the Restatement is that, at this stage in the development of the law, it remains helpful to state the weak version of the defence separately from change of position, even if it is a more specific manifestation of that wider defence.

Stevens, 'Why Do Agents "Drop Out"?' [2005] LMCLQ 101 has powerfully argued that, where the unjust factor is failure of consideration, there is often no right to restitution from an agent (even if one rejects the strong version of the agency defence) because a failure of consideration as regards the principal does not necessarily mean that there has been a failure of consideration as regards the agent. This can be illustrated as follows:

Example 3

P agrees to paint C's house for £1,000 payable in advance. C pays £1,000 into P's account at A bank. P refuses to carry out the work. C has a right to restitution of £1,000 from P for failure of consideration. But even if the weak version of the agency defence applies, C has no right to restitution from A bank because there is no failure of consideration vis-à-vis A bank (ie as far as the bank is concerned there is no condition relating to the payment of the money).

Having explained s 25(1) and (2), this is the appropriate point at which to explain s 7(4) of the Restatement. This is because, in understanding agency in the law of unjust enrichment, one needs to explain not only why the agent has a defence but also why the principal is liable. Yet it is clear law that, whether or not the agent has a defence, the principal is liable to make restitution (subject—although this has rarely, if ever, been stated—to avoiding double recovery from both agent and principal: see s 5(3)(c)). This can be seen both from the cases that apply the strong version of the defence so that *only* the principal can be sued (eg *Sadler v Evans* (1766) 4 Burr 1984; *Duke of Norfolk v Worthy* (1808) 1 Camp 337; *Ellis v Goulton* [1893] 1 QB 350, CA); and from cases applying the weaker version of the defence so that both the principal and the agent can be sued subject to the agent's 'payment over' defence (eg *Coulthurst v Sweet* (1866) LR 1 CP 649, in which it was held that the principal was liable to repay money even though the agent had no defence). It would seem that the best explanation for the principal's liability is that the agency relationship precisely rests on the common intention of the principal and agent that the agent's obtaining of a benefit is to be treated as (also) being the principal's obtaining of a benefit.

Example 4

C mistakenly overpays A £10,000 on a contract with P. A has throughout been acting as P's agent in relation to the contract. A fails to pay the £10,000 over to P. C has a right to restitution from P (and, on the weak version of the agency defence, also has a claim against A). P is liable even if A has disappeared with the £10,000 or is insolvent. It is also most unlikely that P would have a change of position defence because, vis-à-vis C, its position cannot be neatly separated from that of its agent A so that, eg, P is caught by the 'bad faith' of A.

Example 5

C enters into a contract with P for the purchase of land from P. C pays A, P's agent (who is a solicitor) a deposit of £50,000. P breaks the contract by refusing to go ahead with the conveyance. C has a right to restitution of £50,000 from

P for failure of consideration. (Assuming C has an unjust factor as regards A, A has a defence at least if it has paid the money over to P (or done something equivalent) without notice of C's claim.)

Example 6

C enters into a contract with P for the purchase of soya beans and, as requested, C pays £20,000 as part of the price in advance to P's agent, A. P breaks the contract by failing to supply soya beans. C has a right to restitution of £20,000 from P for failure of consideration. (Assuming C has an unjust factor as regards A, A has a defence at least if it has paid the money over to P (or done something equivalent) without notice of C's claim.)

26 Counter-restitution

(1) The defendant has a defence if it is impossible for there to be counter-restitution of reciprocal benefits conferred on the claimant by the defendant.
(2) The defendant normally has a set-off defence for counter-restitution of reciprocal benefits conferred on the claimant by the defendant.

26(1)

The term 'counter-restitution' was used by the Court of Appeal in *Halpern v Halpern* [2007] EWCA Civ 291, [2008] QB 195 as the English equivalent of *restitutio in integrum*. It underpins the traditional bar to rescission that '*restitutio in integrum* is impossible'. The rationale of this bar is that *the claimant* must be able to make restitution of what it has itself received from the defendant otherwise, by reversing the defendant's unjust enrichment, the law will produce the result that the claimant is itself left unjustly enriched at the defendant's expense. Therefore, if counter-restitution cannot be made—counter-restitution is impossible—the claimant should be denied restitution. The case law shows that the bar has been successfully invoked where the claimant has consumed, or disposed of, the benefit obtained: see, eg, *Vigers v Pike* (1842) 8 Cl & Fin 562, HL; *Clarke v Dickson* (1858) EB & E 148; *Ladywell Mining Co v Brookes* (1887) 35 Ch D 400, CA.

Example 1

C and D enter into a contract compromising an inheritance dispute. Under the agreement, C is to transfer substantial assets to D in return for D destroying certain documents (that might have assisted D in any proceedings against C). C now seeks to rescind the contract for duress by D. Applying the traditional bar, C cannot rescind and have restitution from D because C cannot make counter-restitution of the benefit that C has derived from the destruction of the documents by D. (This example is based on the facts of *Halpern v Halpern* [2007] EWCA Civ 291, [2008] QB 195.)

However, the modern trend is for the courts to allow rescission provided counter-restitution can be achieved in a rough-and-ready way by a monetary award, even if precise counter-restitution is impossible: see, eg, *Erlanger v New Sombrero Phosphate Co* (1878) 3 App Cas 1218, HL (non-disclosure); *O'Sullivan v Management Agency and Music Ltd* [1985] QB 428, CA (undue influence). Moreover, it can be strongly argued that, in principle, the traditional bar focusing on the impossibility of counter-restitution is needlessly extreme because counter-restitution by a monetary equivalent, while sometimes raising difficult issues of assessment, is *never* impossible. If that argument were to be accepted—and it was considered, but not ruled on, in *Halpern v Halpern*—the weaker version of this defence, which effectively recognises counter-restitution as a set-off defence, would still apply. This weaker version is embodied in s 26(2).

26(2)

As we have just seen, the modern trend is for the courts to allow rescission provided counter-restitution can be achieved in a rough-and-ready way by a monetary award even if precise counter-restitution is impossible. The idea of counter-restitution also underpins the situation where, eg, under a void contract requiring payments both ways, the claimant is entitled to restitution of money paid but subject to giving credit—counter-restitution—for the sums it has itself received: see, eg, *Westdeutsche Landesbank Girozentrale v Islington BC* [1994] 4 All ER 890, 941 (per Hobhouse J). Expanding beyond those situations, counter-restitution should be recognised as a general proportionate defence to restitution of an unjust enrichment. In essence, it appears that one is recognising that the defendant has a counterclaim/set-off for the enrichment it has conferred on the claimant which is unjust most obviously because of failure of consideration (ie the basis upon which the *defendant* rendered the benefit to the *claimant* has been removed). The importance of this defence would become even more obvious if the Restatement's position were fully accepted that a failure of consideration need not be total in order to trigger restitution: a claimant seeking restitution of money paid for failure of consideration, comprising the partial performance of services by the defendant, would need to give counter-restitution of the value of the services rendered. Although one might regard counter-restitution as already embraced by the wider defence of change of position, it seems preferable to treat it separately not only because, in principle, it has a separate rationale, but also because there is at least one practical difference, namely that there is no bad faith disqualification. See, eg, *Spence v Crawford* [1939] 3 All ER 271 at 288–9, HL (per Lord Wright). This can be illustrated as follows:

Commentary: Part 4

Example 2

D induces a contract for the sale of a car to C (C is the purchaser) by a fraudulent misrepresentation to C. C is entitled to rescind the contract and to have restitution of the price paid subject to giving counter-restitution to D of the car or its value. It is not a bar to D's entitlement to counter-restitution that D was acting in bad faith in transferring the car to C.

One might further argue that, because it operates as a set-off defence, counter-restitution should not be afforded separate status as a defence. That is, one might view the defence as merely an aspect of the general defence of set-off rather than being a defence of counter-restitution; and a set-off to a claim for restitution of an unjust enrichment could operate (applying the standard law on counterclaims and set-offs) in situations that have nothing to do with counter-restitution (eg D may be entitled to set off a contractual claim for money owed to D by C against the restitution owed by D to C). But set-off by counter-restitution will be very common as a defence to restitution for unjust enrichment because it will apply wherever benefits have passed both ways, and for that reason it seems appropriate to highlight it as a separate defence while recognising that set-off other than by counter-restitution is also a possible defence to restitution for unjust enrichment (although not one that has been included in the Restatement because the general law on counterclaims and set-offs applies without there being anything specific to, or worthy of comment in relation to, the context of unjust enrichment.)

The word 'normally' has been included in s 26(2) as recognition that, in some limited situations, counter-restitution should not be required. There was some discussion of this in *Halpern v Halpern* [2007] EWCA Civ 291, [2008] QB 195 at [74]. Although this is by no means certain, it would appear that the principle is that counter-restitution is not required where the usual elements of unjust enrichment cannot be established in relation to the counter-restitution. So, for example, this will be so where the claimant cannot be said to have been enriched because it did not freely choose the benefit.

Example 3

D demands £2,000 for retiling C's roof, threatening 'unpleasant consequences' if C does not agree. D does the work and C pays £2,000. Assuming C is entitled to restitution of the £2,000 for duress, there will usually be no set-off defence of counter-restitution for the value of the retiling work. This is because C cannot be said to be enriched by the retiling of the roof (unless, for example, the retiling has enhanced the value of the house and C has sold the house and realised that enhanced value).

A counter-example, where C is clearly enriched so that there is a set-off for counter-restitution, is as follows:

Example 4

D demands that C pays him £1m for a Rembrandt worth £800,000, threatening 'unpleasant consequences' if C does not agree. C buys the picture for £1m. C can have restitution of the £1m for duress but must give counter-restitution to D of the Rembrandt or its value.

Another possible example where set-off for counter-restitution may be denied is where the defendant's illegality is such that it would be a defence to a counterclaim for restitution by the defendant. This is supported by *Kasumu v Babe-Egbe* [1956] AC 539, PC (no counter-restitution required by claimant borrower when rescinding an illegal moneylending contract). But for an earlier contrary decision, also in the context of an illegal moneylending contract, see *Lodge v National Union Investment Co Ltd* [1907] 1 Ch 300.

---

27 Purchaser in good faith, for value and without notice
(1) The defendant has a defence if the defendant—
   (a) is a purchaser in good faith of the benefit for value, without notice of the claimant's right to restitution, from a person other than the claimant, and
   (b) can rely on an exception to the rule that no person can give a better title than the person has.
(2) The defendant normally has a defence if the defendant has obtained the benefit from a person who satisfies paragraphs (a) and (b) of subsection (1).

27(1)

There is a continuing dispute as to what role, if any, is played in the law of unjust enrichment by the defence of bona fide purchase from a third party. Clearly the defence is well established as a defence in property law whereby it provides a wide-ranging exception to the general rule that 'no person can give better title than the person has' (*nemo dat quod non habet*). Some would seek to confine the defence to that role within the law of property and would argue that it has no relevance to the law of unjust enrichment: see, eg, Lord Millett's speech in *Foskett v McKeown* [2001] 1 AC 102 at 129. But as we have seen above (commentary on s 9), the reasoning in that case (arguing that the trust was explicable in terms of 'vindicating property rights' as opposed to being created by unjust enrichment) is unsatisfactory and Lord Millett's obiter dicta on the bona fide purchase defence are tainted in the same way. The preferable view is that bona fide purchase from a third party may be a defence to both personal and proprietary restitution for unjust enrichment (albeit that, as one is here concerned with restitution from a defendant who has obtained the benefit from a third party, an initial substantial hurdle facing the claimant will be to establish that the enrichment is 'at the expense of' the indirect provider (the claimant) rather than the direct provider (the third party): see ss 8–9).

As regards personal restitution, the leading case is *Lipkin Gorman v Karpnale Ltd* [1991] 2 AC 548, in which it was accepted that bona fide purchase from a third party is a defence to a personal restitutionary claim. On the facts the defence failed because, although in one sense value was given by the defendant club to Cass (by exchanging money for gambling chips or in paying out winnings on money gambled), it was held that that value did not count for the purposes of the defence because it was given under a void wagering contract. Had the contract been a valid one (as it would be now by reason of the Gambling Act 2005) the defence would have succeeded.

Example 1

X, a partner in a firm of solicitors (C), draws £2,000 from the partnership account without C's authority and uses it to stay at The Ritz (D). D is acting in good faith without notice that the £2,000 has been taken from C. Assuming that C has a prima facie claim against D in unjust enrichment, D has the defence that it is a bona fide purchaser for value of the £2,000 without notice.

It should be interjected here that, although the reasoning of the House of Lords in *Lipkin Gorman* was clear that there can be no relevant value for the purposes of this defence if the contract is void, that is controversial and it can be strongly argued that, provided factual value has been given, it should be irrelevant whether the contract is valid or void. After all, 'purchaser' in the context of real property has historically extended beyond contracts to gifts, which explains the need for the additional words 'for value': see Harpum, Bridge and Dixon, *Megarry and Wade's The Law of Real Property* (8th edn, 2012) para 5-008.

As regards proprietary restitution, it is clear that bona fide purchasers for value without notice, as opposed to innocent volunteers, have a defence to the recognition of rights in property after tracing (see, eg, *Sinclair Investments (UK) Ltd v Versailles Trade Finance Ltd* [2011] EWCA Civ 347, [2011] 3 WLR 1153; *Independent Trustee Services Ltd v GP Noble Trustees Ltd* [2012] EWCA Civ 195, [2012] 3 All ER 210; Hanbury and Martin, *Modern Equity* (19th edn, 2012) para 23-069); and it is also well established that, where the claimant is rescinding a contract (eg for misrepresentation or undue influence), the fact that the defendant is a bona fide purchaser for value without notice prevents the claimant revesting its proprietary rights in property that has subsequently been transferred to the defendant: *Cundy v Lindsay* (1878) 3 App Cas 459 at 463–4; *Morley v Loughnan* [1893] 1 Ch 736. (The conventional view is that bona fide purchase is a bar to rescission of the contract. If correct, bona fide purchase would have the further impact of preventing a successful claim for restitution of an unjust enrichment because the benefit has been conferred under a voidable contract that, unless and until rescinded, remains binding: see s 3(6). But for powerful criticism of the conventional view, and for the better interpretation being that bona fide purchase does not bar rescission of the contract as such, see Häcker, 'Rescission and Third Party Rights' [2006] RLR 21 esp at 36; O'Sullivan, Elliott, and Zakrzewski, *The Law of Rescission* (2008) ch 20.)

For a discussion of the meaning of 'notice' for the defence, including the point that it extends to constructive notice, see *Sinclair Investments (UK) Ltd v Versailles Trade Finance Ltd* [2011] EWCA Civ 347, [2011] 3 WLR 1153 at [97]–[128].

As made clear in *Lipkin Gorman v Karpnale Ltd*, the bona fide purchase defence is an all-or-nothing defence and therefore fundamentally differs from the change of position defence which operates proportionately. So if the contract between Cass and the club had been a valid one, it would have given a defence to the club irrespective of the quantum of value given by the club under the contract.

Example 2

X steals £1,000 from C and uses it to buy a car from D. Although X pays D £1,000 for the car, it is in fact worth only £400. Assuming that C has a prima facie claim against D in unjust enrichment, D has the defence that it is a bona fide purchaser for value without notice. That is an all-or-nothing defence. In contrast, a change of position defence would merely protect D to the extent that it is worse off than if it had not received the money in the first place: and D is worse off only to the extent of £400 so that, if one were merely to apply a change of position defence, D would be bound to make restitution of £600.

Assuming that the above is correct, and that the bona fide purchase defence is a defence (and a defence to personal as well as proprietary restitution) within the law of unjust enrichment, the question becomes: what is the precise justification and scope of this defence? The best answer appears to be that the defence is concerned to avoid a clash between the law of unjust enrichment and the well-established application of the bona fide purchase defence within the law of property (in which it operates as a wide-ranging exception to the *nemo dat* rule). What the defence seeks to avoid is the indirect recipient taking good title to the property, as a bona fide purchaser, and yet simultaneously being made liable in unjust enrichment (eg to make restitution of the value of the property) to the original owner. The defence therefore has a 'parasitic' justification, which reads across from property law to unjust enrichment: hence s 27(1)(b). Where the defence would apply in the law of property it will apply in unjust enrichment; where the defence would not apply in the law of property it will not apply in unjust enrichment.

Example 3

X steals £1,000 from C. X uses that £1,000 to buy a car from D. D is a bona fide purchaser of the £1,000 for value without notice. As a matter of property law, D takes good title to the £1,000 as an exception to the *nemo dat* rule. C would have a prima facie claim against D in the law of unjust enrichment for personal (or proprietary) restitution of the £1,000. But, by reason of s 27(1), the bona fide purchase by D would be a defence to that claim. This would prevent the law of unjust enrichment undermining the law of property by which it has been decided (in resolving the conflict between security of receipt and sanctity of transactions) that D has good title to the £1,000.

Example 4

X steals a car from C. X sells the car to D for £5,000. Although D is a bona fide purchaser for value without notice, as a matter of property law D does not take good title to the car because as regards goods (other than money) the *nemo dat* rule here applies and C retains his title to the car. C would also have a claim against D in the law of unjust enrichment for personal restitution of the £5,000 and here, applying s 27(1), there would be no defence of bona fide purchase. The defence tracks the defence in property law and hence granting restitution would, in this example, not undermine the approach taken in the law of property.

There is an argument that this defence should be expanded so as to have a wider rationale. This is the argument that the bona fide purchase defence should break free from its 'proprietary' limitations so as to provide a defence where the defendant was contractually entitled to the relevant enrichment under a valid contract with a third party. For this argument see, eg, Barker, 'After Change of Position: Good Faith Exchange in the Modern Law of Restitution' in Birks (ed) *Laundering and Tracing* (1995) 191. If that were to occur, one would be protecting the sanctity of the contract between the defendant and the third party in a similar way to where unjust enrichment is denied in a two-party case because the enrichment was owed to the defendant by the claimant under a valid contract (see s 3(6)). However, acceptance of this argument would appear to involve abandoning the present insistence on purchase 'for value' so as to include an unexecuted contractual promise (that a party promising to pay money is not a purchaser for value until he pays over money is long established: see, eg, *Story v Lord Windsor* (1743) 2 Atk 630). And, arguably, the need for the defendant to be acting bona fide without notice would also need to be abandoned on the ground that it would be sufficient that the contract with the third party was valid (and, applying the normal objective approach in contract, knowledge of, for example, the other party's mistake is irrelevant).

Example 5

X steals a car from C. X sells the car to D, who has no notice of the theft, for £10,000. As we have seen in Example 4 above, D has no defence under s 27(1) to an unjust enrichment claim by C for the value of the car. But if the wider contractual justification were applied, D would have a defence because D is entitled to the car under a valid contract with X (at least where D has no notice of the theft by X).

Closely linked to this is the argument that, alongside the bona fide purchase defence, English law should recognise a defence of 'good consideration' or 'discharge for value'. This would apply where the defendant (D) in good faith obtained a benefit from the claimant (C) that D was entitled to under a valid obligation owed by a third party (X). Support for the existence of this defence may be derived from one interpretation of the following: *Aiken v Short* (1856) 1 H & N 210; Robert Goff J's judgment (his qualification 2(b)) in *Barclays Bank Ltd v WJ Simms, Son and Cook (Southern) Ltd* [1980] QB 677, 695; and *Lloyds Bank plc v Independent Insurance Co Ltd* [2000] QB 110, CA. However, it is very controversial whether there is such a defence and, at least at this stage of development, it has not been included in the Restatement. This is particularly because the above cases are probably open to better interpretations. So, for example, in the *Lloyds Bank* case (see Example 17 in the commentary to s 8(3) above), Waller LJ, giving the leading judgment, appeared to regard the defence of change of position as the best explanation for the decision (ie as D (the creditor) had accepted the discharge of the liability of the third party customer (X), D would be in a worse position than before the payment from C (the bank) if the money was repaid to C: and that would clearly have been so unless X's liability was revived if D repaid C). Moreover, the denial of restitution on the facts of a case like *Lloyds Bank* case is best explained, although this was not part of the reasoning, by s 8(3): so it has been forcefully argued by, for example, Birks, *Unjust Enrichment* (2nd edn, 1995) 90, that the 'at the expense of' interpretation must be correct because it was irrelevant whether the payment by C to D was made to discharge a liability of X to D or to effect a gift from X to D.

27(2)

Applying the rationale of not undermining, by means of the law of unjust enrichment, the application of the bona fide purchase defence in the law of property, the defence also normally applies where the defendant has obtained the benefit from a bona fide purchaser (who itself has a defence). The most obvious application of this is where tracing is being relied on to establish that the defendant has been enriched *at the claimant's expense* (see s 9 above) and there has been an intermediate purchase by a bona fide purchaser for value without notice.

Example 6

C transfers a ring under a fundamental mistake to X so that title does not pass to X. X transfers the ring to Y in exchange for a watch. X transfers the watch to Z in exchange for a necklace. Z gives the watch to D. D now has the watch. Although one can say that C can trace from the ring to the watch, and although C had title to the ring immediately prior to its substitution by the watch, C has no right to restitution from D. This is because D has obtained the watch from Z, who was a bona fide purchaser of the watch for value without notice and acquired good title to it.

The word 'normally' has been included in s 27(2) because there are some limited situations where an exception to this aspect of the bona fide purchase defence has been recognised. See, eg, *Wilkes v Spooner* [1911] 2 KB 473, 483, CA, per Vaughan Williams LJ; and *Independent Trustee Services Ltd v GP Noble Trustees Ltd* [2012] EWCA Civ 195, [2012] 3 All ER 210, at [49] per Patten LJ, which recognise exceptions where the defendant, although deriving title from a bona fide purchaser, has been acting fraudulently or in breach of trust.

28   Illegality as a defence
(1) The defendant has a defence if the claimant's conduct has been illegal.
(2) Conduct is illegal if—
    (a) it constitutes a crime or a civil wrong, or
    (b) it is contrary to public policy.
(3) But the defendant does not have this defence if—
    (a) the unjust factor is concerned with illegality (see section 20), or
    (b) the unjust factor excuses the illegality (as, for example, where the claimant was acting under duress or, because of a mistake, did not know of the illegality), or
    (c) the denial of restitution would be a disproportionate response to the illegality, taking into account in particular the following aims—
        (i) furthering the purpose of the rule which the illegal conduct has infringed;
        (ii) avoiding inconsistency in the law;
        (iii) deterring illegal conduct;
        (iv) ensuring that the claimant does not profit from the illegal conduct.

Illegality as a defence

28(1)–(2)

As made clear by s 28(2), illegality as a defence embraces conduct that not only constitutes a legal wrong, whether a crime or civil wrong (including a statutory wrong), but also conduct that is contrary to public policy. In the context of illegal contracts, conduct that has been regarded as contrary to public policy has included sexual immorality, restraint of trade, and interfering with the administration of justice. See, generally, Peel, *Treitel on the Law of Contract* (13th edn, 2011) ch 11; Law Commission Consultation Paper CP No 154, *Illegal Transactions: The Effect of Illegality on Contracts and Trusts* (1999) paras 1.4–1.11.

28(3)

The law on illegality as a defence to restitution for unjust enrichment is, in some respects, unclear and difficult to rationalise. Two Latin maxims are often used without greatly illuminating the legal position: *ex turpi causa non oritur actio* ('no action arises from a disgraceful cause') and *in pari delicto potior est conditio defendentis* ('where both parties are equally in the wrong the position of the defendant is the stronger'). In very general terms it can be said that: (i) illegality is normally a defence to restitution for total failure of consideration (see, eg, the denial of restitution in *Parkinson v College of Ambulance Ltd and Harrison* [1925] 2 KB 1; *Berg v Sadler and Moore* [1937] 2 KB 158, CA; *Boissevain v Weil* [1950] AC 327, HL; and *Awwad v Geraghty & Co* [2001] QB 570, CA); (ii) illegality is rarely a defence to restitution for mistake or duress (*Oom v Bruce* (1810) 12 East 225; *Hughes v Liverpool Victoria Friendly Society* [1916] 2 KB 482, CA; *Kiriri Cotton Co v Dewani* [1960] AC 192, PC; *Re Cavalier Insurance Co Ltd* [1989] 2 Lloyd's Rep 43 (all granting restitution for mistake despite illegality); *Astley v Reynolds* (1731) 2 Stra 915; *Smith v Bromley* (1760) 2 Doug KB 696n; *Smith v Cuff* (1817) 6 M & S 160; and *Davies v London and Provincial Marine Insurance Co* (1878) 8 Ch D 469 (all granting restitution for duress despite illegality).

The muddled state of the law on illegality has led to calls for reform by commentators and by the Law Commission. This is not only in the law of unjust enrichment but also in relation to tort and contract and especially in respect of claims based on pre-existing title (where, as established in the leading cases of *Bowmakers Ltd v Barnet Instruments Ltd* [1945] KB 65, CA, and *Tinsley v Milligan* [1994] 1 AC 340, HL, the courts apply the formalistic and unwarranted approach of asking whether the claimant is, or is not, *relying* on the illegality to establish its claim). The Law Commission's final report, *The Illegality Defence* (Law Com No 320, 2010), argued that (leaving aside the 'reliance principle' for which statutory reform was recommended) satisfactory development of the law was within the interpretative reach of the courts so that legislation was not needed. In its earlier consultation paper, CP No 189, *The Illegality Defence, A Consultative Report* (2009) esp at paras 2.35,

3.142, and 4.44, the Law Commission proposed that the way forward was for the courts to articulate and balance the various polices in play in deciding the central question of whether the denial of the claimant's normal rights was a proportionate response to the claimant's illegality. The policies articulated were furthering the purpose of the rule which the illegal conduct has infringed, consistency, that the claimant should not profit from his or her own wrong, deterrence, and maintaining the integrity of the legal system. Very importantly, in its final report, the Commission saw support for this approach from the House of Lords in the tort case of *Gray v Thames Trains Ltd* [2009] UKHL 33, [2009] 1 AC 1339. Lord Hoffmann said at [30]: 'The maxim ex turpi causa expresses not so much a principle as a policy. Furthermore that policy is not based upon a single justification but on a group of reasons which vary in different situations.' This was cited with approval by Lord Phillips in *Stone & Rolls Ltd v Moore Stephens* [2009] UKHL 39, [2009] 1 AC 1391 at [25] (by a 3–2 majority it was held that illegality barred the contract and tort claim of the company against its auditors). It is also noteworthy that both those decisions (and *Safeway Stores Ltd v Twigger* [2010] EWCA Civ 1472, [2011] 1 Lloyd's Rep 462) endorsed the importance of the policy of avoiding inconsistency within the legal system, or maintaining 'the integrity of the legal system' as it was termed by McLachlin J in the Supreme Court of Canada in *Hall v Hebert* [1993] 2 SCR 159 at 176. This is the same idea as not 'stultifying the law', which was the language used by Lord Radcliffe in *Boissevain v Weil* [1950] AC 327 and was the terminology relied on heavily by Birks, *Unjust Enrichment* (2nd edn, 2005) 247–50.

That approach has recently been explicitly approved and applied by the Court of Appeal in *Les Laboratoires Servier v Apotex Inc* [2012] EWCA Civ 593 esp at [66], [73] and [75]. The leading judgment was given by Etherton LJ, who was Chair of the Law Commission at the time of much of its work on illegality. The claim was for damages under a cross-undertaking in damages given by Servier, who had been granted an injunction against Apotex to restrain infringement of a patent. It transpired that Servier should not have been granted that injunction because it had no valid patent in this jurisdiction. The question was whether Apotex's illegality, by acting in breach of a valid Canadian patent, constituted a defence to Apotex's claim for damages under the cross-undertaking. It was held that, in the light of the policies in play and, taking into account in assessing those policies whether the illegality was trivial or inadvertent, the illegality should not be a defence, so that Apotex was entitled to damages.

Section 28(3)—which, it is believed (especially in the light of *Les Laboratoires Servier v Apotex Inc*) sets out a position that can be reached by the courts and reflects the explicit policy emphasis that has recently been endorsed by the cases referred to above—draws on much of the thinking of the Law Commission and of the Court of Appeal in the *Apotex* case, albeit that one is here putting forward a formulation that is specific to restitution for unjust enrichment.

Illegality as a defence

The first exception in s 28(3)(a) is to ensure that there is no inconsistency with an entitlement to restitution under s 20. That is, one cannot say, on the one hand, that C is entitled to restitution so as to encourage abandonment of an illegal purpose or to protect C as a member of a particular class and then go on to say, on the other hand, that there is a defence of illegality.

The second exception in s 28(3)(b) is very close to the application of the *non in pari delicto* idea but removes any importance being attached to the relative fault of the parties. It ties in directly with illegality not normally being a defence to duress or mistake.

Example 1

C pays money to D to remove D's threat to prosecute X, a friend of C's, for suspected theft. Although C's contract with D is illegal as being concerned to stifle a prosecution, the illegality is not a defence to C's claims against D for restitution for duress. (This is based on *Davies v London and Provincial Marine Insurance Co* (1878) 8 Ch D 469.)

Example 2

C enters into a contract with D (an insurer) to insure goods that are being transported from a country that is at war with England. C knows nothing about the outbreak of war and pays premiums under the policy. The contract is illegal as involving trading with an enemy. But the illegality is not a defence to C's mistake claim for restitution of the premiums. (This is based on *Oom v Bruce* (1810) 12 East 225.)

Example 3

C and D enter into a contract whereby C pays D for him to ensure that C is given a knighthood. D fails to bring this about (and indeed does not have the power to do so). C seeks restitution for mistake, the mistake being that C thought D had the power to arrange a knighthood. Illegality *is* a defence because C's mistake does not excuse, by 'masking', the illegality: ie C still knows that he is entering into an illegal contract. This is based on the facts of *Parkinson v College of Ambulance Ltd and Harrison* [1925] 2 KB 1 (see also the commentary on s 20 above, especially Example 2).

The third exception in s 28(3)(c) is more broad-ranging and, in particular, enables the courts to reach decisions on whether illegality should bar restitution for failure of consideration more openly and rationally than has traditionally occurred in the past. (Note that of the five specific policies articulated by the Law Commission, 'maintaining the integrity of the legal system' has not been included because that is synonymous with, and is covered by, 'avoiding inconsistency in the law'.) Although some may fear that an open weighing of policies will produce uncertainty, it is believed that this is an unwarranted fear and that uncertainty has pervaded this area precisely because, until recently, there has been no clear articulation of the underlying issues of policy involved.

Example 4

C and D enter into a contract whereby C pays D for him to ensure that C is given a knighthood. D fails to bring this about (and indeed does not have the power to do so). C seeks restitution for failure of consideration. Illegality is a defence and denial of restitution is a proportionate response, not least because of the need to deter such payments. This is based on the facts of *Parkinson v College of Ambulance Ltd and Harrison* [1925] 2 KB 1.

Example 5

C contracts to pay D £10,000 to murder X. C pays the money but D refuses to carry out the murder. C is not entitled to restitution for failure of consideration. Denial of restitution is a proportionate response to the extreme illegality involved. Moreover, far from deterring such illegality, to allow restitution for failure of consideration might encourage D to carry out the murder (so as to be entitled to the money) and might encourage people like C to enter into such contracts (in the knowledge that one is entitled to restitution if the murder is not carried out).

Example 6

C loans £50,000 to D under a contract that is illegal as involving an excessively high rate of interest. D fails to repay. C has been fined for the offence in question and C is not entitled to enforce the loan because of the illegality. C seeks restitution of the money paid for failure of consideration. In deciding whether illegality should apply as a defence, the courts should take into account that, on the one hand, the sanction of C 'losing' £50,000 plus the fine appears excessive for the illegality in question and, in that sense, does not further the purpose of the relevant rule. On the other hand, to allow restitution would, on the face of it, be inconsistent with the contractual invalidity and, rather than deterring such illegality, granting restitution might tend to encourage creditors to make such loans knowing that, if not repaid, they would be entitled to restitution. At least if C did not know of the illegality, the former considerations probably outweigh the latter, and, if so, illegality would not be a defence in this example.

It should be noted, finally, that no separate treatment is afforded in the Restatement to the equitable maxim that 'he who comes to equity must come with clean

Resolved disputes

hands'. Although potentially applicable to equitable restitutionary rights (such as rescission for innocent misrepresentation or rectification or an equitable lien) there appears to be no case in the context of unjust enrichment where this bar has been applied. In any event, in principle there is no good reason why one should recognise a defence for the claimant's bad conduct that goes beyond the defence of illegality.

29 Resolved disputes

The defendant has a defence if—

(a) there has been a judgment or contract of compromise which dealt with the unjust enrichment and has not been reversed or set aside, or

(b) the claimant is seeking restitution in respect of a payment made by the claimant to stop legal proceedings that were initiated against the claimant in good faith.

29

A claimant with a right to restitution of an unjust enrichment may lose that right because the dispute has been resolved and cannot be reopened. The policy is one of ensuring finality to disputes. Traditionally treated under labels such as *res judicata* and compromise, it is a wide-ranging defence that is not exclusive to unjust enrichment (outside this Restatement, the underlying dispute might be about, eg, a right in contract or tort).

Section 29(a) can be illustrated as follows:

Example 1

C has paid D £1,000 under alleged duress and claims restitution. There has been a judgment in D's favour to the effect that C was not acting under duress. C regards the judgment as incorrect. C cannot revert to its original claim provided the judgment is valid and has not been overturned on an appeal. (It appears that a judgment is invalid if, eg, it is ultra vires the court or has been obtained by fraud.)

Example 2

C has paid D £10,000 by mistake, although D disputes that C was mistaken and in any event is arguing that it has partly changed its position. The parties enter into a contract of compromise whereby C gives up any claim it may have in return for a payment of £2,500. C cannot revert to a claim to restitution provided the contract of compromise is valid.

Commentary: Part 4

As an alternative to talking about a policy of finality one could say that the right to restitution has been merged in the judgment or that the claimant has given up that right by a contractual waiver.

Although the underlying claim was not one for unjust enrichment, it is worth mentioning here a leading modern case on compromises: *Brennan v Bolt Burdon* [2004] EWCA Civ 1017, [2005] QB 303. Here a compromise (of a personal injury claim) had been reached on the assumption that the claim had been validly struck out. In a subsequent decision in a different case, the law was 'changed' so that the striking out was invalid. The Court of Appeal accepted that, while a common mistake of law can render a contract of compromise void in the same way as any other contract, the courts would be reluctant to find a contract of compromise void for common mistake precisely because a claimant takes various risks, including that the law may be 'changed', when entering into a compromise.

Section 29(b) covers a situation more specifically tied to unjust enrichment. It deals with where, even though there has been no judgment that would need to be reversed or set aside, a payment has been made *after* legal proceedings have been initiated in good faith demanding that payment. Although at first sight one might regard this as merely an aspect of the law of duress (as illustrating the principle that a threat to sue is not normally illegitimate) it is more wide-ranging and is also a defence to a claim for, eg, mistake. It is therefore best seen alongside judgments and compromises as justified by the merits of bringing finality to disputes. This may be referred to as a 'submission to an honest claim' but that terminology is sometimes used in a wider sense to include a contract of compromise and also, misleadingly, where a non-contractual payment is made *before* legal proceedings have been started (the latter usage is misleading because there should be no defence in that situation).

Example 3

C pays for goods bought from D. D later demands payment again, and initiates legal proceedings in good faith, alleging that C has not paid. C cannot find the receipt for the first payment and pays again. When C subsequently finds the receipt, C seeks restitution of the second payment as paid by duress or mistake. Applying s 29(b), there is no right to restitution. (These were the facts in *Marriot v Hampton* (1797) 7 Term Rep 269.)

Example 4

D demands payment from C for street improvements. A summons is issued. C pays but then discovers that a mistake has been made because his house does not abut the street in question so that he was not liable to pay for the improvements. Applying s 29(b), there is no right to restitution. (These were the facts in *Moore v Vestry of Fulham* [1895] 1 QB 399, CA.)

Limitation

It should be noted that the important distinction between the facts in *Moore v Vestry of Fulham* and those in *Woolwich Equitable Building Soc v IRC* [1993] AC 70, HL (see s 21 above) is that, in the former, but not the latter, the payment was made *after* legal proceedings had been initiated.

30 Limitation

(1) The rules set out in subsections (2) to (7) are largely derived from the Limitation Act 1980.

(2) Subject to the exceptions in subsections (3) to (9), there is a limitation period of 6 years to enforce a restitutionary right which runs from when the cause of action accrues.

The cause of action in unjust enrichment accrues when the defendant is unjustly enriched at the claimant's expense.

(3) If the unjust factor is mistake, the limitation period does not start to run until the claimant has discovered, or could reasonably have discovered, the mistake; but this postponement does not apply to the restitution of tax paid to Her Majesty's Revenue and Customs under a mistake of law.

(4) If any fact relevant to the claimant's cause of action has been deliberately concealed from the claimant by the defendant, the limitation period does not start to run until the claimant has discovered, or could reasonably have discovered, the concealment.

(5) The limitation period does not run where the claimant is under 18 or lacks mental capacity.

(6) If—
   (a) an action in unjust enrichment has accrued to recover any debt or other liquidated pecuniary claim, and
   (b) the defendant acknowledges the claim or makes any part payment in respect of it,

the cause of action is to be treated as having accrued on the date of the acknowledgement or part payment.

(7) There are statutory provisions which displace the 6 year limitation period to enforce a restitutionary right running from the date of the accrual of the cause of action.

(8) Under the doctrine of laches—
   (a) the enforcement of restitutionary rights which are equitable may be barred because of the prejudice to the defendant caused by an unreasonable delay of the claimant in commencing the claim;

> (b) there can be no unreasonable delay for the purposes of paragraph (a) until—
>   (i) the claimant has discovered, or could reasonably have discovered, that the defendant has been unjustly enriched at the claimant's expense, and
>   (ii) if the enrichment was unjust because of impairment of consent under any of sections 11 to 14, the impairment no longer exists;
> (c) the enforcement of a restitutionary right may be barred if—
>   (i) a limitation period mentioned in any of subsections (2) to (7) has not ended, or
>   (ii) there is no limitation period.
> (9) In general (but subject, for example, to subsections (4) and (5)) the terms of a contract may govern—
>   (a) the limitation period to enforce a restitutionary right, and
>   (b) when that period starts to run.

30

The law on limitation ensures that, usually after a fixed period of time but sometimes where there has been unreasonable delay by the claimant in commencing its claim, an action or 'remedy' is barred. The legal burden of proving that the claim falls within a limitation period is on the claimant—see s 4(3)—albeit that, as explained in the commentary to s 4(3), the defendant must plead limitation.

30(1)

The relevant law for restitution of an unjust enrichment is largely statutory, with the main statute being the Limitation Act 1980. It may therefore be thought odd to include in the Restatement legal rules that are already in statutory form. In truth, however, the 1980 Act does not clearly set out the law on limitation for restitution for unjust enrichment and reflects an earlier era when this cause of action was seen as an adjunct to contract ('quasi-contract'). In any event, the 1980 Act is not comprehensive so that, for example, the equitable doctrine of laches is still relevant. For these reasons, it has been thought helpful to set out in the Restatement in an uncluttered form, albeit without every detail, the law on limitation for restitution for unjust enrichment.

30(2)

Although there is no clear single formulation of a limitation period for unjust enrichment in the 1980 Act, the general position is that there is a limitation period of six years from the accrual of the cause of action. So it is that s 5 of the 1980 Act ('An action founded on simple contract shall not be brought after the expiration of six years from the date on which the cause of action accrued') has been pressed into service to cover common law ('quasi-contractual') restitution: obiter dicta in *Re Diplock* [1948] Ch 465, 514, CA; *Kleinwort Benson Ltd v Sandwell BC* [1994] 4 All ER 890 at 942–3; *Kleinwort Benson Ltd v Lincoln CC* [1999] 2 AC 349, HL (in which this was implicitly accepted, albeit that the issue in dispute concerned the operation of s 32(1)(c) on mistake). A six-year period from the accrual of the cause of action also applies, by reason of s 9 of the 1980 Act ('actions for sums recoverable by statute'), to restitution under the Law Reform (Frustrated Contracts) Act 1943; and under s 21(3) of the 1980 Act to an action by a beneficiary to recover trust property or in respect of any breach of trust (unless, by reason of s 21(1)(a), the trustee was fraudulent).

The date when a cause of action accrues in unjust enrichment is essentially a matter of common law. As regards payments, this will normally be the date when the payment is made (see *Kleinwort Benson Ltd v Sandwell BC* [1994] 4 All ER 890 at 978) but it may be later than this, as where the unjust factor is failure of consideration (see, eg, *BP Exploration Co (Libya) Ltd v Hunt (No 2)* [1983] 2 AC 352, HL, and *Guardian Ocean Cargoes Ltd v Banco do Brasil* [1994] 2 Lloyd's Rep 152, CA, which were failure of consideration cases dealing with the accrual of the cause of action for the purposes of interest). The correct principle therefore is that the cause of action accrues at the date of the unjust enrichment of the defendant at the claimant's expense. That there is no need for a demand before action is shown by *Baker v Courage & Co* [1910] 1 KB 56 and *Fuller v Happy Shopper Ltd* [2001] 2 Lloyd's Rep 49.

A limitation period of six years from the unjust enrichment is the general position. It is subject to numerous exceptions, which are set out in the Restatement in s 30(3)–(9). Of these, s 30(3)–(7) are set out in statute, s 30(8) refers to the equitable doctrine of laches, and s 30(9) deals with contractually agreed limitation periods.

30(3)

Under s 32(1)(c) of the Limitation Act 1980, where 'the action is for relief from the consequences of a mistake' the running of the limitation period is postponed until the claimant 'discovered the...mistake...or could with reasonable diligence have discovered it'.

Example 1

C pays D £5,000 by mistake in 2002. C did not discover, and could not reasonably have discovered, the mistake until June 2010. C has until June 2016 to commence an action for restitution of the £5,000.

Commentary: Part 4

In *Test Claimants in the FII Group Litigation v Revenue and Customs Commissioners* [2012] UKSC 19, [2012] 2 WLR 1149, it was authoritatively confirmed that s 32(1)(c) of the 1980 Act should be narrowly construed so that, in the context of unjust enrichment, the subsection covers only cases where mistake is an essential element of the cause of action (ie where mistake is the unjust factor). The claimants could not therefore rely on s 32(1)(c) of the 1980 Act as regards their claims to restitution based on the *Woolwich* principle even though, on the facts, they had made a mistake of law in making the payments.

Section 32(1)(c) of the 1980 Act has been at the forefront of attention in leading cases on the law of unjust enrichment such as *Kleinwort Benson Ltd v Lincoln CC* [1999] 2 AC 349, HL, and *Deutsche Morgan Grenfell Group plc v Inland Revenue Commissioners* [2006] UKHL 49, [2007] 1 AC 558, HL, in which claimants seeking the restitution of overpaid tax have framed their claims on the ground of mistake (rather than the *Woolwich* principle) in order to take advantage of the postponement of the limitation period by reason of s 32(1)(c). The success of those mistake claims has led to legislative reform (hence the last part of s 30(3) of the Restatement): the Finance Act 2004, s 320, and the Finance Act 2007, s 107, have abolished the application of s 32(1)(c) to claims for the restitution of tax paid to the Revenue by a mistake of law. So, eg, s 320(1) of the 2004 Act reads: 'Section 32(1)(c) of the Limitation Act 1980... (extended period for bringing an action in case of mistake) does not apply in relation to a mistake of law relating to a taxation matter under the care and management of Her Majesty's Revenue and Customs.' (In *Test Claimants in the FII Group Litigation v Revenue and Customs Commissioners* [2012] UKSC 19, [2012] 2 WLR 1149, it was decided that, on the facts of that case, where the claimants had an accrued EU law right to restitution, s 107 of the 2007 Act was invalid (being retrospective without transitional provisions) and the validity of s 320 of the 2004 Act would be referred to the European Court of Justice.)

30(4)

The postponement of the running of time for deliberate concealment is set out in s 32(1)(b) of the Limitation Act 1980 (using marginally different wording from that in s 30(4) of the Restatement) and may be just as relevant to restitution for unjust enrichment as to any other claim. In contrast, it has been thought unnecessary to include in the Restatement the postponement for 'an action based upon the fraud of the defendant' in s 32(1)(a) of the 1980 Act because as a practical matter, in the context of unjust enrichment (as opposed to, for example, a claim in tort), s 32(1)(c) swallows up s 32(1)(a). (But note that in the highly unlikely event of an action for restitution for mistake of law being based upon the fraud of Her Majesty's Revenue and Customs, s 32(1)(a) of the 1980 Act could be relied on despite the removal of s 32(1)(c) by the Finance Act 2004, s 320.)

30(5)

By reason of s 28 of the Limitation Act 1980, time does not run while the claimant is under a 'disability'; and by s 38 of the 1980 Act a person is treated as under a disability 'while he is an infant, or lacks capacity within the meaning of the Mental Capacity Act 2005 to conduct legal proceedings'.

30(6)

The fresh accrual of a cause of action from the date of an acknowledgement or part payment by the defendant is embodied in s 29(5) of the Limitation Act 1980 (using marginally different wording from that in s 30(6) of the Restatement). The words 'debt or liquidated pecuniary claim' have been given a wide meaning so as to include, in the context of unjust enrichment, a *quantum meruit* (*Amantilla Ltd v Telefusion Ltd* (1987) 9 Con LR 139). In the terminology of this Restatement, s 29(5) of the 1980 Act should therefore be read as applying to any claim for a 'monetary restitutionary award'. By s 30(1) of the 1980 Act, the acknowledgement 'must be in writing and signed by the person making it'.

30(7)

This makes clear that the Restatement is merely intended to set out the main relevant limitation provisions for restitution of an unjust enrichment. There are statutory provisions, both in the 1980 Act and in other statutes, that are not here mentioned which depart from the general rule of 'six years from the date of the unjust enrichment'. So, eg, by s 10(1) of the 1980 Act contribution claims under the Civil Liability (Contribution) Act 1978 have a two-year limitation period running from when the right accrued (as defined in s 10(2)–(4)); for claims to a share of a deceased's estate, s 22(a) of the 1980 Act lays down a twelve-year limitation period, which runs from when the right to receive the share accrued; the extremely complex s 21 of the 1980 Act deals with actions in respect of trust property; and under several taxing statutes there is a limitation period of four years for restitution of overpaid tax running from, eg, the end of the relevant tax year or accounting period (see, eg, s 33 and Sch 1AB, Taxes Management Act 1970).

30(8)(a)

By the flexible doctrine of laches (sometimes referred to as the 'lapse of time bar') equitable 'remedies' may be barred where there would be injustice to the defendant caused by the unreasonable delay of the claimant in commencing its claim. In the context of unjust enrichment, relevant 'remedies' include: rescission (in equity) of executed contracts for innocent misrepresentation or undue influence; rectification of executed contracts for mistake; equitable liens; trusts imposed by law; and equitable contribution. For a classic formulation of the doctrine, see *Lindsay*

Petroleum Co v Hurd (1874) LR 5 PC 221, at 239–40, HL. For consideration of the correct approach to limitation for (equitable) subrogation, see Mitchell and Watterson, *Subrogation Law and Practice* (2007) paras 7.137–7.162, 10.114–10.115.

In contrast to proving that a claim falls within a limitation period, the burden of proving laches is on the defendant (as indicated by *Lindsay Petroleum Co v Hurd* (1874) LR 5 PC 221 at 241): see s 4(2)–(3) above.

30(8)(b)

In contrast to the standard position under the Limitation Act 1980 where time runs from the accrual of the cause of action, under the doctrine of laches the delay can only be unreasonable, and therefore only runs, from when the claimant discovered, or should reasonably have discovered, the unjust enrichment: *Lindsay Petroleum Co v Hurd* (1874) LR 5 PC 221, PC (misrepresentation); *Erlanger v New Sombrero Phosphate Co* (1878) 3 App Cas 1218, HL (non-disclosure); *Alec Lobb (Garages) Ltd v Total Oil (GB) Ltd* [1985] 1 WLR 173, CA (exploitation of weakness). Moreover, in respect of duress, undue influence, exploitation of weakness, or incapacity—and assuming that one is seeking an equitable 'remedy' so that laches applies—time will not run until the removal of the impairment: see, in the context of undue influence, *Allcard v Skinner* (1887) 36 Ch D 145 at 187, CA. (But note that, under the present law, there is no such postponement in respect of duress at common law: see Mitchell, Mitchell, and Watterson (eds), *Goff and Jones on the Law of Unjust Enrichment* (2011) para 33-39.)

30(8)(c)

The interrelationship between the doctrine of laches and the periods prescribed by the Limitation Act 1980 is not entirely clear. The only oblique reference to this in the Limitation Act 1980 is in s 36(2), which reads: 'Nothing in this Act shall affect any equitable jurisdiction to refuse relief on the ground of acquiescence or otherwise.' There is, of course, no difficulty where there is no limitation period prescribed by statute because then the doctrine of laches alone applies. This appears to be the case for, for example, rescission (in equity) or rectification of an executed contract (or, outside the law of unjust enrichment, where compensatory or restitutionary remedies are sought for the equitable wrong of breach of confidence). However, where there is a limitation period (although the authorities are not consistent) it would appear that the doctrine of laches can apply even where the statutory limitation period has not expired (see for this approach, albeit outside the context of unjust enrichment, *P & O Nedlloyd BV v Arab Metals Co, The UB Tiger* [2006] EWCA Civ 1717, [2007] 1 WLR 2288: specific performance of a contract can be barred by laches even if there is a statutory limitation period of six years and the claimant is within that period). So if a limitation period applies to the enforcement of an equitable restitutionary right in unjust enrichment (eg by reason of s 21 of the

Special statutory defences: passing on and prevailing practice

1980 Act in respect of trust property), the laches doctrine may nevertheless still be applied to bar the enforcement of the right.

30(9)

Although nothing in the Limitation Act 1980 explicitly allows the parties to set their own limitation periods and starting point, it is generally accepted that this is possible. For a general discussion, see the Law Commission CP No 151, *Limitation of Actions* (1998) paras 9.7–9.11 and Law Commission, *Limitation of Actions* (Law Com No 270, 2001) paras 3.170–3.175. Section 30(9) applies this to the law of unjust enrichment.

Example 2

By a term in a contract it is agreed that any claim for mistaken overpayments under the contract are to be brought within twelve months of payment. Although the normal limitation period would be six years from when the mistake was discovered or could reasonably have been discovered, this term is valid (subject to any statutory restriction on unfair terms) so that claims for restitution for mistake cannot be brought after the period agreed.

As the Law Commission recognised, this contractual freedom is subject to the general law on the validity of the contract term (eg the controls in the Unfair Contract Terms Act 1977 and the Unfair Terms in Consumer Contracts Regulations 1999). The words in brackets in s 30(9) acknowledge that it would also be inappropriate, as the Law Commission again accepted, for there to be contractual modification of the postponement of a limitation period under what, in this Restatement, are subsections 30(4) and (5) (and there may conceivably be other examples where a contractually agreed limitation period or starting point is inappropriate).

31 Special statutory defences: passing on and prevailing practice
(1) Passing on of a loss by the claimant to a third party is not a defence at common law to restitution for unjust enrichment, but, in the case of particular taxes, there are statutory defences of a similar nature.
(2) In the case of a payment made under a mistake of law, payment in accordance with prevailing practice or the settled understanding of the law is not a defence at common law but, in the case of particular taxes, there are statutory defences of a similar nature.

31(1)

Passing on—where the claimant has passed on its loss to a third party and thereby avoided that loss—was rejected as a defence at common law in *Kleinwort Benson Ltd v Birmingham CC* [1997] QB 380, CA. In contrast, some English tax statutes (most importantly, the Value Added Tax Act 1994, s 80, for the recovery of overpaid VAT) require the application of a defence of passing on or, as it is usually termed in legislation, that restitution would 'unjustly enrich *the claimant*'.

31(2)

In *Kleinwort Benson Ltd v Lincoln CC* [1999] 2 AC 349 the dissenting Law Lords (Lord Browne-Wilkinson and Lord Lloyd) favoured the acceptance of a defence to a claim for the restitution of a payment made by mistake of law that the payment was made in accordance with a settled understanding of the law. However, that defence was rejected by the majority so that the defence has no application at common law. In contrast, some English tax statutes (see para 2(8) of Sch 1AB to the Taxes Management Act 1970, on mistakenly paid income tax and capital gains tax, and para 51A(8) of Sch 18 to the Finance Act 1998, on mistakenly paid corporation tax) do include a defence where 'liability was calculated in accordance with the practice generally prevailing at the time'.

32 Contractual or statutory exclusion

The defendant has a defence if the defendant's liability is excluded (in whatever terms) by a contract or by statute.

32

(i) Contractual exclusion

Just as the parties to a contract are free to exclude their contractual or tortious liability as between themselves (subject to any statutory restriction such as the Unfair Contract Terms Act 1977 or the Unfair Terms in Consumer Contracts Regulations 1999), so they can exclude by contract the liability in unjust enrichment that would otherwise arise. The exclusion may be express or implied. As we have seen in the commentary on s 15(4)(b), contractual exclusion is one explanation for the denial of restitution to a contract-breaker for failure of consideration where there is a forfeiture or non-refundable clause or where a clause is construed as being an 'entire obligation' clause. Another example is provided by *BP Exploration Co (Libya) Ltd v Hunt (No 2)* [1983] 2 AC 352, HL, in which the main issue for the House of Lords was whether the relevant clause (which stated, inter alia, that 'Hunt shall have no personal liability to repay the sums required') constituted a

Contractual or statutory exclusion

contracting out of restitution (as is permitted by s 2(3) of the Law Reform (Frustrated Contracts) Act 1943). It was decided that the clause, as a matter of construction, did not cover the event that had actually occurred.

Example

By a clause in a contract between C and D, C agrees that D 'shall have no liability to repay money paid under the contract in the event of the contract being terminated for breach or frustration'. Such a clause excludes the right to restitution that would otherwise arise for failure of consideration.

The perhaps obvious point should be emphasised that the contractual exclusion of restitution only applies if the contractual exclusion is valid. Apart from statutes that control exclusion clauses (such as the Unfair Contract Terms Act 1977 and the Unfair Terms in Consumer Contracts Regulations 1999) there are some directly relevant common law doctrines in particular equitable relief against forfeiture of benefits conferred (see, eg, *Stockloser v Johnson* [1954] 1 QB 476, CA; *Galbraith v Mitchenhall Estates Ltd* [1965] 2 QB 473; *Workers Trust and Merchant Bank Ltd v Dojap Investments Ltd* [1993] AC 573, PC).

Although it is hard to find examples of this in the case law, in principle the relevant contractual exclusion may be of only some of the restitutionary rights which the claimant would otherwise have, rather than all restitutionary rights. Although not dealt with in the Restatement, it is also the case that in principle a claimant may 'waive' its claim in unjust enrichment other than by a contract.

Contractual exclusion is, at root, one aspect of the general subsidiarity of unjust enrichment to contract. Two other aspects of that general subsidiarity are: first, that as set out in s 3(6), an unjust factor does not normally render the enrichment at the claimant's expense unjust where the enrichment was owed to the defendant by the claimant under a valid contractual obligation; and, secondly, that as set out in s 29 (a), a valid contractual compromise dealing with the unjust enrichment shuts out restitution. But for the view that it is unhelpful to talk of subsidiarity in discussing the relationship between unjust enrichment and contract, see Mitchell, Mitchell, and Watterson (eds), *Goff and Jones on The Law of Unjust Enrichment* (8th edn, 2011) paras 2-01–2-04.

(ii) Statutory exclusion

In principle, a statute may exclude all liability in unjust enrichment. A rare but excellent example of this is provided by the now-repealed s 127(3) of the Consumer Credit Act 1974 as interpreted in *Dimond v Lovell* [2002] 1 AC 384, HL. While the courts were given a general discretion to enforce improperly executed agreements, that discretion did not apply unless the debtor had signed a document containing certain prescribed terms. The House of Lords decided that, where that formality had not been complied with, to permit the creditor a claim in unjust enrichment for the use value of the hire car obtained by the debtor would conflict with the statute. Parliament in this situation had impliedly excluded all liability in unjust enrichment.

More commonly, a statute sets up its own regime of restitution for unjust enrichment (rather than excluding all liability in unjust enrichment). Such a statutory regime may sit alongside the common law of unjust enrichment or it may, expressly or impliedly, replace the common law. The examples most relevant to the general law of unjust enrichment have already been referred to. So, for example, under s 21(5) we have seen that taxing statutes generally replace, expressly or impliedly, the common law but that there are residual situations where the common law of unjust enrichment applies. We have also seen in s 15(6) that the common law of unjust enrichment in relation to contracts terminated by frustration is displaced by the Law Reform (Frustrated Contracts) Act 1943 (unless s 2(5) of that Act applies).

Although not relevant to statutory exclusion as such, in thinking about the impact of statutes it is worth noting that a statute may also be important in countering the force of an unjust factor. This is where the relevant benefit was owed to the defendant (eg tax payable to HMRC) under a valid statutory obligation (see commentary to s 3(6) above, especially Example 3).

33 Affirmation

The defendant has a defence if the claimant has affirmed the contract, gift or other transaction under which the benefit was obtained.

33

One can regard the law on affirmation as merely part of a more wide-ranging doctrine of election or waiver that applies across many areas of the law. However, it has been thought appropriate to include affirmation within this Restatement essentially because one of the most important and well-established 'bars' to enforcing one of the most important restitutionary rights, namely, revesting title by rescission of an executed contract, is affirmation; and one can generalise from that to say that affirmation is a general defence to restitution for unjust enrichment.

Affirmation applies where a party, who is entitled, for example, to rescind a contract or other transaction, unequivocally manifests an intention to stick with the transaction (after being free from the effects of any factor impairing consent). The idea behind this defence is that a party cannot 'blow hot and cold' and, having made a choice, is bound by it. No detrimental reliance by the other party is required.

Affirmation

So, eg, a person who is induced by misrepresentation to buy goods cannot rescind if, after discovering the truth, she uses them (as in *United Shoe Machinery Co of Canada v Brunet* [1909] AC 330, PC). For a leading discussion of the requirements of affirmation, in which it was decided on the facts that there was no affirmation so that the claimant had validly rescinded an executed contract for fraudulent misrepresentation, see *Clough v London and North Western Rly Co* (1871) LR 7 Exch 26. For well-known decisions that affirmation barred rescission on the facts, in situations where the claimant had become free of the impaired consent, see *Allcard v Skinner* (1887) 36 Ch D 145, CA (undue influence) and *North Ocean Shipping Co Ltd v Hyundai Construction Co Ltd, The Atlantic Baron* [1979] QB 705 (duress). In *Peyman v Lanjani* [1985] Ch 457, CA, it was controversially held (in the context of termination for breach of contract) that a claimant must know of its legal right to rescind or terminate before it can be held to have affirmed a transaction. For an excellent discussion of affirmation in the context of rescission, see O'Sullivan, Elliott, and Zakrzewski, *The Law of Rescission* (2008) ch 23. (That chapter draws a conceptual distinction between affirmation by election, where there are alternative inconsistent rights, and affirmation by waiver, where there need be no alternative inconsistent right: applying that distinction, affirmation by election cannot apply to a unilateral contract or gift as opposed to a bilateral contract.)

Example

D, a ship-builder, threatens to break its contract with C to build a ship unless paid 10 per cent more to complete the work. C pays the extra demanded. When the ship is completed, C takes delivery of it and makes no protest about the extra money it has paid. Over six months later, C brings a claim for restitution of the extra money paid as having been paid under economic duress. The claim is barred because of C's affirmation of the contract. (This example is based on *North Ocean Shipping Co Ltd v Hyundai Construction Co Ltd, The Atlantic Baron* [1979] QB 705.)

PART 5
RESTITUTIONARY RIGHTS

> **34 Personal right to a monetary restitutionary award**
> (1) A personal right to a monetary restitutionary award (see section 5(2)(a)) is a right, enforceable only against the defendant or the defendant's representatives, to recover the value of the defendant's enrichment.
> (2) The value of the defendant's enrichment is normally the market value of the benefit at the time it is obtained by the defendant unless it is shown (for example, by the terms of a request) that a lower value is more appropriate.

34(1)

We have explained above (see the commentary to s 5(2)(a) that the term 'monetary restitutionary award' is being used in the Restatement in preference to the many differently labelled 'remedies', enforcing the personal right to restitution for the value of the enrichment received, that have historically been adopted. The opportunity will now be taken to explain that more fully in relation to each of the unjust factors in turn.

34(1): mistake

Nearly all cases on mistake have concerned payments made to the defendant. A straightforward monetary restitutionary award has usually been made—namely an award of money had and received to the use of the claimant—which enforces a personal right to restitution for the value of the enrichment received by the defendant. Where a contract is voidable for misrepresentation (or non-disclosure), the monetary restitutionary award enforcing a personal right to restitution for the value of the enrichment received has been a monetary award that is part of the process of, and consequent on, rescission: see, eg, *Redgrave v Hurd* (1881) 20 Ch D 1, CA (restitution of deposit paid).

34(1): duress

Nearly all cases on duress have concerned payments made to the defendant. Where the payment has not been made under a contract, the monetary restitutionary award has been a straightforward award of money had and received to the use of the claimant which enforces a personal right to restitution for the value of the enrichment received by the defendant. But where the payment has been contractual, so that the contract has first had to be rescinded for duress, the monetary restitutionary award enforcing a personal right to restitution for the value of the enrichment received has been a monetary award that has usually simply been viewed as part of the process of, and consequent on, rescission (cf *North Ocean Shipping Co Ltd v Hyundai Construction Co Ltd* [1979] QB 705 at 714, where Mocatta J talked of both rescission and the award of money had and received).

34(1): undue influence

Almost invariably the benefit has been obtained under a voidable transaction, whether a contract or gift, which the claimant has been seeking to rescind. So the monetary restitutionary award for undue influence standardly given to enforce a personal right to restitution for the value of the enrichment received by the defendant has been a monetary award that is part of the process of, and consequent on, rescission: see, eg, *Cheese v Thomas* [1994] 1 WLR 129, CA.

34(1): exploitation of weakness

Almost invariably the benefit has been obtained under a voidable contract, which the claimant has been seeking to rescind. So the monetary restitutionary award for exploitation of weakness, which has standardly been given to enforce a personal right to restitution for the value of the enrichment received by the defendant, has been a monetary award that is part of the process of, and is consequent on, rescission: see, eg, *The Port Caledonia and The Anna* [1903] P 184.

34(1): incapacity of the individual

Most cases on incapacity have concerned payments and a straightforward monetary restitutionary award has been made—an award of money had and received to the use of the claimant—which enforces a personal right to restitution for the value of the enrichment received by the defendant. However, where 'rescission' has been involved, the monetary restitutionary award enforcing a right to restitution for the value of the enrichment received has usually been viewed as part of the process of, and consequent on, rescission.

34(1): failure of consideration

In most cases of restitution for failure of consideration, a straightforward monetary restitutionary award has been made—namely, an award of money had and received to the use of the claimant or, where services have been rendered, a *quantum meruit*—which enforces a personal right to restitution for the value of the enrichment received by the defendant.

34(1): ignorance or powerlessness or a fiduciary's lack of authority

At common law, in most cases of restitution for ignorance or powerlessness or a fiduciary's lack of authority a straightforward monetary restitutionary award has been made—namely, an award of money had and received to the use of the claimant—which enforces a personal right to restitution for the value of the enrichment received by the defendant: see, eg, *Lipkin Gorman v Karpnale Ltd* [1991] 2 AC 548. In equity, the equivalent monetary restitutionary award has usually been an account of money received or an account of the value of an asset received: see, eg, *Ministry of Health v Simpson (Re Diplock)* [1951] AC 251, HL (and, in so far as one interprets the 'knowing receipt' cases as implicitly embodying an unjust enrichment claim, it should be noted that the award in those cases has been an account of money received or an account of the value of an asset received, although this has sometimes been obscured by references to the defendant being 'liable as a constructive trustee').

34(1): legal compulsion

The main 'remedies' for this unjust factor, enforcing a personal right to restitution for the value of the enrichment received by the defendant, have historically been as follows: where restitution of the whole sum paid is being awarded, an award of money paid to the defendant's use or an indemnity or, described at a higher level of generality, recoupment; where restitution of part of the sum paid is being awarded, an award of contribution (although this is also used at a higher level of generality to contrast with recoupment). These are all subsumed within the Restatement's simplifying term 'monetary restitutionary award'.

It should be noted that, because the enrichment in play is the discharge of another's liability, 'subrogation to extinguished rights' (see s 36(2) below) can be used, indirectly, to achieve the same effect as a direct monetary restitutionary award. An excellent example of this is provided by *Niru Battery Manufacturing Co v Milestone Trading Ltd (No 2)* [2004] EWCA Civ 487, [2004] 2 Lloyd's Rep 319, where the same restitution was effected by 'recoupment', by '100% contribution', and by subrogation. The important point is that subrogation is in this context superfluous. It adds nothing to the direct 'remedies'. Under the Restatement, there is here no need, and it is of no advantage, to go through subrogation reasoning to arrive at the monetary restitutionary award.

34(1): necessity

Traditionally, the monetary restitutionary award, enforcing a personal right to restitution for the value received by the defendant, has been the award of money paid to the defendant's use (often referred to, in this context, as reimbursement) or a *quantum meruit* (often referred to, in this context, as remuneration). The former has covered money paid to a third party and the latter has been for the value of services rendered.

In the maritime salvage cases, the award has included an element of reward so as to encourage successful rescue. Professional salvors have been held entitled to more generous awards than those who act on the spur of the moment; the intervention must have been successful; and the value of the property saved, the skill used, and the degree of danger involved have also been important considerations in fixing the size of the award. See generally Kennedy and Rose, *Law of Salvage* (7th edn, 2009) paras 1.042–1.048, ch 16. There is some difficulty in analysing the nature of the 'reward'. One might argue that it is *sui generis* and, like compensation, not tied to the enrichment. If that is correct, maritime salvage probably belongs outside this Restatement. An alternative view, favoured here, and which puts maritime salvage within this Restatement, is that the reward is a generous restitutionary award reflecting the desire to encourage successful intervention.

34(1): factors concerned with illegality

In most past cases of withdrawal during the *locus poenitentiae* and of class protection, the enrichment has been money paid to the defendant. The monetary restitutionary award, enforcing a personal right to restitution for the value received by the defendant, has been a straightforward award of money had and received to the use of the claimant or the award of money paid under an illegal contract.

34(1): unlawful obtaining or conferral of a benefit by a public authority

In all past cases, one has been concerned with payments made to the defendant. In line with this, the monetary restitutionary award, enforcing a personal right to restitution for the value received by the defendant, has been a straightforward award of money had and received to the use of the claimant.

34(2)

We have already encountered the notion of 'subjective devaluation' in determining whether the defendant has been enriched (see the commentary to s 7(3)). That one is concerned with the benefit *to the defendant* carries through to the valuation stage so that the valuation can be lower than the market value. This explains why the rate of compound interest awarded in *Sempra Metals Ltd v Inland Revenue Commissioners* [2007] UKHL 34, [2008] 1 AC 561 was lower than the market rate; the defendant, as an arm of government, was able to borrow at lower rates than a typical commercial borrower.

Example 1

C and D are negotiating a contract for C to landscape D's garden. D has requested the work but has made it clear that she will not agree to pay more than two-thirds of the standard market price for the work and needs the work finished within a month. Before the contract is made (and, although the parties have agreed on the work, they have not agreed the precise price, or the date of completion or about guarantees of the work) C starts and completes within a month the work that has been requested. Assuming that C has no contractual right but does have the right to restitution based on D's unjust enrichment, the measure of restitution should not be more than two-thirds of the market price because that was all that D was willing to pay as made clear by her request.

It remains undecided whether 'subjective overvaluation' (sometimes called 'subjective revaluation') also applies where there is evidence that the particular defendant valued the services, etc at higher than the market rate. For discussion, see *Benedetti v Sawiris* [2010] EWCA Civ 1427. The correct view is probably that, without a valid contract, the claimant should not be entitled to overvaluation. In other words, and as reflected in the Restatement, restitution allows downward subjectivity only so as to protect a defendant. That there should be no subjective overvaluation may be illustrated as follows:

Example 2

C enters into a contract for the carriage of D's goods by sea. D is most anxious to secure the services of C and therefore agrees to pay twice the market rate. After C completes two-thirds of the journey, the contract of carriage is frustrated when war breaks out and the ship is requisitioned. The goods are unloaded and D is able to complete, at a cheaper rate, their carriage by a different route. Assuming that C is entitled to a restitutionary monetary award (*quantum meruit*) for the value of C's services based on unjust enrichment, it would seem that the assessment should be based on the market rate. C would only be entitled to the agreed higher rate if it could bring a contractual action.

Example 3

C mistakenly delivers heating oil to D (rather than D's neighbour) just before Christmas. D's neighbour had plenty of oil and was just topping up out of an abundance of caution. By contrast, D was running on near-empty, facing a houseful over Christmas, and would have happily paid double the market rate. Without a valid contract with D, it is hard to see that C should be entitled to restitution for the enhanced value of the oil to D. Rather in a claim in unjust enrichment, C would be entitled to a restitutionary award against D for the value of the oil assessed at the market rate.

As regards the date when value is assessed, this will normally be the date when the benefit is obtained. So, for example, the value of services (for a *quantum meruit*) or goods (for a *quantum valebat*) is assessed at the date the services are rendered or goods are received even though the market value has subsequently increased or decreased. Sometimes there is an enrichment newly accruing from day to day (eg use value represented by interest) but one can still say that the relevant date of assessment is the date of the continuing obtaining of the benefit. However, there

Other restitutionary rights

may be some exceptions to valuation at the date when the benefit is obtained. For example, on rescission of a contract for misrepresentation or duress or undue influence under which rights in goods have been transferred, and a monetary award of the value of the goods consequent on rescission is being made—rather than a revesting of the goods—it may be that the higher or lower value of the goods at the time of the rescission should be awarded (although note that a decrease in value might in any event be covered by the change of position defence).

35 Other restitutionary rights

(1) The rights referred to in section 5(2)(b) are—
   (a) if the benefit obtained is directly linked to an asset retained by the defendant, the right to have a monetary restitutionary award secured by a lien over that asset;
   (b) if the benefit obtained is the discharge of a secured liability of the defendant, the right to be subrogated to the discharged security;
   (c) if the benefit obtained is a right in property retained by the defendant, the right to revest, or to have revested, that right in property, by rescission or rectification of a contract, gift or other transaction;
   (d) if the benefit obtained is a right in property retained by the defendant, the right to be a beneficiary of that right in property under a trust imposed by law.
(2) The following restrictions on the rights mentioned in subsection (1) apply in relation to particular cases of unjust enrichment—

unjust factor	*restrictions on rights*
failure of consideration (section 15)	the subsection (1)(a), (b) and (d) rights are available only in limited circumstances
	the subsection (1)(c) right is not available
legal compulsion (section 18)	the subsection (1)(a), (c) and (d) rights are not available
necessity (section 19)	the subsection (1)(c) and (d) rights are not available
factors concerned with illegality (section 20)	the subsection (1)(a), (b) and (d) rights are not available
unlawful obtaining or conferral of a benefit by a public authority (section 21)	the subsection (1)(b) and (c) rights are not available

(3) The claimant does not have a right mentioned in subsection (1) if—
   (a) the claimant has, as part of a bargain, taken the risk of being unsecured or inadequately secured, and
   (b) the right would give the claimant better security than the claimant bargained for,

unless the unjust factor undermines the consent of the claimant to the taking of the risk.
(4) In this Restatement, "a right in property" means—
   (a) a right in tangible property (whether money, goods or land), or
   (b) intangible property (such as intellectual property, receivables or shares).
(5) In this Restatement "rescission" and "rectification" include any consequential order necessary to revest a right in property, such as rectification of a register.

35

It has been explained in outline in the commentary to s 5(2)(b) above that, in addition to the standard personal restitution, there is 'proprietary restitution'; that 'proprietary restitution' is most likely to be in issue where the defendant is insolvent; and that four kinds of right are involved in relation to 'proprietary restitution'. The details concerning these rights will now be fully explained.

We shall begin by looking at the four kinds of right in general before moving on to examine, across both s 35(1) and (2), the incidence of, and restrictions on, those rights in relation to each unjust factor in turn.

35(1)(a): general

This recognises that an equitable lien (ie a charge) may be used to secure monetary restitutionary awards although when this will be so is not entirely clear. Standard examples of equitable liens being imposed that fall within s 35(1)(a) are where an asset has been traced into its substitute and the equitable lien is seen as an alternative 'remedy' to a trust: see, eg, *Re Hallett's Estate* (1888) 13 Ch D 696, CA. Another example is where the claimant has mistakenly improved another's land: see *Cooper v Phibbs* (1867) LR 2 HL 149, HL. It would appear that a necessary requirement for the equitable lien in these instances is that the enrichment is directly linked to an asset retained by the defendant. While the lien in question will almost always be an equitable non-possessory lien, it is conceivable that, where the claimant has possession of the defendant's property, a common law possessory lien could also be used to secure a monetary restitutionary award. An example of a common law possessory lien is a repairer's lien (and see the recognition of a common law lien, securing a *quantum meruit* in unjust enrichment, in *Spencer v S Frances Ltd* [2011] EWHC 1269 (QB)).

35(1)(b): general

Very similar to what is dealt with in s 35(1)(a), and falling within s 35(1)(b), is where a surety has a right to be subrogated to a discharged security because it has enriched D by discharging the secured debt (see the Mercantile Law Amendment Act 1856, s 5) or where a lender, C, has a right to be subrogated to a discharged security because C has enriched D by providing the loan that has been used to pay off D's debt (see, eg, *Butler v Rice* [1910] 2 Ch 277). For subrogation, see s 36.

35(1)(c): general

Rescission of a contract, gift, or other transaction reverses an enrichment and is therefore restitutionary where it revests rights in property retained by the defendant. Those rights in property may be rights in, eg, goods, land, or intellectual property (see s 35(4)). The process of rescission includes, as made clear in s 35(5), a consequential order necessary to revest rights, such as rectification of the land register or rectification of a register of shares. Leading examples of such rescission are *Car and Universal Finance Co Ltd v Caldwell* [1965] 1 QB 525, CA (fraudulent misrepresentation inducing sale of a car); and *O'Sullivan v Management Agency and Music Ltd* [1985] QB 428, CA (undue influence inducing transfer of intellectual property and goods). Unjust enrichment is here therefore creating a right to rescind (by revesting rights in property) rather than creating a personal right to restitution of value received.

Some commentators regard it as necessary to uphold the historical distinction between, on the one hand, common law rescission for fraudulent misrepresentation and duress and, on the other hand, equitable rescission for, for example, innocent misrepresentation, undue influence, exploitation of weakness and, as regards rescinding gifts, unilateral mistake. It can be argued that rescission in equity, as opposed to rescission at common law, is not a self-help remedy, has a less restrictive approach to the need for *restitutio in integrum* to be possible and, most importantly for present purposes, brings about a resulting trust. On that approach, it is the trust that is restitutionary and this situation would be covered by s 35(1)(d) rather than s 35(1)(c). But, although there are cases that support that trust analysis of equitable rescission (see, eg, *Allcard v Skinner* (1887) 13 Ch D 145 per Cotton LJ, and, in relation to fraudulent misrepresentation, *Lonrho plc v Fayed (No 2)* [1992] 1 WLR 1, 11–12; *El Ajou v Dollar Land Holdings plc* [1993] 3 All ER 717 at 734; *Bristol and West Building Society v Mothew* [1996] EWCA Civ 533, [1998] Ch 1 at 22–3; *Ciro Citterio Menswear plc v Thakrar* [2002] EWHC 662 (Ch), [2002] 1 WLR 2217 at [32]–[41]; *Shalson v Russo* [2003] EWHC 1637 (Ch), [2005] Ch 281 at [106]–[127]) there are many other cases of equitable rescission that revest rights in property without mention of a trust (see, eg, *Tate v Williamson* (1866) 2 Ch App 55, CA; *Lady Hood of Avalon v Mackinnon* [1909] 1 Ch 476; *O'Sullivan v Management Agency and Music Ltd* [1985] QB 428, CA; and *Re Griffiths* [2008] EWHC 118 (Ch), [2009] Ch 162). One should also note that most of the above modern cases adopting a trust analysis in relation to equitable rescission have been concerned with tracing where, applying the traditional unsatisfactory approach (referred to in the commentary on s 9(4) above), it has been thought necessary to find a trust or fiduciary duty in order to allow equitable tracing. Given the uncertainty in the law, and that it is hard to see the rationale of an interim trust analysis if the ultimate purpose of the rescission (including any consequential rectification of a register) is to revest rights in property, the preferable view is that the trust analysis is best avoided. The Restatement therefore takes the view that, as regards rights in property retained by the defendant, rescission, whether at common law or in equity, has the effect of revesting rights in the claimant (if necessary with a consequential order such as rectification of a register). See generally on these issues, O'Sullivan, Elliott, and Zakrzewski, *The Law of Rescission* (2008) esp at 11.55, 11.100, 14.21–14.28, 15.04–15.13, 16.18–16.38.

Equitable rectification of a transaction is also restitutionary where it revests rights in property retained by the defendant (if necessary with a consequential order such as rectification of a register): see, eg, as regards land mistakenly conveyed, *Beale v Kyte* [1907] 1 Ch 564; *Blacklocks v JB Developments (Godalming) Ltd* [1982] Ch 183. (Rectification of wills—governed by the Administration of Justice Act 1982, s 20—falls outside the Restatement: see commentary under s 1 (5) above.)

Nothing said here is intended to deny that the rescission of an *executory* contract is best viewed as non-restitutionary because it does not reverse an enrichment. Nor is anything here intended to deny that, after a contract has been rescinded, there will be a personal right to restitution of value received by the defendant. The unjust factor triggering that personal right to restitution is most naturally viewed as the same as that which created the right to rescind (eg mistake (induced by misrepresentation) or duress or undue influence) and the 'remedy' enforcing that personal right is a monetary restitutionary award consequent on rescission.

35(1)(d): general

Instead of revesting rights in property retained by the defendant through rescission or rectification, the rights in property retained by the defendant may sometimes be made the subject-matter of a trust (whether constructive or resulting) with the claimant as beneficiary. The imposition of that trust is restitutionary and, on the best analysis, reverses the unjust enrichment of the defendant (who is enriched by retaining the rights in property) at the claimant's expense. Unjust enrichment is here creating a trust under which the claimant has a beneficiary's right to the rights in property retained by the defendant. Examples of such trusts are those imposed after tracing (see, eg, *Re Diplock* [1948] Ch 465, CA, in respect of funds to which the 'first-in first-out' rule was not applied; *Barlow Clowes International Ltd v Vaughan* [1992] 4 All ER 22, CA; *Foskett v McKeown* [2001] 1 AC 102, HL, although the House of Lords there reasoned, with respect unsatisfactorily, that the trust was explicable in terms of 'vindicating property rights' as opposed to being a trust created by unjust enrichment); the trust imposed for a mistake in *Chase Manhattan Bank NA v Israel-British Bank (London) Ltd* [1981] Ch 105 (although this must be read in the light of the explanation of it given in *Westdeutsche Landesbank Girozentrale v Islington London BC* [1996] AC 669, HL, which required knowledge by the defendant of the mistake); for an inevitable failure of consideration (see, eg, *Neste Oy v Lloyds Bank plc* [1983] 2 Lloyd's Rep 658); or where an express trust has failed (see, eg, *Re Ames' Settlement* [1946] Ch 217).

There is a long-standing debate as to the point in time at which the trust arises. According to one view, most forcefully advocated by Häcker, 'Proprietary Restitution after Impaired Consent Transfers: a Generalised Power Model' [2009] CLJ 324, the claimant has a 'power' to have a trust imposed once there has been an unjust enrichment. It is analogous to the 'power' to rescind (and the cases on rescission—see, eg, *Reese River Silver Mining Co v Smith* (1869) LR 4 HL 64—indicate that the effect of rescission is retrospective to the extent that, on rescission, the revesting of rights is deemed to have occurred from the date that the claimant elected to rescind). Although this is an attractive view, it contrasts with, on the one hand, the analysis that the trust only arises once a court has ordered it (as if it were a judicial remedy like an injunction) or, on the other hand, the analysis that the trust arises as soon as there has been an unjust enrichment prior to any exercise of choice by the claimant. A great practical advantage of the 'power' (or judicial remedy) analysis of the trust, as against the immediately vested interest analysis, is that it makes it easier to protect third party creditors (ie in line with the law on rescission, the 'power' to revest title would be barred where this would conflict with the rights of bona fide purchasers for value without notice).

35(1)–(2): the particular unjust factors

It has been explained in the commentary to s 5(2)(b) that proprietary restitution is more restricted than personal restitution not only because the rights in question are intrinsically more restricted (being dependent on the retention of an asset or a right in property or on the discharge of a secured liability) but also because they are not available in respect of all unjust factors. It falls to s 35(2) to set out in relation to the unjust factors the restrictions that appear to apply under the present law (and s 35(3) then sets out a general restriction). In considering restrictions, the opportunity is taken in the commentary that follows to focus on the case law under each unjust factor that positively illustrates the recognition of the right in property in question. The picture that emerges is that, as regards the 'consent-based' unjust factors (see s 3(2)(a)), restrictions apply to failure of consideration but not otherwise. As regards the 'policy-motivated' unjust factors (see s 3(2)(b)) there are restrictions which reflect the factual circumstances in which the specific reason for restitution arises.

Commentary: Part 5

35(1)–(2): mistake

In the context of mistake, an example of s 35(1)(a) is *Cooper v Phibbs* (1867) LR 2 HL 149, HL (equitable lien over improved land for work done). An example analogous to s 35(1)(b) is *Banque Financière de la Cité v Parc (Battersea) Ltd* [1999] 1 AC 221, HL (subrogation for mistaken lender so as to give it priority as against a subsequent lender, albeit not against all creditors because that would give the lender better security than it bargained for). In the context of mistake, examples of s 35(1)(c) are *Car and Universal Finance Co Ltd v Caldwell* [1965] 1 QB 525, CA (rescission, revesting title to a car, for fraudulent misrepresentation); *Lady Hood of Avalon v Mackinnon* [1909] 1 Ch 476 and *Re Griffiths* [2008] EWHC 118 (Ch), [2009] Ch 162 (rescission of gifts for mistake); *Blacklocks v JB Developments (Godalming) Ltd* [1982] Ch 183 (rectification where wrong area of land conveyed). As regards mistake, the best example of s 35(1)(d) is *Chase Manhattan Bank NA v Israel-British Bank (London) Ltd* [1981] Ch 105 (constructive or resulting trust imposed where mistaken double payment). Although that decision seems correct, it was explained in *Westdeutsche Landesbank Girozentrale v Islington London BC* [1996] AC 669, HL, as turning on the fact that the defendant knew of the mistake while still having the money. One can strongly argue that, in principle, that emphasis on the defendant's knowledge should be irrelevant to determining whether or not there should be proprietary restitution.

In relation to s 35(1)(c), it is worth reiterating that, as regards contracts, it is not every causal mistake that allows rescission or rectification (and this is reflected in s 10(6) by which, in general, an enrichment is not unjust if the contract is valid.) The basic position is that rescission of a contract is available for all types of misrepresentation (whether fraudulent, negligent, or purely innocent) and for non-disclosure in those limited circumstances where there is a duty to disclose (eg where the contract is one of insurance or is made between a fiduciary and its beneficiary). Rescission of a contract is not available for mistake in itself, whether the mistake is common or unilateral. In contrast, a written contract can be rectified for common or unilateral mistake subject to certain requirements. Rescission or rectification of a gift is available for mistake in itself, although there may be a requirement of seriousness in addition to causation: see s 10(4) (cf rectification of wills which, outside the Restatement, is governed by the Administration of Justice Act 1982, s 20).

35(1)–(2): duress

The additional rights referred to in s 35(1) cannot yet be illustrated from the case law on duress but rest on principle and on drawing an analogy to undue influence (and mistake). As regards an equitable lien for duress (see s 35(1)(a)), the following example may be helpful.

Example 1

D threatens C that D will pay C nothing for work C is carrying out in renovating D's house unless C does extra work for nothing. C reluctantly does the extra work, which is worth £10,000. Assuming that C can establish duress, C is entitled to a monetary restitutionary award (a *quantum meruit*) of £10,000. C should have the right to have that award secured by an equitable lien over D's house.

35(1)–(2): undue influence

The additional rights covered by s 35(1) cannot be illustrated, as regards s 35(1)(a), (b) and (d), from the case law but rest on principle and on drawing an analogy to mistake. But there are a number of examples of s 35(1)(c), where rescission for undue influence (if necessary with consequential rectification of a register: see s 35(5)) involves the revesting of rights in property retained by the defendant: see, eg, *Tate v Williamson* (1866) 2 Ch App 55, CA (sale of land); *Allcard v Skinner* (1887) 13 Ch D 145, CA (shares); *Goldsworthy v Brickell* [1987] Ch 378, CA (lease of land); *Crédit Lyonnais Bank Nederland NV v Burch* [1997] 1 All ER 144 (charge over land); *O'Sullivan v Management Agency and Music Ltd* [1985] QB 428, CA (copyright and rights in master tapes); *Royal Bank of Scotland v Etridge (No 2)* [2001] UKHL 44, [2002] 2 AC 773 (charge over land).

35(1)–(2): exploitation of weakness

The additional rights covered by s 35(1) cannot be illustrated, as regards s 35(1)(a), (b) and (d), from the case law on exploitation of weakness but rest on principle and on drawing an analogy to mistake. But there are a number of examples of s 35(1)(c) where rescission for exploitation of weakness (if necessary with consequential rectification of a register: see s 35(5)) involves the revesting of rights in property retained by the defendant: see, e.g. *Fry v Lane* (1888) 40 Ch D 312 (sale of land); *Creswell v Potter* [1978] 1 WLR 255n (transfer of share in land); *Boustany v Pigott* (1995) 69 P & CR 298, PC (lease of land).

35(1)–(2): incapacity of the individual

The additional rights covered by s 35(1) cannot be illustrated, as regards s 35(1)(a), (b) and (d), from the case law on incapacity but rest on principle and on drawing an analogy to mistake.

As regards s 35(1)(c), in relation to mental incapacity the most straightforward view is that the contract or gift is voidable for the mental incapacity. Although sometimes speaking of the gift being void, *Daily Telegraph Newspaper Co Ltd v McLoughlin* [1904] AC 776, *Re Beaney* [1978] 1 WLR 770, and *Simpson v Simpson* [1992] 1 FLR 601 are all best viewed as examples of rescission for mental incapacity revesting rights in property. See also Example 2 in the commentary on s 14(3) above.

It would appear that a gift can be rescinded for infancy but, if the gift is rendered void rather than voidable, the wording of s 35(1)(c) will be inapplicable because the defendant never acquires a right in property that needs revesting. The use of the term *rescission* in relation to minors' contracts is a simplification of the present law. This is because, although it is appropriate to describe the second category of invalid minors' contracts—for the two categories, see the commentary on s 14(2) above—as voidable and liable to be rescinded, that is marginally inaccurate as a description of the first category: the minor is not required to 'rescind' a contract that is unenforceable because of infancy under the first category. However, in practice the process of seeking to revest a right in property under a contract that is unenforceable and revesting a right in property by rescission of a contract are very similar so that, with care, one may think of revesting by rescission in both. Although denying restitution, and applying the flawed requirement of total failure of consideration, both *Steinberg v Scala (Leeds) Ltd* [1923] 2 Ch 452, CA, and *Pearce v Brain* [1929] 2 KB 310 should have involved revesting of rights in property retained by the defendants (shares and goods respectively): see the commentary on s 14(2) above.

Example 2

C, who is 15, contracts to sell a motorbike and shares to D, an adult, for £200. Six months later, C seeks restitution of the motorbike and the shares. C will be entitled to revest title to the bike and the shares by 'rescinding' the contract (the process of 'rescission' will require rectification of the share register). This will be subject to any counter-restitution for the £200 to which D is entitled.

35(1)–(2): failure of consideration

In the context of failure of consideration, it is clear that, in general, there is no proprietary restitution: see, eg, *Re Goldcorp Exchange Ltd* [1995] 1 AC 74, PC; *Westdeutsche Landesbank Girozentrale v Islington London BC* [1996] AC 669, HL.

Example 3

C pays £1,000 to D for work to be done by D. D fails to carry out the work. D still has the £1,000 or a traceable substitute (ie D retains the right in property). Apart from C's claim to damages for breach of contract, C has a personal right to restitution of £1,000 for failure of consideration. But C does not have a right to have that monetary restitutionary award secured by an equitable lien over the retained right in property. Nor does C have a right to be a beneficiary of the right in property under a trust imposed by law.

Other restitutionary rights

Example 4

C, under a contract for the sale of goods, delivers goods to D. There is no retention of title clause. D fails to pay the price. C has a contractual right to payment of the price. In principle, on the better view (but cf *Taylor v Motability Finance Ltd* [2004] EWHC 2619), C also has a personal right to restitution for the value of the goods on the ground of failure of consideration (although, as this will be measured by the contract rate so as to reflect D's request, this offers no advantage to C compared to the contractual action for the price). What C does not have is either a right to have the monetary restitutionary award secured by an equitable lien over the goods or a right to be a beneficiary of the goods under a trust imposed by law.

The justification for the distinction between this general denial of proprietary restitution for failure of consideration and the willingness to allow proprietary restitution for, for example, mistake and undue influence has been explained in various ways by commentators. For example, Birks, *Unjust Enrichment* (2nd edn, 2005) ch 8 esp 181-2, and Chambers, *Resulting Trusts* (1997) 110, 155-70, have argued that, where the failure of consideration is subsequent (rather than initial), proprietary restitution through a trust is inconsistent with the defendant having had full beneficial entitlement to the enrichment. One might perhaps elaborate on that by saying that, while there has been a failure of consideration in relation to the transfer of value, there has been no failure of consideration in relation to the transfer of the right in property. An alternative justification is to focus on insolvency (as the most important practical consequence of proprietary restitution) and to argue that, in contrast to the mistaken payor, the payor who pays for a consideration that fails takes the risk of the defendant's insolvency. Certainly if the law were otherwise, many unsecured creditors would automatically be given security through proprietary restitution, thereby undermining the present insolvency regime.

However, there are some limited exceptions where a right to restitution for failure of consideration does comprise one of the rights set out in s 35(1)(a), (b), and (d) (although s 35(1)(c) does not arise because rescission or rectification is never triggered by failure of consideration). Most importantly, as regards s 35(1)(b), where the enrichment is a discharged secured liability of the defendant, there is the right to have the monetary restitutionary award secured by being subrogated to the discharged security. This is subject to the general restriction in s 35(3) below that this does not give a lender better security than it bargained for: see *Re Wrexham, Mold and Connah's Quay Rly Co* [1899] 1 Ch 440; *Butler v Rice* [1910] 2 Ch 277; *Paul v Speirway Ltd* [1976] Ch 220; *Boscawen v Bajwa* [1996] 1 WLR 328, CA; *Cheltenham & Gloucester plc v Appleyard* [2004] EWCA Civ 291.

As regards s 35(1)(d), one can also regard trusts imposed on the failure of express trusts, because events do not turn out as specified, as illustrating restitution for a failure of consideration in its non-promissory sense: see, eg, *Re Ames' Settlement* [1946] Ch 217 (trust set up on son's marriage, which was subsequently annulled); *Re Abbott Fund Trusts* [1900] 2 Ch 326; *Re Gillingham Bus Disaster Fund* [1958] Ch 300; *Re West Sussex Constabulary Widows' Children and Benevolent (1930) Fund Trusts* [1971] Ch 1 (subsequent failure of purpose trusts). (In contrast, a *Quistclose* trust, as established in *Barclays Bank Ltd v Quistclose Investments Ltd* [1970] AC 567, HL, is probably best viewed as a form of express trust resting on intention rather than as an illustration of proprietary restitution for failure of consideration.) The reasoning in *Neste Oy v Lloyds Bank plc* [1983] 2 Lloyd's Rep 658 (see also *Re Farepak Food and Gifts Ltd* [2006] EWHC 3272, [2007] 2 BCLC 1, although there it was suggested that the decision in *Neste Oy* might be better explained as one based on a known mistake) was that the trust was being imposed because, at the time of payment, the recipient knew that the failure of consideration was inevitable. The emphasis on knowledge is controversial and, in principle, it should be sufficient that the failure of consideration was inevitable at the time of payment.

In relation to s 35(1)(a), see *Spence v S Frances Ltd* ([2011] EWHC 1269 (QB)) in which a common law lien was recognised securing a restitutionary *quantum meruit* in unjust enrichment: the unjust factor is probably best rationalised as failure of consideration (although that language was not used by Thirlwall J).

35(1)–(2): ignorance or powerlessness or fiduciary's lack of authority

Where the unjust factor is ignorance or powerlessness or a fiduciary's lack of authority, s 35(1)(a) and (d) are well illustrated by many cases on unauthorised substitution: see s 9(2)–(7) above. So equitable liens were imposed over an asset traceably retained by the defendant, in, eg, *Re Hallett's Estate* (1880) 13 Ch D 696 and *Re Oatway* [1903] 2 Ch 356: see Example 6 in the commentary to s 9(6) above. Trusts were imposed under which the claimant was a beneficiary (with a proportionate share) of a right in property, traceably retained by the defendant, in, eg, *Re Diplock* [1948] Ch 465, CA (as regards, eg, the funds of the Royal Sailors Orphan Girls' School and Home); *Barlow Clowes International v Vaughan* [1992] 4 All ER 22, CA; *Foskett v McKeown* [2001] 1 AC 102, HL: and see Example 5 in the commentary to s 9(5) above. Although in this context there appears to be no reported case illustrating s 35(1)(b), that there can be subrogation to a discharged security where the unjust factor is ignorance or powerlessness or a fiduciary's lack of authority follows by analogy from mistake. As regards s 35(1)(c), there is a helpful discussion in Mitchell, Mitchell, and Watterson (eds), *Goff and Jones on the Law of Unjust Enrichment* (8th edn, 2011) paras 8-94–8-107 of (admittedly rare)

Other restitutionary rights

situations in which rescission involving a revesting of a right in property could arise where there has been a fiduciary's lack of authority. (For the contrary view that rescission does not arise in this context—and making the clearly correct point that a void but ratifiable contract is not voidable in the sense of 'liable to be rescinded'—see O'Sullivan, Elliott and Zakrzewski, *The Law of Rescission* (2008) paras 1.52–1.83, esp 1.63–1.71.)

35(1)–(2): legal compulsion

There are no case law examples of s 35(1)(a), (c), or (d) in the context of legal compulsion and it is hard to imagine circumstances in which they might arise. However, subrogation to extinguished secured rights, as set out in s 35(1)(b), is an important illustration of proprietary restitution to avoid an undeserved escape from legal liability. The leading category of cases in which this has been applied has been where a surety has paid off another's liability (see, eg, *Forbes v Jackson* (1882) 19 Ch D 615); and the right of a surety to take over a creditor's security by subrogation is statutorily enshrined in s 5 of the Mercantile Law Amendment Act 1856. Reasoning by analogy from the surety cases would indicate that subrogation to extinguished secured rights should always be available for legal compulsion where there has been the discharge of another's liability (whether the claimant is a surety or not) subject to the general limiting principle (see s 35(3)) that a lender should not have better security than it bargained for (although it is unsatisfactory that s 5 of the 1856 Act appears to ignore such a limitation).

35(1)–(2): necessity

There have been no cases in which the rights in s 35(1)(c) and (d) have been relevant and it is hard to envisage circumstances in which they could be relevant. But as regards s 35(1)(a), it is noteworthy that, although salvage is a specialised area, salvors are entitled to a maritime lien, which is a common law possessory lien (superior to other liens, such as those securing wages) over the defendant's salvaged property, in order to secure their award: Kennedy and Rose, *Law of Salvage* (7th edn, 2009) ch 14. Although some of the hostility to restitution in the context of necessity has been in the precise context of liens being sought (see, eg, *Falcke v Scottish Imperial Insurance Co* (1886) 34 Ch D 234, CA) the policy of encouraging intervention would seem to indicate that, by analogy to the maritime lien, the necessitous intervener should be entitled to a lien over the asset that has been saved as security for the monetary restitutionary award. For similar reasons, although there is no case exemplifying this, if the necessitous intervention comprises discharging the defendant's secured liability, the claimant should in principle be entitled to be subrogated (by 'subrogation to extinguished rights') to the discharged security (under s 35(1)(b)).

Commentary: Part 5

35(1)-(2): factors concerned with illegality

There have been no case-law examples of the rights in s 35(1)(a), (b), or (d) in this context. But as regards s 35(1)(c)—albeit that the terminology of 'rescission' has not generally been used—withdrawal during the *locus poenitentiae* allows the claimant, in effect, to rescind the contract so that rights in property will be revested (as in, eg, *Taylor v Bowers* (1876) 1 QBD 291); and class protection rendering a contract illegal also gives the claimant, in effect, a right to revest a right in property by rescission (see *Lodge v National Union Investment Co Ltd* [1907] 1 Ch 300).

35(1)-(2): unlawful obtaining or conferral of a benefit by a public authority

As regards claims against a public authority, there has been no discussion of proprietary restitution in the English cases and, as a practical matter, the question of proprietary restitution is unlikely to arise because public authorities are unlikely to become insolvent. Nevertheless, if there were a practical advantage in securing a monetary restitutionary award by imposing a lien over a traced asset (or an asset to which the benefit is otherwise directly linked) retained by the defendant or in imposing a trust where the benefit obtained is a right in property retained by the defendant, furtherance of the reason underlying this unjust factor would indicate that a lien or trust should be imposed; and that would be consistent with the law on mistake. Moreover, that a trust is a possibility in this context is supported by the Canadian decision of Barr J in *Zaidan Group Ltd v City of London* (1987) 36 DLR (4th) 443 (albeit that this was overturned by the Ontario Court of Appeal on a different point (1990) 64 DLR (4th) 514).

As regards claims by a public authority, the possible insolvency of the payee may mean that proprietary restitution becomes relevant. Furtherance of the policy of protecting public funds indicates that, where the defendant retains a traced (or otherwise directly linked) asset or where the benefit obtained is a right in property retained by the defendant, it would be appropriate to impose a lien or a trust; and it is perhaps significant in support of this that Lord Goff in *Woolwich Equitable Building Soc v Inland Revenue Commissioners* [1993] AC 70, at 177, interpreted Lord Haldane's reference to 'tracing' in *Auckland Harbour Board v R* [1924] AC 318, PC, as meaning that the claim was 'proprietary in nature'.

35(3)

This general restricting principle (sometimes referred to as the '*Paul v Speirway* principle') has been most obviously applied in the context of a lender's non-contractual subrogation to discharged secured rights. In a number of cases it has been made clear that the lender should not by means of subrogation be given better

Subrogation

security than it bargained for (the unjust factor usually being failure of consideration or mistake): see *Re Wrexham, Mold and Connah's Quay Rly Co* [1899] 1 Ch 440; *Butler v Rice* [1910] 2 Ch 277; *Paul v Speirway Ltd* [1976] Ch 220; *Boscawen v Bajwa* [1996] 1 WLR 328, CA; *Banque Financière de la Cité v Parc (Battersea) Ltd* [1999] 1 AC 221, HL; *Cheltenham & Gloucester plc v Appleyard* [2004] EWCA Civ 291. The Restatement reflects the point that this idea has force beyond the context of subrogation and lenders and, in principle, operates as a limiting restriction on proprietary restitution generally. In essence, one is here accepting the idea that restitution should not allow a claimant to escape from the risk that it has taken of being unsecured or inadequately secured (ie the risk of the defendant's insolvency). However, the restriction does not apply where the unjust factor undermines the claimant's consent to the taking of that risk (ie the unjust factor outweighs the taking of the risk) as, for example, where a lender was induced to enter into the contract by duress or undue influence or where the mistake made by a lender extended to (ie 'masked') the credit risk. See Mitchell, Mitchell, and Watterson (eds), *Goff and Jones on the Law of Unjust Enrichment* (8th edn, 2011) paras 37-17–37-18.

35(4)

A right in property is defined so as to include intangible property, thereby extending beyond rights to things.

35(5)

As has been explained above in the commentary on s 35(1)(c), rescission or rectification includes any consequential order necessary to revest a right of property, most obviously rectification of a register.

36 Subrogation

(1) Subrogation is the process by which, either by contract or by operation of law but without an assignment, a claimant may take over, or be treated as having taken over, some or all of a person's former or present rights against another person; but in this Restatement "subrogation" means subrogation by operation of law.

(2) In connection with sections 34 and 35(1)(b)—

   (a) if the defendant's enrichment is the discharge of a liability of the defendant to another person, the claimant may be treated as having taken over some or all of that person's former rights against the defendant, in order to reverse that enrichment;

   (b) if a liability of one defendant to another person has been discharged at the claimant's expense, the claimant may be treated as having taken over some or all of that person's former rights against that defendant in order to reverse the resulting enrichment of another defendant.

(3) If the claimant has indemnified the defendant against a loss under a contract of indemnity (for example, a contract of indemnity insurance), the claimant may take over some or all of the defendant's present rights (or the fruit of those rights) against another person so that, in conjunction with that person's liability not being discharged—
   (a) the unjust enrichment, by over-indemnification, of the defendant at the claimant's expense is reversed or prevented, and
   (b) the claimant's loss is recouped.
(4) Subsection (3) is not exhaustive as to the situations in which the claimant may take over some or all of the defendant's present rights against another person in order to reverse the unjust enrichment of the defendant at the claimant's expense.
For example subrogation may be available where a claimant has not been paid for supplying goods or services to a business carried on by a defendant trustee.

36(1)

This explains what the term 'subrogation' means. Subrogation allows one party (without an assignment) to 'step into the shoes' of another party as regards some or all of that party's extinguished or subsisting rights.

Although subrogation is usually described by judges as a remedy, it is probably better seen as a legal process or means of getting to particular rights (or, some might add, remedies). So to describe a claimant as seeking subrogation against the defendant is less accurate than describing the claimant as seeking subrogation *to* particular rights against the defendant.

It can be seen immediately that the whole concept of subrogation rests on an element of metaphor and fiction. The underlying truth is that the claimant is being given rights which it did not previously have and one might argue that one should recognise that truth directly without going through the deemed substitution involved in subrogation. The fiction is particularly clear where the rights in question have been extinguished so that the claimant is treated as if 'taking over' rights that no longer exist. However, at least at this stage in the development of the law—when the role of subrogation within the law of unjust enrichment has only recently been accepted by the courts—there is a danger of causing more confusion than enlightenment by seeking to abandon the idea and language of subrogation. The Restatement has therefore preferred the approach of continuing to use the language of subrogation, as the courts do, while explaining, as transparently as possible, what lies behind that language.

Subrogation

The law on subrogation is complex and, until recently, was poorly understood. Traditionally, it was viewed as a *sui generis* area of the law, occasionally resting on contract, but primarily being seen as a pocket of 'equity' without any further doctrinal explanation. Relying on the work of academic commentators, a major advance was made by the House of Lords in *Banque Financière de la Cité v Parc (Battersea) Ltd* [1999] 1 AC 221 at 231–2, 228 (hereinafter 'the *BFC* case') in recognising a clear divide between contractual subrogation, which rests on the intention of the parties, and subrogation by operation of law (traditionally arising in equity) which rests on reversing, or preventing, unjust enrichment. Contractual subrogation (as, for example, where there are subrogation clauses in insurance contracts) plainly lies outside this Restatement and within the law of contract. Subrogation by operation of law lies within this Restatement.

Mitchell and Watterson, *Subrogation Law and Practice* (2007) make a helpful division, as regards subrogation by operation of law, between 'subrogation to extinguished rights' and 'subrogation to subsisting rights'. This distinction was explicitly relied on by Vos J in *Ibrahim v Barclays Bank plc* [2011] EWHC 1897 (Ch), [2012] 1 BCLC 33 (upheld, on a different point, [2012] EWCA Civ 640). The distinction is reflected in the Restatement by the division between s 36(2) and s 36(3)–(4). Section 36(2) concerns 'subrogation to extinguished rights'; ss 36(3) and (4) concern 'subrogation to subsisting rights'.

36(2)

This type of subrogation ('subrogation to extinguished rights') was in issue in the *BFC* case and, for the purposes of this Restatement, it is the more important type of subrogation because it potentially applies across a wide field. The usual situation is that set out in s 36(2)(a). Any of the unjust factors may be in play, although most commonly the unjust factors will be legal compulsion, failure of consideration, or mistake. It is exemplified by the (non-contractual) subrogation rights of a surety (*Forbes v Jackson* (1882) 19 Ch D 615; Mercantile Law Amendment Act 1856, s 5) or of a lender (*Butler v Rice* [1910] 2 Ch 277; *Boscawen v Bajwa* [1996] 1 WLR 328, CA; the *BFC* case [1999] 1 AC 221, HL; *Cheltenham & Gloucester plc v Appleyard* [2004] EWCA Civ 291) or of a banker (*B Liggett (Liverpool) Ltd v Barclays Bank Ltd* [1928] 1 KB 48). In some recent cases (eg *Niru Battery Manufacturing Co v Milestone Trading Ltd (No 2)* [2004] EWCA Civ 487, [2004] 2 Lloyd's Rep 319; *Primlake Ltd v Matthews Associates* [2006] EWHC 1227 (Ch)) this type of subrogation has been cut free from those traditional categories so that it potentially applies wherever there has been an unjust enrichment and the enrichment comprises the discharge of another's obligation.

This type of subrogation plainly rests on a fiction precisely because there are no subsisting rights for the claimant to 'take over'. This was recognised by Lord Hoffmann in the *BFC* case when his Lordship said ([1999] 1 AC 221 at 236) that one is treating the situation '*as if* the benefit... had been assigned to [the claimant]'. In the Restatement this is captured by the words, 'may be treated as having taken over...'.

It is important to appreciate that the rights 'taken over' through subrogation to extinguished rights may be personal or 'proprietary'. Hence the cross-reference at the start of s 36(2) to s 34 and s 35(1)(b). The right to be subrogated to a discharged security, where the enrichment is a discharged secured liability of the defendant, is one of the four main types of proprietary restitution (see s 35(1)(b)).

Example 1

C lends £5,000 to D so as to enable D to pay off his debt to X (a bank) which is secured by X's charge over D's house. C lends the money on the understanding that repayment is to be secured by D arranging for C to have a charge over the house but D fails to arrange this and fails to repay the loan. C is entitled to be subrogated to X's extinguished rights against D (including X's charge over the house) so as to effect restitution of the £5,000.

That a claimant who has bargained for repayment should not be entitled to security, by subrogation, where it would give the claimant better security than the claimant bargained for is exemplified by cases on a lender's subrogation rights (see s 35(3) above). In line with that restriction, the *BFC* case also made clear that the extinguished rights of X that C is treated as if it has taken over, in order to reverse D's unjust enrichment, need not be taken over in full and can be modified. So on the facts the claimant had mistakenly thought that it had security as against OOL (the second charge-holder) but not against all Parc's creditors. The claimant's loan was used to pay off the first charge, over Parc's land, held by RTB. To give the claimant the first charge of RTB would have gone beyond the secured position that the claimant mistakenly thought it had. The House of Lords therefore adjusted the extinguished rights of RTB to be treated as taken over by the claimant so as to limit them to giving the claimant priority as against OOL.

Subsection 36(2)(b) has been included primarily because, although sometimes overlooked, the leading *BFC* case ultimately involved the enrichment not of the defendant whose liability had been discharged (Parc) but of the second charge-holder (OOL). So, on the facts, the dispute in the *BFC* case was, in practice, not between BFC (which had lent the money to discharge Parc's debt to RTB, the first charge-holder) and Parc but rather, because Parc was insolvent, between BFC and OOL (the second charge-holder). In deciding on the appropriate extent of the extinguished rights of RTB that BFC should be treated as if it had taken over, the

Subrogation

House of Lords focused on the unjust enrichment of OOL rather than the unjust enrichment of Parc (Mitchell and Watterson, *Subrogation Law and Practice* (2007) refer to this, at para 4.09, as a secondary enrichment of a remoter party). So, applying s 36(2)(b) to the facts of the *BFC* case, the claimant is BFC, Parc is 'one defendant', RTB is 'another person' and OOL is 'another defendant'.

36(3)

The type of subrogation in issue here is 'subrogation to subsisting rights'. The most important feature distinguishing this type of subrogation from that in s 36(2) is that here no liability has been discharged by C's payment. Rather the relevant liability of the third party to the defendant remains alive in the defendant's name.

The most important example of this type of subrogation is an indemnity insurer's non-contractual subrogation (*Mason v Sainsbury* (1782) 3 Doug KB 61; *Lord Napier & Ettrick v Hunter* [1993] AC 713, HL; and see the discussion in *Esso Petroleum Co Ltd v Hall, Russell & Co Ltd* [1989] AC 643 at 662-3 per Lord Goff, where the tanker owners' oil pollution agreement was a contract of indemnity). Although subrogation will usually be provided for in the contract of indemnity, whether by an express or implied term (indeed Diplock J in *Yorkshire Insurance Co Ltd v Nisbet Shipping Co Ltd* [1962] 2 QB 330 at 339-40 and, arguably, Lord Hoffmann in the *BFC* case indicated that an insurer's subrogation is exclusively contractual), it appears (see *Lord Napier and Ettrick v Hunter* [1993] AC 713 at 743-4 per Lord Goff) that, even if there is no such contractual term, subrogation arises by operation of law.

In *Lord Napier and Ettrick v Hunter* money had already been paid by the third party to the insured. As in many other cases, the insurer's rights in respect of that money were treated as an aspect of the subrogation rights of the insurer. Strictly speaking, where money has already been paid to the insured, the insurer is not taking over subsisting rights, so much as the 'fruit' of the rights that the insured had against the third party and this explains the inclusion of the words in brackets 'or the fruit of those rights'. Indeed, one can strongly argue that subrogation is here clearly superfluous in that the claimant has a direct right to a monetary restitutionary award for the insured's accrued unjust enrichment. However, subrogation to the insured's subsisting rights often operates *before* the relevant unjust enrichment (ie before payment by the third party to the insured). So the best analysis of an insurer's subrogation rights is that the insurer takes over the rights of the insured against a third party in order to reverse or *prevent* the insured's unjust enrichment at the insurer's expense. See generally on prevention of an anticipated unjust enrichment, s 6.

The injustice involved is the very specific one of adhering to the principle of indemnity by avoiding the over-indemnification of the insured/indemnified party, while at the same time ensuring that the ultimate burden of paying falls on the third party rather than the insurer: see Mitchell and Watterson, *Subrogation Law and Practice* (2007) paras 1.07–1.08. There is also the incidental purpose—albeit in practice this may appear to be the primary purpose—of enabling the insurer to recoup its loss. As this unjust factor is so specific, and tied entirely to subrogation in the context of a contract of indemnity, it has been thought preferable to refer to it in the Restatement here rather than including in Part 3 an unjust factor of avoiding the insured's over-indemnification. (Note that this area does not fall within s 18 (legal compulsion) because the insurer's payment to the insured does not discharge the liability of the third party so that there is no question of the insured seeking restitution from the third party on the ground that, as between the two of them, the third party had the primary liability.)

Example 2

C insures D against damage to D's property. X tortiously damages D's property. C pays out £10,000 to D for the loss in accordance with the insurance policy. Irrespective of any contractual subrogation, C can be subrogated to D's subsisting rights (in tort) against X. The subrogation operates to prevent D's unjust enrichment, by over-indemnification, at C's expense.

Example 3

Same facts as Example 2 except that D first recovers £8,000 from X. C is entitled to the £8,000 (i.e. C is subrogated to the 'fruit' of D's rights against X) so as to reverse D's unjust enrichment, by over-indemnification, at C's expense.

In *Lord Napier and Ettrick v Hunter* it was laid down that, in exercising its subrogation rights to payments received by the insured, the insurer has not merely a personal right to restitution but also an equitable lien over the payments received to secure the monetary award: see s 35(1)(a). So applying this to the facts of Example 3, C would have an equitable lien over the £8,000 to secure payment.

36(4)

'Subrogation to subsisting rights' is the type of subrogation applied in some other specialised situations, most obviously the subrogation rights of creditors of a business carried on by trustees (*Re Johnson* (1880) 15 Ch D 548 at 552; *Re Oxley* [1914] 1 Ch 604). A creditor can take over the right (on this right, see the Trustee Act 2000, s 31(1)) that a trustee has against the beneficiary of the trust to be reimbursed for properly incurred expenses so as to reverse the unjust enrichment of the trustee at the creditor's expense. The most obvious unjust factor is failure of consideration in that the creditor has not been paid.

Subrogation

Example 4

D, a trustee, fails to pay C £20,000 owed for financial advice in relation to the trust assets. X is the beneficiary under the trust. C can be subrogated to D's right to be reimbursed by X for properly incurred expenses so as to reverse D's unjust enrichment (with the unjust factor being failure of consideration) at C's expense.

TABLE OF STATUTES

Administration of Justice Act 1982,
   s 20... 29, 162, 164
Apportionment Act 1870... 91
Civil Liability (Contribution) Act 1978... 102, 103, 147
   s 10(2)–(4)... 147
Consumer Credit Act 1974
   s 127(3)... 151
   ss 140A, 140B... 110
Customs and Excise Management Act 1979
   s 137A(5)... 114
Equality Act 2010
   s 199... 108
Finance Act 1998
   Sch 18, para 51A(8)... 150
Finance Act 200... 4
   s 320... 146
   s 320(1)... 146
Finance Act 2007
   s 107... 146
Forfeiture Act 1982... 28
Gambling Act 2005... 132
Infants Relief Act 1874... 83
Inheritance Tax Act 1984
   s 241... 114
Insolvency Act 1986
   ss 238, 239... 110
   s 423... 110
Law of Property Act 1925
   s 1(6)... 84
Law Reform (Frustrated Contracts) Act 1943... 13, 16, 86, 88, 92, 117, 122, 145, 152
   s 1(2)... 16, 117, 122
   s 1(3)... 16, 117
   s 1(3)(a)... 122
   s 1(3)(b)... 122
   s 2(3)... 151
   s 2(5) 13... , 86, 88, 92, 122, 152
Limitation Act 1980... 18, 33, 143–45, 147–49
   s 5... 144
   s 9... 145
   s 10(1)... 147
   s 10(2)–(4)... 147
   s 21... 147, 148

s 21(1)(a)... 145
s 21(3)... 145
s 22(a)... 147
s 28... 147
s 29(5)... 147
s 30(1)... 147
s 32(1)(a), (b)... 146
s 32(1)(c)... 112, 145, 146
s 35... 26
s 36(2)... 148
s 38... 147
Mental Capacity Act 2005... 147
   s 2(1)... 85
   s 7... 104
Mercantile Law Amendment Act 1856
   s 5... 102, 161, 169, 173
Minors' Contracts Act 1987... 83, 84
   s 3(1)... 36
Proceeds of Crime Act 2002... 28
Sale of Goods Act 1979
   s 3(2)... 104
   s 30(1)... 91
Senior Courts Act 1981
   s 35A... 38
Social Security Administration Act 1992
   s 71... 115
Statute of Frauds 1677... 89
Taxes Management Act 1970
   s 33... 114, 147
   Sch 1AB... 114, 147
   Sch 1AB, para 2(8)... 150
Torts (Interference with Goods) Act 1977
   s 6(1)... 64
Trustee Act 2000
   s 31(1)... 176
Unfair Contract Terms Act 1977... 149–51
Unfair Terms in Consumer Contracts Regulations 1999... 149–51
Value Added Tax Act 1994
   s 80... 51, 114, 150
   s 80(7)... 50, 114
Wills Act 1837... 29
   s 7... 85

EUROPEAN UNION
Reg 864/2007 ('Rome II' Regulation)... 30

TABLE OF CASES

Abbott Fund Trusts, Re [1900] 2
  Ch 326... 168
Abou-Rahman v Abacha [2006]
  EWCA Civ 1492, [2007] 1 All ER
  (Comm) 827... 121
Agip (Africa) Ltd v Jackson [1990]
  Ch 265, aff'd [1991] Ch 547,
  CA... 60, 96, 125
Aiken v Short (1856) 1
  H & N 210... 135
Alev, The [1989] 1 Lloyd's Rep 138... 71, 72
Alf Vaughan & Co Ltd v Royscot Trust plc,
  [1999] 1 All ER (Comm) 856... 72
Alexander v Rayson [1936]
  1 KB 169, CA... 108
Allcard v Skinner (1887) 36
  Ch D 145, CA... 76, 77, 148,
  153, 161, 165
Allen v Flood [1898] AC 1, HL... 95
Amantilla Ltd v Telefusion plc (1987) 9
  Con LR 139... 147
Ames' Settlement, Re [1946]
  Ch 217... 163, 168
Amin v Amin [2010] EWHC
  528 (Ch)... 46
Amministrazione delle Finanze dello
  Stato v SpA San Giorgio: 199/82 [1983]
  ECR 3595, ECJ... 111, 122
Armstrong DLW GmbH v Winnington
  Networks Ltd [2012] EWHC 10 (Ch), [2012]
  3 All ER 425... 58
Astley v Reynolds (1731)
  2 Stra 915... 71, 72, 137
Atlas Express Ltd v Kafco
  (Importers and Distributors) Ltd [1989]
  QB 833... 72
A-G v Blake [2001] 1 AC 268, HL... 27, 89
A-G v Guardian Newspapers Ltd (No 2) [1990]
  1 AC 109, HL... 27
Auckland Harbour Board v R [1924] AC 318,
  PC... 113, 115, 170
Austin v Gervas (1614) Hobart 77... 84
Avon County Council v Howlett [1983]
  1 WLR 605, CA... 123
Awwad v Geraghty & Co (a firm) [2001]
  QB 570, CA... 137
Aylesford (Earl) v Morris (1873)
  8 Ch App 484... 80

B & S Contracts and Design Ltd v
  Victor Green Publications Ltd [1984]
  ICR 419, CA... 71, 72
BP Exploration Co (Libya) Ltd v
  Hunt (No 2) [1979] 1 WLR 783,
  affd [1983] 2 AC 352,
  HL... 42, 122, 145, 150
Backhouse v Backhouse [1978]
  1 WLR 243... 81
Baker v Courage & Co [1910] 1 KB 56... 145
Baker (GL) Ltd v Medway Building and
  Supplies Ltd [1958] 2 All ER 532, [1958]
  1 WLR 1216, CA... 98
Bank of Credit and Commerce International
  (Overseas) Ltd v Akindele [2001] Ch 437,
  CA... 97
Banque Belge pour L'Etranger v Hambrouck
  [1921] 1 KB 321, CA... 59
Banque Financière de la Cité v Parc
  (Battersea) Ltd [1999] 1
  AC 221, HL... 25, 40, 164, 171, 173–75
Barclays Bank Ltd v Quistclose Investments
  Ltd [1970] AC 567, HL... 168
Barclays Bank Ltd v WJ Simms, Son
  and Cook (Southern) Ltd [1980]
  QB 677... 64, 65, 67, 135
Barclays Bank plc v O'Brien [1994]
  1 AC 180, HL... 69, 74, 77, 79, 116
Barlow Clowes International Ltd v Vaughan
  [1992] 4 All ER 22, CA... 60, 62, 162, 168
Barros Mattos Junior v MacDaniels
  [2004] EWHC 1188 (Ch), [2005]
  1 WLR 247... 121
Barton v Armstrong [1976]
  AC 104, PC... 65, 71, 74
Barton v County NatWest Ltd [1999]
  EWCA Civ 1826, [1999] Lloyd's
  Rep Bank 408, CA... 65
Baylis v Bishop of London [1913]
  1 Ch 127, CA... 124
Beale v Kyte [1907] 1 Ch 564... 162
Beaney, Re [1978] 1 WLR 770... 85, 165
Benedetti v Sawiris [2009] EWCA
  Civ 1427... 43, 158
Berg v Sadler and Moore [1937]
  2 KB 158, CA... 137
Berkeley Applegate (Investment Consultants)
  Ltd, Re [1989] Ch 32... 104

Table of Cases

Bigos v Bousted [1951] 1 All ER 92... 108
Bishopsgate Investment Management Ltd v Homan [1995] Ch 211, CA... 61, 62
Blacklocks v JB Developments (Godalming) Ltd [1982] Ch 183... 162, 164
Boardman v Phipps [1964] 1 WLR 993, HL... 27
Boissevain v Weil [1950] AC 327, HL... 137, 138
Bonner v Tottenham and Edmonton Permanent Investment Building Society [1899] 1 QB 161, CA... 100
Boscawen v Bajwa [1996] 1 WLR 328, CA... 60, 167, 171, 173
Boustany v Pigott (1993) 69 P & CR 298, PC... 81, 165
Bowmakers Ltd v Barnet Instruments Ltd [1945] KB 65, CA... 137
Boyter v Dodsworth (1796) 6 Term Rep 681... 51, 96
Bradford Corpn v Pickles [1895] AC 587, HL... 95
Brennan v Bolt Burdon [2004] EWCA (Civ) 1017, [2005] QB 303... 142
Bridgeman v Green (1755) Wilm 58... 78, 79
Bristol and West Building Society v Mothew (t/a Stapley & Co) [1998] Ch 1, CA... 161
British Steel Corpn v Cleveland Bridge and Engineering Co Ltd [1984] 1 All ER 504... 87
British Steel plc v Customs and Excise Comrs [1997] 2 All ER 366, CA... 113
Brook's Wharf and Bull Wharf Ltd v Goodman Bros [1937] 1 KB 534, CA... 101, 102
Brown and Davis Ltd v Galbraith [1972] 1 WLR 997, CA... 52
Browning v Morris (1778) 2 Cowp 790... 110
Butler v Rice [1910] 2 Ch 277... 51, 161, 167, 171, 173
CTN Cash and Carry Ltd v Gallaher Ltd [1994] 4 All ER 714, CA... 32, 72
Car and Universal Finance Co Ltd v Caldwell [1965] 1 QB 525, CA... 161, 164
Carillion Construction Ltd v Felix (UK) Ltd [2001] BLR 1... 72
Cavalier Insurance Co Ltd, Re [1989] 2 Lloyd's Rep 430... 137
Chandler Bros Ltd v Boswell [1936] 3 All ER 179, CA... 91

Chaplin v Leslie Frewin (Publishers) Ltd [1966] Ch 71, CA... 84
Charles Terence Estates Ltd v The Cornwall Council [2011] EWHC 2542 (QB), [2012] 1 P & CR 2... 113
Charter plc v City Index Ltd [2007] EWCA Civ 1382, [2008] Ch 313... 102, 103
Chase Manhattan Bank NA v Israel-British Bank (London) Ltd [1981] Ch 105... 163, 164
Cheese v Thomas [1994] 1 WLR 129, CA... 118, 155
Cheltenham & Gloucester plc v Appleyard [2004] EWCA Civ 291... 167, 171, 173
Chief Constable of the Greater Manchester Police v Wigan Athletic AFC Ltd [2008] EWCA Civ 1449, [2009] 1 WLR 1580... 25, 31, 42, 43
China-Pacific SA v Food Corpn of India, The Winson [1982] AC 939, HL... 104, 107
Ciro Citterio Menswear plc (in administration), Re Ciro Citterio Menswear plc v Thakrar [2002] EWHC 293 (Ch), [2002] 1 WLR 2217... 161
Clarke v Dickson (1858) EB & E 148... 128
Clayton's Case (1816) 1 Mer 572... 60
Clough v London and North Western Rly Co (1871) LR 7 Exch 26... 153
Cobbe v Yeoman's Row Management Ltd [2008] UKHL 55, [2008] 1 WLR 1752... 47, 87
Commerzbank AG v Gareth Price-Jones [2003] EWCA Civ 1663... 118, 120, 121
Commerzbank Aktiengesellschaft v IMB Morgan plc [2004] EWHC 2771 (Ch), [2005] 2 All ER (Comm) 564... 60
Cooper v Phibbs (1867) LR 2 HL 149... 160, 164
Coulthurst v Sweet (1866) LR 1 CP 649... 127
Craig, Re [1971] Ch 95... 78
Crantrave Ltd v Lloyd's Bank plc [2000] EWCA Civ 127, [2000] QB 917... 100
Crédit Lyonnais Bank Nederland NV v Burch [1997] 1 All ER 144, CA... 78, 165
Cressman v Coys of Kensington (Sales) Ltd [2004] EWCA Civ 47, [2004] 1 WLR 2775... 25, 42, 43, 64, 65, 117, 120
Cresswell v Potter [1978] 1 WLR 255n... 81, 165
Criterion Properties plc v Stratford UK Properties plc [2004] UKHL 28, [2004] 1 WLR 1846... 97

Table of Cases

Cundy v Lindsay (1878) 3 App Cas 459... 132
DSND Subsea Ltd v Petroleum Geo-Services ASA [2000] EWHC 185 (TCC), [2000] BLR 530... 72, 73
Daily Telegraph Newspaper Co Ltd v McLaughlin [1904] AC 776, PC... 85, 165
Davies v London and Provincial Marine Insurance Co (1878) 8 Ch D 469... 137, 139
Dawood (Ebrahim) Ltd v Heath (Est 1927) Ltd [1961] 2 Lloyd's Rep 512... 89
Deering v Earl of Winchelsea (1787) 2 Bos & P 270... 102
Deglman v Guaranty Trust Co of Canada and Constantineau [1954] 3 DLR 78, SCC... 35
Deutsche Bank (London Agency) v Beriro & Co (1895) 73 LT 669, CA... 123
Deutsche Morgan Grenfell Group plc v Inland Revenue Commissioners [2006] UKHL 49, [2007] 1 AC 558... 28, 32, 34, 39, 64, 66, 68, 112, 114, 146
Dextra Bank and Trust Co Ltd v Bank of Jamaica [2002] 1 All ER (Comm) 193, PC... 67, 120, 121
Dies v British and International Mining and Finance Corpn Ltd [1939] 1 KB 724... 91
Dimond v Lovell [2002] 1 AC 384, HL... 151
Dimskal Shipping Co SA v International Transport Workers' Federation, The Evia Luck (No 2) [1992] 2 AC 152, HL... 71, 74
Diplock, Re see Ministry of Health v Simpson
Dubai Aluminium Co Ltd v Salaam [2002] UKHL 48, [2003] 2 AC 366... 102, 103
Duke of Norfolk v Worthy (1808) 1 Camp 337... 125, 127
ENE Kos 1 Ltd v Petroleo Brasileiro SA (No 2) [2012] UKSC 17, [2012] 2 WLR 976... 104
Edgington v Fitzmaurice (1885) 29 Ch D 459, CA... 65
Edwards v Lee's Administrator 96 SW 2d 1028 (1936)... 94
El Ajou v Dollar Land Holdings plc [1993] 3 All ER 717, CA... 161
Ellis v Goulton [1893] 1 QB 350, CA... 125, 127
Erlanger v New Sombrero Phosphate Co (1878) 3 App Cas 1218, HL... 129, 148
Esso Petroleum Co Ltd v Hall Russell & Co Ltd [1989] AC 643, HL... 175
Evans v Llewellin (1787) 1 Cox Eq Cas 333... 80, 81
Exall v Partridge (1799) 8 Term Rep 308... 101, 103
F v West Berkshire Health Authority [1990] 2 AC 1, HL... 105, 106
Falcke v Scottish Imperial Insurance Co (1886) 34 Ch D 234, CA... 104, 169
Farepak Food and Gifts Ltd, Re [2006] EWHC 3272, [2007] 2 BCLC 1... 168
Ferguson (D O) & Associates (a firm) v Sohl (1992) 62 BLR 95, CA... 88
Fibrosa Spolka Akcyjna v Fairbairn Lawson Combe Barbour Ltd [1943] AC 32, HL... 34, 87, 91
Forbes v Jackson (1882) 19 Ch D 615... 169, 173
Fortis Bank SA v Indian Overseas Bank [2011] EWHC 538 (Comm), [2011] 2 Lloyd's Rep 190... 100
Foskett v McKeown [2001] 1 AC 102, HL... 56–60, 62, 131, 162, 168
Friends' Provident Life Office v Hillier Parker May & Rowden (a firm) [1997] QB 85, CA... 103
Fry v Lane (1888) 40 Ch D 312... 81, 165
Fuller v Happy Shopper Markets Ltd [2001] 2 Lloyd's Rep 249... 145
Galbraith v Mitchenall Estates Ltd [1965] 2 QB 473... 151
Gamerco SA v ICM/Fair Warning (Agency) Ltd [1995] 1 WLR 1226... 122
Gebhardt v Saunders [1892] 2 QB 452... 100
Gibb v Maidstone and Tunbridge Wells NHS Trust [2010] EWCA Civ 678, [2010] IRLR 786... 32, 41
Giedo Van der Garde BV v Force India Formula One Team Ltd [2010] EWHC 2373 (QB)... 88
Giles v Edwards (1797) 7 Term Rep 181... 34, 87, 91
Gillingham Bus Disaster Fund, Re, Bowman v Official Solicitor [1958] Ch 300... 168
Goldcorp Exchange Ltd, Re [1995] 1 AC 74, PC... 61, 166
Goldsworthy v Brickell [1987] Ch 378... 78, 165
Goodman v Pocock (1850) 15 QB 576... 90
Goring, The [1987] QB 687, HL... 104
Goss v Chilcott [1996] AC 788, PC... 121
Gowers v Lloyds and National Provincial Foreign Bank Ltd [1938] 1 All ER 766, CA... 125

Table of Cases

Gray v Thames Trains Ltd [2009] UKHL 33, [2009] 1 AC 1339... 138
Great Northern Rly Co v Swaffield (1874) LR 9 Exch 132... 104
Great Western Rly Co v Sutton (1869) LR 4 HL 226... 71
Greenwood v Bennett [1973] QB 195, CA... 64
Griffiths, Re [2008] EWHC 118 (Ch), [2009] Ch 162... 65, 67, 161, 164
Guardian Ocean Cargoes Ltd v Banco do Brasil SA [1994] 2 Lloyd's Rep 152, CA... 145
Hain Steamship Co Ltd v Tate and Lyle Ltd [1936] 2 All ER 597, HL... 91
Hall v Hebert [1993] 2 SCR 159, SCC... 138
Hallett's Estate, Re (1880) 13 Ch D 696, CA... 60, 160, 168
Halpern v Halpern [2007] EWCA Civ 291, [2008] QB 195... 128, 129, 130
Hart v O'Connor [1985] AC 1000, PC... 85
Haugesund Kommune v Depfa ACS Bank [2010] EWCA Civ 103 6, [2012] 2 WLR 199... 27, 117, 121, 122
Henderson v Merrett Syndicates Ltd [1995] 2 AC 145, HL... 28
Holiday v Sigil (1826) 2 C & P 176... 94
Holland v Russell (1861) 1 B & S 424, affd (1863) 4 B & S 14... 125
Holt v Markham [1923] 1 KB 504, CA... 123
Hughes v Liverpool Victoria Legal Friendly Society [1916] 2 KB 482, CA... 137
Huyton SA v Peter Cremer GmbH & Co [1999] 1 Lloyd's Rep 620... 72, 74
Hyundai Heavy Industries Co Ltd v Papadopoulos [1980] 2 All ER 29, HL... 323, 355
Ibrahim v Barclays Bank plc [2011] EWHC 1897 (Ch), [2012] 1 BCLC 33; affd [2012] EWCA Civ 640... 100, 173
Imperial Loan Co v Stone [1892] 1 QB 599, CA... 85
Inche Noriah v Shaik Allie Bin Omar [1929] AC 127, PC... 78
Independent Trustee Services Ltd v GP Noble Trustees Ltd [2012] EWCA Civ 195, [2012] 3 All ER 210... 132, 136
Investment Trust Companies v HMRC [2012] EWHC 458 (Ch)... 25, 48, 50
Jenkins v Tucker (1788) 1 Hy Bl 90... 104
Johnson, Re (1880) 15 Ch D 548... 176
Johnson v Royal Mail Steam Packet Co (1867) LR 3 CP 38... 101

Jones v Churcher [2009] EWHC 722 (QB), [2009] 2 Lloyd's Rep 94... 121, 125, 126
Kasumu v Babe-Egbe [1956] AC 539, PC... 131
Kelly v Solari (1841) 9 M & W 54... 64, 65, 67
Kiriri Cotton Co Ltd v Dewani [1960] AC 192, PC... 110, 137
Kleinwort Benson Ltd v Birmingham City Council [1997] QB 380, HL... 46, 150
Kleinwort Benson Ltd v Lincoln City Council [1999] 2 AC 349, HL... 31, 33, 64, 145, 146, 150
Kleinwort Benson Ltd v Sandwell Borough Council [1994] 4 All ER 890... 145
Kleinwort Benson Ltd v Vaughan [1996] CLC 620, CA... 101
Kleinwort Sons & Co v Dunlop Rubber Co (1907) 97 LT 263, HL... 125
Kolmar Group AG v Traxpo Enterprises Pvt Ltd [2010] EWHC 113 (Comm), [2010] 2 Lloyd's Rep 653... 72, 74
Kwei Tek Chao (t/a Zung Fu Co) v British Traders and Shippers Ltd [1954] 2 QB 459... 90
Lady Hood of Avalon v Mackinnon [1909] 1 Ch 476... 66, 161, 164
Ladywell Mining Co v Brookes (1887) 35 Ch D 400, CA... 128
Lancashire Loans Ltd v Black [1934] 1 KB 380, CA... 77
Les Laboratoires Servier v Apotex Inc [2012] EWCA Civ 593... 138
Leslie (R) Ltd v Sheill [1914] 3 KB 607, CA... 36
Liggett (B) (Liverpool) Ltd v Barclays Bank Ltd [1928] 1 KB 48... 173
Lindsay Petroleum Co v Hurd (1874) LR 5 PC 221... 147, 148
Lipkin Gorman (a firm) v Karpnale Ltd [1991] 2 AC 548, HL... 25, 27, 49, 57–59, 96–98, 117, 119–21, 132, 133, 156
Lister v Hodgson (1867) LR 4 Eq 30, 15 WR 547... 52
Littlewoods Retail Ltd v Revenue and Customs Commissioners [2010] EWHC 1071 (Ch), [2010] STC 2072... 46
Lloyds Bank Ltd v Bundy [1975] QB 326, CA... 78
Lloyds Bank plc v Independent Insurance Co Ltd [2000] QB 110, CA... 53, 64, 135
Lobb (Alec) (Garages) Ltd v Total Oil GB Ltd [1985] 1 WLR 173, CA... 81, 148
Lodder v Slowey [1904] AC 442, PC... 89

Table of Cases

Lodge v National Union Investment Co Ltd [1907] 1 Ch 300... 110, 131, 170
Lonrho plc v Fayed (No 2) [1992] 1 WLR 1... 161
Louth v Diprose (1992) 175 CLR 621, HCA... 80
Lumbers v W Cook Builders Pty Ltd [2008] HCA 27, (2008) 232 CLR 635, HCA... 53
MacDonald Dickens & Macklin v Costello [2011] EWCA Civ 930, [2011] 3 WLR 1341... 53
Macmillan Inc v Bishopsgate Investment Trust plc (No 3) [1996] 1 WLR 387, CA... 28
Marine Trade SA v Pioneer Freight Co Ltd BVI [2009] EWHC 2656 (Comm), [2010] 1 Lloyd's Rep 631... 68
Marriot v Hampton (1797) 7 Term Rep 269... 142
Maskell v Horner [1915] 3 KB 106, CA... 71
Mason v Sainsbury (1782) 3 Doug KB 61... 175
Matheson v Smiley [1932] 2 DLR 787, SCC... 105, 106
Mayson v Clouet [1924] AC 980... 90
Medina, The (1876) 1 PD 272, affd (1876) 2 PD 5, CA... 81
Metropolitan Police District Receiver v Croydon Corpn [1957] 2 QB 154, CA... 100
Ministry of Defence v Ashman (1993) 66 P & CR 195, CA... 27
Ministry of Health v Simpson (Re Diplock) [1948] Ch 465, CA; affd [1951] AC 251, HL... 29, 52, 60, 96, 97, 145, 156, 162, 168
Mitchell v Homfray (1881) 8 QBD 587, CA... 77
Monro v Revenue and Customs Commissioners [2008] EWCA Civ 306, [2009] Ch 69... 114
Moore v Vestry of Fulham [1895] 1 QB 399, CA... 142, 143
Moriarty v Regent's Garage Co [1921] 1 KB 423, CA... 91
Morley v Loughnan [1893] 1 Ch 736... 132
Moule v Garrett (1872) LR 7 Exch 101... 101
Mutual Finance Ltd v John Wetton & Sons Ltd [1937] 2 KB 389... 72
Napier and Ettrick (Lord) v Hunter [1993] AC 713, HL... 175, 176
National Westminster Bank plc v Somer International (UK) Ltd [2001] EWCA Civ 970, [2002] QB 1286... 123
Neate v Harding (1851) 20 LJ Ex 250... 94

Neste Oy v Lloyds Bank plc, The Tiiskeri, Nestegas and Ensken [1983] 2 Lloyd's Rep 658... 163, 168
Nicholson v Chapman (1793) 2 Hy Bl 254... 106
Niru Battery Manufacturing Co v Milestone Trading Ltd [2002] EWHC 1425 (Comm), [2002] 2 All ER (Comm) 705... 50, 101, 120
Niru Battery Manufacturing Co v Milestone Trading Ltd (No 2) [2004] EWCA Civ 487, [2004] 2 Lloyd's Rep 319... 101, 102, 156, 173
North Ocean Shipping Co Ltd v Hyundai Construction Co Ltd, The Atlantic Baron [1979] QB 705... 72, 153, 155
Norton v Haggett 85 A 2d 571 (1952)... 100
Nott and Cardiff Corpn, Re [1918] 2 KB 146, CA... 100
Oatway, Re [1903] 2 Ch 356... 60, 168
Ogilvie v Littleboy (1897) 13 TLR 399, CA, affd (1899) 15 TLR 294, HL... 66
Olanda, The [1919] 2 KB 728n, HL... 90
Oom v Bruce (1810) 12 East 225... 137, 139
Opel (Adam) GmbH v Mitras Automotive (UK) Ltd [2007] EWHC 3481 (QB)... 72
O'Rorke v Bolingbroke (1877) 2 App Cas 814, HL... 81
O'Sullivan v Management Agency and Music Ltd [1985] QB 428, CA... 78, 129, 161, 165
Owen v Tate [1976] QB 402, CA... 102
Oxley, Re [1914] 1 Ch 604, CA... 176
P & O Nedlloyd BV v Arab Metals Co, The UB Tiger [2006] EWCA Civ 1717, [2007] 1 WLR 2288... 148
Pan Ocean Shipping Co Ltd v Creditcorp Ltd, The Trident Beauty [1994] 1 WLR 161, HL... 54
Pao On v Lau Yiu Long [1980] AC 614, PC... 72, 74
Parkinson v College of Ambulance Ltd and Harrison [1925] 2 KB 1... 109, 137, 139, 140
Paul v Speirway Ltd [1976] Ch 220... 167, 170, 171
Pavey & Matthews Pty Ltd v Paul (1986) 162 CLR 221, HCA... 35
Pearce v Brain [1929] 2 KB 310... 166
Peyman v Lanjani [1985] Ch 457, CA... 153
Philip Collins Ltd v Davis [2000] 3 All ER 808... 119
Pitt v Holt [2011] EWCA Civ 197, [2012] Ch 132... 66, 67
Plowright v Lambert (1885) 52 LT 646... 77

Table of Cases

Polly Peck International plc v Nadir (No 2) [1992] 4 All ER 769, CA... 97
Port Caledonia, The and The Anna [1903] P 184... 81, 155
Portman Building Society v Dusangh [2000] 2 All ER (Comm) 221, CA... 81
Portman Building Society v Hamlyn Taylor Neck [1998] 4 All ER 202, CA... 32, 124, 126
Prager v Blatspiel, Stamp and Heacock Ltd [1924] 1 KB 566... 106
Primlake Ltd v Matthews Associates [2006] EWHC 1227 (Ch)... 173
Progress Bulk Carriers Ltd v Tube City IMS LLC [2012] EWHC 273 (Comm) [2012] 1 Lloyd's Rep 501... 72
R v A-G for England and Wales [2003] UKPC 22... 72
R v Secretary of State for Work and Pensions [2010] UKSC 54, [2011] 2 AC 15... 115
Redgrave v Hurd (1881) 20 Ch D 1, CA... 154
Reese River Silver Mining Co v Smith (1869) LR 4 HL 64... 163
Rhodes, Re, Rhodes v Rhodes (1890) 44 Ch D 94, CA... 107
Richardson, Re [1911] 2 KB 705, CA... 40
Richmond Gate Property Co Ltd, Re [1964] 3 All ER 936... 90
Rogers v Price (1829) 3 Y & J 28... 104
Roscoe (James) (Bolton) Ltd v Winder [1915] 1 Ch 62... 61
Rover International Ltd v Cannon Film Sales Ltd (No 3) [1989] 1 WLR 912, CA... 87, 88, 91
Rowe v Vale of White Horse DC [2003] EWHC 388 (Admin), [2003] 1 Lloyd's Rep 418... 42, 43
Rowland v Divall [1923] 2 KB 500, CA... 88
Roxborough v Rothmans of Pall Mall Australia Ltd (2001) 208 CLR 516, HCA... 34, 87, 90, 92
Royal Bank of Scotland v Etridge (No 2) [2001] UKHL 44, [2002] 2 AC 773... 69, 74–79, 81, 116, 122, 165
Royal Brompton Hospital NHS Trust v Hammond [2002] UKHL 14, [2002] 1 WLR 1397... 103
Ruabon Steamship Co v London Assurance [1900] AC 6, HL... 54
Rusden v Pope (1868) LR 3 Ex 269... 52
Russell-Cooke Trust Co v Prentis [2002] EWHC 2227 (Ch), [2003] 2 All ER 478... 60

Sadler v Evans (1766) 4 Burr 1984... 124, 127
Safeway Stores Ltd v Twigger [2010] EWCA Civ 1472, [2011] 1 Lloyd's Rep 462... 138
Scottish Equitable plc v Derby [2001] EWCA Civ 369, [2001] 3 All ER 818... 119, 120, 123
Sempra Metals Ltd v Inland Revenue Commissioners [2007] UKHL 34, [2008] 1 AC 561... 38, 42, 46, 64, 157
Shalson v Russo [2003] EWHC 1637 (Ch), [2005] Ch 281... 62, 161
Sharma v Simposh Ltd [2011] EWCA Civ 1383, [2012] 1 P & CR 12... 88
Shell UK Ltd v Total UK Ltd [2010] EWCA Civ 180, [2011] QB 86... 50
Siboen and The Sibotre, The [1976] 1 Lloyd's Rep 293... 72
Siddell v Vickers (1892) 9 RPC 152, CA... 27
Simpson v Simpson [1992] 1 FLR 601... 85, 165
Sinclair v Brougham [1914] AC 398, HL... 36, 60
Sinclair Investments (UK) Ltd v Versailles Trade Finance Ltd [2011] EWCA Civ 347, [2011] 3 WLR 1153... 132, 133
Smith v Bromley (1760) 2 Doug KB 696n... 137
Smith v Cuff (1817) 6 M & S 160... 137
Smith v Hughes (1871) LR 6 QB 597... 69
South Tyneside Metropolitan Borough Council v Svenska International plc [1995] 1 All ER 545... 113
Spence v Crawford [1939] 3 All ER 271, HL... 129
Spencer v S Frances Ltd [2011] EWHC 1269 (QB)... 160, 168
Steinberg v Scala (Leeds) Ltd [1923] 2 Ch 452, CA... 84, 166
Stevenson v Mortimer (1778) 2 Cowp 805... 50
Stockloser v Johnson [1954] 1 QB 476, CA... 90, 151
Stocznia Gdanska SA v Latvian Shipping Co [1998] 1 WLR 574, HL... 87, 88
Stone & Rolls Ltd v Moore Stephens [2009] UKHL 39, [2009] 1 AC 1391... 138
Story v Lord Windsor (1743) 2 Atk 630... 134
Sumpter v Hedges [1898] 1 QB 673, CA... 90
Tappenden v Randall (1801) 2 B & P 467... 109
Tate v Williamson (1866) 2 Ch App 55, LR CA... 78, 161, 165

Table of Cases

Taylor v Bowers (1876) 1 QBD 291, CA... 108, 109, 170
Taylor v Johnston (1882) 19 Ch D 603... 84
Taylor v Motability Finance Ltd [2004] EWHC 2619... 89, 167
Taylor v Plumer (1815) 3 M & S 562... 59
Test Claimants in the FII Group Litigation v Revenue and Customs Commissioners [2008] EWHC 2893 (Ch); on appeal [2010] EWCA Civ 103; on appeal [2012] UKSC 19, [2012] 2 WLR 1149... 31, 33, 111, 112, 114, 117, 121, 122, 146
Thomas v Brown (1876) 1 QBD 714... 87, 89
Tinsley v Milligan [1994] 1 AC 340, HL... 137
Tito v Waddell (No 2) [1977] Ch 106... 77
Transvaal and Delagoa Bay Investment Co Ltd v Atkinson [1944] 1 All ER 579... 124, 125
Tribe v Tribe [1996] Ch 107, CA... 108
Trustee of the Property of FC Jones & Sons v Jones [1997] Ch 159, CA... 59
UCB Corporate Services Ltd v Williams [2002] EWCA Civ 555, [2003] 1 P & CR 12... 76
Ulmer v Farnsworth 15 A 65 (1888)... 55, 95
United Australia Ltd v Barclays Bank Ltd [1941] AC 1, HL... 27, 29
United Overseas Bank v Jiwani [1976] 1 WLR 964... 123
United Shoe Machinery Co of Canada v Brunet [1909] AC 330, PC... 153
Universe Tankships Inc of Monrovia v International Transport Workers Federation, The Universe Sentinel [1983] 1 AC 366, HL... 71
Uren v First National Home Finance Ltd [2005] EWHC 2529 (Ch)... 32, 49

Vigers v Pike (1842) 8 Cl & Fin 562, HL... 128
West Sussex Constabulary's Widows, Children and Benevolent (1930) Fund Trusts, Re, Barnett v Ketteringham [1971] Ch 1... 168
Westdeutsche Landesbank Girozentrale v Islington London Borough Council [1996] AC 669, HL... 27, 36, 87, 129, 163, 164, 166
Wilkes v Spooner [1911] 2 KB 473, 483, CA... 135
Wilkinson v Lloyd (1845) 7 QB 27... 89
William Lacey (Hounslow) Ltd v Davis [1957] 1 WLR 932... 87
Williams v Bayley (1866) LR 1 HL 200... 72
Williams v Roffey Bros & Nicholls (Contractors) Ltd [1991] 1 QB 1, CA... 73
Woolwich Equitable Building Society v IRC [1993] AC 70, HL... 34, 71, 111–14, 122, 143, 146, 170
Workers Trust and Merchant Bank Ltd v Dojap Investments Ltd [1993] AC 573, PC... 151
Wrexham, Mold and Connah's Quay Rly Co, Re [1899] 1 Ch 440, CA... 167, 171
Wright v Carter [1903] 1 Ch 27, CA... 77
Yorkshire Insurance Co Ltd v Nisbet Shipping Co Ltd [1962] 2 QB 330... 175
Zaidan Group Ltd v City of London (1987) 36 DLR (4th) 443; on appeal (1990) 64 DLR (4th) 514, Ontario CA... 170
Zouch d Abbot v Parsons (1765) 3 Burr 1794... 84

INDEX

absence of basis approach xii, 31–2
affirmation 19, 152–3
  application of 152
  bilateral contracts 153
  breach of contract 153
  context of rescission, in the 153
  duress 153
  by election 153
  gifts 153
  misrepresentation 153
  requirements of 153
  undue influence 153
  unilateral contracts 153
  by waiver 153
agency 7–8, 17, 41, 44, 124–8
  as a defence 17, 36, 40, 43, 124–8
    agent's authority 124
    banks 126, 127
    breach of fiduciary duty 124
    civil wrongs 124
    common law 124
    dishonest assistance 124
    double recovery 127
    equity 124
    failure of consideration 126–8
    good faith 126
    law of agency 50, 124
    'ministerial receipt' 124
    payment over 126
    principal, the 125, 127
    strong version of 125
    tort of deceit 124
    weak version of 125–7
  agency of necessity 104, 106
  at the expense of 44, 50
  enrichment 41, 43, 127–8
  restitutionary rights against 7, 37, 40, 127–8
  third party misrepresentation, duress or undue influence in making contract 10–11, 63, 69–70, 75, 79
at the claimant's expense xii, 5, 7–9, 30, 44–62
  causation, 44
  from the claimant 7, 44

  distinguished from consequential gain 46–48
  no need for (equivalent) loss 45–6
  objective loss 45–6
  subtraction 45
  transfer of value 45
  from the claimant directly 7, 44
    contract for the benefit of a third party 8, 44, 53
    direct providers only rule 48–51
    exceptions 49–52
    interceptive subtraction 51–2
    'leapfrogging' 49, 51
    stolen money 49
    subrogation 44, 51
    'trust' exception 8, 49–50
    usurpation of office 51
  incidental benefit 8, 44, 54–5, 94
  purchaser in good faith 135–6
  tracing, see **tracing**

bad faith
  change of position 121
  counter-restitution 129–30
  duress 73
  exploitation of weakness 81
  illegality 110
bailment 104
benefits 7, 41–3
  defendant's 43
  demanding or taking of a 43
  free acceptance 7, 43
  incidental 8, 44, 54–5, 94
  incontrovertible 42–3
breach of confidence 27, 148
breach of contract
  affirmation 153
  failure of consideration 89–92
  restitution for 27
  threatened 72–3
breach of fiduciary duty
  agency 124
  enrichment and 52
  restitution for the equitable wrong of 27
  undue influence 77

Index

breach of trust, *see also* breach of fiduciary duty
  limitation 145
  purchaser in good faith 136
'but for' test 9–10, 63, 70
  duress 10, 70, 74
  exploitation of weakness 80
  incapacity of the individual 83
  mistake 9, 63–6
  undue influence 76

causation, *see* at the claimant's expense; 'but for' test; reason/present in the claimant's mind test
cause of action
  accrual, *see* limitation
  unjust enrichment as a 26–7, 35–6, 91, 117, 145
change of position 16, 117–22
  anticipatory reliance 119–20
  causally relevant loss 119–20
  disenrichment 118
  disqualification from 120–2
    bad faith 121
    criminal illegality 121
    good faith 120–2
    loaned money 121–2
    public authority 122
    Woolwich principle 122
    wrongdoing 121
  establishing loss 118–19
  executed contract, rescission of 118
  fiduciary's lack of authority 97
  frustration 122
  gift for undue influence 118
  Law Reform (Frustrated Contracts) Act 1943 122
  loss incurred in 'anticipatory reliance' 119–20
  mistaken payments 117
    personal right to restitution 117–18
  proprietary restitution 117–18
  restitutionary rights 159
  risk 23, 117, 121
  trusts 118
  unjust enrichment 117–18
  unjust factors 117
  Woolwich principle 117
civil wrong 5, 25, 27, 71, 94–6, 121, 124, 136–7

compulsory discharge of another's liability, *see* legal compulsion
concurrent liability 28, 94
conflict of laws, *see* private international law
constructive notice 10–12, 15–16
  concept of 116
  duress 115–16
  financial institutions and 15–16, 115–16
  misprepresentation 115–16
  undue influence 79, 115–116
contractual exclusion, *see* exclusion
counter-performance 88–9
counter-restitution 17, 128–31
  bad faith 129–30
  duress 131
  failure of consideration 129
  illegal moneylending contracts 131
  incapacity of the individual 84
  non-disclosure 129
  restitutio in integrum 128
  set-off defence 130–1
  terminology of 128
  undue influence 129
  unjust enrichment 130
  void contracts 129
  weaker version of 129
crediting a bank account 7, 41–2, 126
crimes
  illegality as a defence, *see* illegality
  restitution for 5, 25, 28

debt 41, 45, 48, 62, 147
  discharge of a 7, 41, 62, 100
defences 6, 16–19, 35–6, 117–53
    see also affirmation; agency; change of position; counter-restitution; estoppel; exclusion; illegality; limitation; purchaser in good faith; resolved disputes
  discharge for value not a defence 36, 135
  fiduciary's lack of authority 97
  good consideration not a defence 36, 135
  incapacity not a defence 36
  infancy 36
  legal burden of proof 36
  special statutory 19, 149–50
    English tax statutes 150
    passing on 150

Index

types of 35–6
ultra vires not a defence 36
direct providers only rule 48–51
disability 147
disenrichment 118
disputes, *see* **resolved disputes**
doctrine of laches 19, 143–4
  defences 36
  limitation 143–9
double recovery 5, 7, 25, 37
  agency 127
  necessity 107
  restitutionary rights 40
  unjust enrichment 28–9
duress 10, 11, 15, 70–4, 115–6
  affirmation 153
  bad faith 73
  benefits in kind rendered under 70–1
  'but for' test 74
  compulsion 71
  counter-restitution 131
  duress of goods 72
  economic duress 71–2, 74–6
    contractual duties 73
    by threatened breach of contract 72–3
  equity 66
  exploitation of weakness 81
  of goods 72
  illegality 139
  illegitimate threats 71–4
  lawful act duress 72
  limitation 148
  mistake 65
  payment of money 70
  reason/ present in the claimant's mind test 74
  resolved disputes 141–2
  restitution for 137
  restitutionary rights 154–5, 159, 162, 164–5, 171
  scope of 74
  third party duress 15, 74, 115–6
  unjust enrichment 33, 40
  unjust factor 74
  unlawful act duress 71
  Woolwich principle 71

enrichment, *see also* **unjust enrichment; value of enrichment**
  benefits 7, 41, 43
  defendant's 42–43
  demanding or taking of a 43
  debt 41
  definition 7, 41
  free acceptance xii, 7, 41, 43
  incontrovertible benefit, an 42–3
  subjective devaluation 42, 157
  subjective overvaluation 158
  two types of 41–2
    rights 41–2
    value 41–2
equity, *see also* **doctrine of laches; wrongs**
  agency 124
  continuing ownership 28
  enrichment and 59, 61
  integrated with common law xii
  subrogation and 173
estoppel 16, 123–4
  proportionate application of 123–4
  requirement of reliance 123
EU law 29, 34, 50–1, 111, 114, 122, 146
exclusion
  contractual 19, 150–1
    common law doctrines 151
    entire obligation clause 150
    failure of consideration 150–1
    forfeiture of benefits 151
    frustration 151
    Law Reform (Frustrated Contracts) Act 1943 151
    personal liability 150
    restitutionary rights 151
    subsidiarity 151
    Unfair Contract Terms Act 1977 150
    Unfair Terms in Consumer Contracts Regulations 1999 150
  statutory 19, 150–2
    Consumer Credit Act 1974 151
    frustration 152
    Law Reform (Frustrated Contracts) Act 1943 152
    unjust enrichment, liability in 151–2
exploitation of weakness 12, 79–82
  acquisition of a right in property 80
  bad faith 81
  'but for' test 80
  compensation for 82
  duress and 81
  illegality 110
  independent advice, absence of 81

Index

exploitation of weakness (*cont.*)
   limitation 148
   payment of money 80
   principle of 80
   reason/ present in the claimant's mind test 80
   reprehensible conduct 81
   restitution for 82
   restitutionary rights 155, 165
   substantive unfairness 81
   undue influence and 81–2
   unjust factor 82
   weakness, types of 80–1
      circumstantial 80–1
      mental 80

failure of consideration 12–13, 20, 86–92, 159
   absence of consideration 87
   agency 126–8
   breach of contract 89–92
   charterparties 92
   contractual exclusion 90–1
   counter-performance 88–9
   counter-restitution 129
   discharge of contract 89–91
   exclusion 150–1
   frustration 88–9, 92
   illegality 108, 137, 140
   Law Reform (Frustrated Contracts) Act 1943 88, 92
   limitation 145
   non-promissory conditions 87–9, 92
   objective approach 88
   restitutionary rights 155, 163, 166–7
   Sale of Goods Act 1979 91
   Statute of Frauds 1677 89
   subrogation and 173, 177
   termination of contract 89–91
   terminology of 86
   unjust factor 87
   void contracts 87
fiduciary's lack of authority xiii, 13–14, 93–8
   absence of consent 94–6
   change of position 97
   concurrent liability 94
   defences 97
   dishonest receipt 97
   ignorance/powerlessness and 93–5

   incidental benefits 94
   knowing receipt 96–7
   lack of authority 96–7
   mistake and 93
   proprietary restitution 97
   restitutionary rights 155–6, 168–9
   strict liability 97–8
   three-party cases 96–7
   trust funds 14, 96–8
   unconscionable retention test 97
   unjust factor 94–5
financial institutions
   constructive notice and 15–16, 115–16
   concept of constructive notice 116
   illegitimate threat 115
   third party's misrepresentation 115
   undue influence 115
first-in, first-out rule 60, 162
forgoing a claim 7, 41
free acceptance xii, 7, 41, 43
frustration
   change of position 122
   exclusion 151–2
   failure of consideration 88–9, 92
   Law Reform (Frustrated Contracts) Act 1943 34, 88, 92, 151–2

gifts
   affirmation 153
   enrichment and 49
   incapacity of the individual 84
   for mistake 66–9
   restitutionary rights 164–6
   for undue influence 78–9, 118
good faith, *see also* purchaser in good faith
   agency 126
   change of position 120–2
   purchaser in 132
   resolved disputes 142
gross turpitude 109

ignorance xiii, 13, 92–6
   restitutionary rights 155–6, 168–9
illegality 15, 17–18, 20, 107–10, 136–41, 159
   as a defence 17–18, 106, 136–41
   administration of justice, interference with 137
   'clean hands' 141
   civil wrongs 137
   contract 137–8

Index

contractual invalidity 140
crimes 137
damages under cross-undertaking 138
denial of restitution 137, 140
deterrence 138
duress 139
equitable restitutionary rights 141
ex turpi causa non oritur actio 137–8
failure of consideration 137, 140
in pari delicto potior est condition defendentis 137
inconsistency 139–40
integrity of the legal system 138
Law Commission, the 137–9
mistake 137, 139
non in pari delicto 139
public policy 137
reliance principle 137
restitution for duress 137
restraint of trade 137
sexual immorality 137
statutory wrongs 137
tort 137–8
uncertainty 140
factors concerned with 15, 107–10
 bad faith 110
 class protection 110
 Consumer Credit Act 1974 110
 exploitation of weakness 110
 failure of consideration 108
 gross turpitude 109
 illegal contracts 108
 Insolvency Act 1986 110
 opportunity for repentance (*locus poenitentiae*) 108–9
 repudiatory breach 109
 right to restitution by withdrawal 108–9
 restitutionary rights 157, 170
 trust 108
 unfairness 110
 unjust factor 108
illegal contracts 108
implied contract fallacy 27, 36
improvements 42, 64, 142
incapacity of the individual 12, 83–5
 beneficial contracts of service 83
 'but for' causation 83
 concept of invalidity 83, 85
 contracts for company shares 83
 contracts for necessaries 83

counter-restitution 84
dementia 85
gifts 84–5
human incapacity 83
Infant Reliefs Act 1874 83
intoxication 85
limitation 148
mental (in)capacity 83, 85
Mental Capacity Act 2005 85, 147
Minors' Contracts Act 1987 83–4
partnership agreements 83
by reason of infancy 83–5
repudiated contracts 83
restitutionary rights 84, 155, 165–6
will-making 85
 Wills Act 1837 85
incidental benefit 8, 44, 54–5, 94
indemnity insurance 21, 35, 40, 175–6
 contract of indemnity 21
 over-indemnification 35, 175–6
 subrogation 21, 35, 40, 172, 175–6
infancy, see **incapacity of the individual**
intellectual property 7, 21, 41, 160
insolvency
 enrichment and 53
 Insolvency Act 1986 110
 restitutionary rights 167, 170–1
intangible property 7, 21, 41, 160, 171
interceptive subtraction 51–2
interest 38
 accrual of cause of action 145
 compound 38, 111, 157
 simple 38
 swap transactions 113
intoxication 12, 83, 85

judgment reversed 32–3
 defence of resolved disputes 18, 141–3

knowing receipt 96–7, 156
 restitutionary rights 156
 strict liability 96–7
 unconscionable retention test 97
 unjust enrichment analysis 96–7, 156
 wrong of 97

lack of authority, see **fiduciary's lack of authority**
lapse of time bar, see **doctrine of laches**
'leapfrogging' 49–51

191

Index

legal compulsion 14, 20, 98–103, 159
  burden of paying 101
  Civil Liability (Contribution) Act 1978 102–3
  common law on contribution 102–3
  compulsory discharge of another's liability 100
  contribution 101
  exercise of 99
  illegality 100
  illegitimate threats 99
  incontrovertible benefit 100
  injustice resulting from 99
  Mercantile Law Amendment Act 1856 102
  monetary restitutionary award 101
  policy-motivated restitution 99
  primary liability 102
  recoupment 100–1
  reimbursement 100–1
  restitution of illegality 100
  restitutionary rights 156, 169
  secondary liability 99, 102
  unjust factor 99, 103
lien 20, 39, 159
  common law 101, 160
  equitable 61, 118, 141, 147, 160, 166, 167, 169, 176
limitation 18, 19, 143–9
  accrual of cause of action 18, 94, 145–8
  breach of trust 145
  Civil Liability (Contribution) Act 1978 147
  common law 148
  debt or liquidated pecuniary claim 147
  disability 147
  doctrine of laches 145–9
  duress 148
  EU law 146
  exploitation of weakness 148
  failure of consideration 145
  Finance Act 2004 146
  Finance Act 2007 146
  fraud 146
  frustration 145
  incapacity 148
  Law Commission 149
  Limitation Act 1980 144–9
  Mental Capacity Act 2005 147
  mistake 146, 149

monetary restitutionary award 147
  period of 144–5, 148–9
  remedies 147–8
  rescission (in equity) 148
  tax, overpayment of 146–7
  tort 146
  trust property 145, 147–9
  undue influence 148
  unjust enrichment 144, 147–9
  Woolwich principle 146
lowest intermediate balance rule 61

maritime salvage 104, 156–7, 169
mental capacity, *see* incapacity of the individual
ministerial receipt, *see* agency
misrepresentation *see also* mistake 9–10, 26, 29, 63, 65, 66, 69, 79, 115, 130, 132, 141, 147–8, 153
  reason/present in claimant's mind (where fraudulent) 9, 63, 65
  tort of deceit 29, 65, 82, 124
  third party misrepresentation 10, 15–6, 63, 69, 115–6
mistake 9–10, 63–9
  'but for' causation test 64–6
  carelessness/negligence 65
  causation 64
  contractual or statutory obligations 69
  doubt 68
  duress 65
  equity 66
  fraudulent misrepresentation 65
  gifts for mistake, rescission of 66–9
  limitation 146, 149
  misprediction 67–8
  mistaken payments 64
  purchaser in good faith 134, 136
  recklessness 63, 65, 68
  requirement of notice (or agency) 69
  resolved disputes 141–2
  restitution for 66
  restitution of non-money benefits 64
  restitutionary rights 154, 163–8
  risk-taking 65, 67–8
  serious 66–7
  subrogation 173
  suspicion 68
  supposed liability 64
  tax consequences of a gift 67

Index

Torts (Interference with Goods) Act 1977 64
will-making 65–6
mixed assets 59, 61
mixed funds 61–2
monetary restitutionary award xii, 6, 20, 37–40, 46–8, 57, 154–7, 162, 165–7, 169–70, 175
  contribution 38, 55, 101–3, 147, 156
  legal compulsion 101
  limitation 147
  money had and received to claimant's use 38, 154, 155, 157
  money paid to defendant's use 38, 155
  personal right to 6, 20, 38–40, 154–8
  quantum meruit 38, 46, 147, 155, 156, 160, 165, 168
  quantum valebat 38, 46, 158
  recoupment 38, 100–3, 156
  reimbursement 100, 106–7, 156
  reward 157
  value of enrichment 20, 37–8, 154

necessity 14, 15, 20, 104–7, 159
  agency of 104, 106
  bailment 104
  common law methodology 104
  compensation 105
  double recovery 107
  duty of care 107
  duty to intervene 107
  emergency 106, 107
  illegality defence 106
  imminent harm 106
  management of the affairs of another 105
  maritime salvage 104
  Mental Capacity Act 2005 104
  mental incapacity 107
  negotiorum gestio 105
  officious intervention 106
  restitutionary rights 156–7, 169
  Sale of Goods Act 1979 104
  suicide 105, 106

passing on 19, 36, 46, 112, 114–15, 149–50
personal right, *see* **monetary restitutionary award**
powerlessness xiii, 13, 92–6
  restitutionary rights 155–6, 168–9

prevailing practice 19, 36, 112, 114–15, 149–50
prevention of anticipated unjust enrichment, *see* **unjust enrichment**
private international law 30
proportionate sharing rule 60–2
proprietary restitution, *see also* **lien; rescission; rectification; subrogation; trust**
  change of position 117–18
  general restricting principle 150
  power model 163
  purchaser in good faith 132–4
  restitutionary rights 39, 160, 163, 166–71
  retention of asset or right in property 39, 163
public authority
  unlawful obtaining or conferral of a benefit 15, 20, 111–15, 157, 159, 170
  change of position 113
  corporation tax 114
  Customs and Excise Management Act 1979 114
  defences 111–13
  demand 15, 111–12
  EU law 111, 112, 114
  Inheritance Tax Act 1984 114
  mistaken payment of tax 114
  principle of unlawfulness 113
  self-assessed tax 112
  Social Security Administration Act 1992 115
  Taxes Management Act 1970 114
  ultra vires tax 112–13
  Value Added Tax Act 1994 114
  Woolwich principle 111–14
purchaser in good faith 17, 131–6
  at the claimant's expense 135–6
  bona fide purchaser 133–6
  breach of trust 136
  change of position 133–5
  discharge for value 135
  fraudulent actions 136
  gifts 135
  good consideration 135
  good faith 132
  mistake 134, 136
  nemo dat quod non habet 131, 134
  'notice,' meaning of 133
  property law 133–4

Index

purchaser in good faith (*cont.*)
  proprietary restitution 132–4
  right to restitution 136
  sanctity of transactions 134
  security of receipt 134
  third parties 131–2, 134–5
  tracing 132
  two-party cases 134
  unjust enrichment 131, 133–5
  valid contracts 134
  for value and without notice 17, 131–6
    property law 131
  voidable contracts 133
  wagering contracts 132

quasi-contract 27, 144–5

reason/present in the claimant's mind test 9, 63, 65, 74, 76, 80
receivables 7, 21, 41, 160
rectification 20–1, 29, 39, 141, 147–8, 161–2, 164–7, 171
remedies 37–8, *see also* **restitutionary rights**
rescission 20–1, 38–9, 41, 66–7, 118, 128, 129, 133, 141, 147–8, 152–5, 159, 161–7, 169–71
resolved disputes 18, 141–3
  compromise 141–2
  contract 141–2
  contractual waiver 142
  duress 141–2
  finality to disputes 142
  good faith 142
  invalid judgments 141
  mistake 141–2
  non-contractual payments 142
  res judicata 141–2
  right to restitution 142
  tort 141–2
  unjust enrichment 141–2
restitution, *see also* **restitutionary rights; unjust enrichment**
  for crimes 5, 25, 28
  founded on agreement or promise 5, 25, 27
  founded on continuing ownership 5, 25, 28
  reversal of enrichment 5, 25, 26, 37, 40
  for unjust enrichment 5, 25–30
  for wrongs (eg breach of contract, breach of fiduciary duty, equitable wrongs, torts) xii, 5, 25, 27
restitutionary rights 6–7, 20–1, 37–40, 154–77
  see also **monetary restitutionary award; proprietary restitution; subrogation**
  personal right to a monetary restitutionary award 20, 37–40 154–8
    duress 154–5, 159
    exploitation of weakness 155
    factors concerned with illegality 157
    failure of consideration 155
    fiduciary's lack of authority 155–6
    ignorance or powerlessness 155–6
    incapacity of the individual 155
    knowing receipt cases 156
    legal compulsion 156
    locus poenitentiae 157
    maritime salvage 156–7
    misrepresentation 159
    mistake 154
    necessity 156–7
    public authority, unlawful obtaining or conferral of benefit by 157
    remedies 154–6
    undue influence 155
  other restitutionary rights xii, 20–1, 159–71
    duress 162, 164, 165, 171
    exploitation of weakness 165
    factors concerned with illegality 170
    failure of consideration 163, 166–7
    fiduciary's lack of authority 168–9
    general restricting principle 170
    gifts 164–6
    ignorance or powerlessness 168–9
    incapacity of the individual 165–6
    insolvency 167, 170–1
    legal compulsion 169
    locus poenitentiae 170
    misrepresentation 164
    mistake 163–8
    necessity 169
    risk of insolvency 167, 170–1
    undue influence 162, 165, 167, 171
  proprietary rights 38–9
  'remedies,' language of 37
  'rights', language of 37

Index

right in property 20–1, 39–40, 57, 75, 80, 84, 118, 163, 166–71
risk-taking 10, 34, 63, 65, 67–8, 88, 125, 142
   change of position 23, 117, 121
   risk of insolvency 20–1, 53, 159–60, 167, 170–1

Scotland 29
services 7, 41, 43, 45–50, 87, 92, 104–7, 155–6, 158
shares 7, 21, 41, 160
statutes 19, 29, 147, 149–52
   see also **frustration; limitation**
statutory exclusion, *see* **exclusion**
strict liability 79, 96–8
subjective devaluation 42, 157
subjective overvaluation 158
subrogation xii, 7–8, 20–1, 159, 171–7
   at the claimant's expense 44, 51
   conceptual meaning of 172
   contractual 173
   equitable lien 176
   equity and 173
   to extinguished rights 172–3
   failure of consideration 173, 177
   indemnity insurance and 21, 35, 40, 175–6
      over-indemnification 175–6
   language of 172
   legal compulsion 173
   legal process rather than remedy 172
   lenders 161, 164, 167, 169, 170–5
   Merchantile Law Amendment Act 1856 173
   mistake 173
   non-contractual, of indemnity insurers 175–6
   non-contractual rights 40
   personal right to restitution and 176
   proprietary restitution and 174
   restitutionary rights 156, 160–1, 164, 167–71
   rights 'taken over' 174–5
   role of 172
   to subsisting rights 172–3, 175–6
   sui generis 173
   surety 160, 169, 173
   third party liability 176
   Trustee Act 2000 176
   trusts 21, 176–7

unjust enrichment and 31, 35, 173, 175, 177
unjust factor 175–7
substitute assets, *see* **tracing**
subsidiarity 151
surety 40, 69, 79, 102, 116, 122
   subrogation 160, 169, 173

tax
   English tax statutes 150
   overpayment of 146–7
tort
   of conversion 64
   of deceit 29, 65, 82, 124
   illegality and 137–8
   liability in 95
   limitation and 146
   mistake and 64
   of negligence 50
   resolved disputes 141–2
   restitution for 27
   Torts (Interference with Goods) Act 1977 6
tracing xii, 8–9, 56–62
   backward 62
   claiming 56–7
   clean substitution 59, 60
   common law 61
   equity 59, 61, 162
   fiction of persistence 57
   fiduciary duty, breach of 52
   first-in, first-out rule 60
   following 56–7
   lowest intermediate balance rule 61
   mixed assets 59, 61
   mixed funds 61–2
   proportionate sharing rule 60–1
   purchaser in good faith 132
   restitutionary rights 162, 170
   substitute assets 58–9
   tracing rules 59–60
   trust 8, 57, 60–1
   vindicating property rights 57
trusts 8, 14, 35, 38–40, 44, 56–7, 60–1, 96–8, 159–68, 170
   at the expense of 8, 44, 49–50, 56
   beneficial interest 28, 38, 57, 64, 158, 163
   change of position 118
   constructive 39, 108, 156
   fiduciary's lack of authority 14, 96–8

Index

trusts (*cont.*)
  illegality 108
  limitation 145, 147–9
  liability as a constructive trustee 156
  power model 163
  restitutionary rights as 35, 38–40, 160–8, 170
  relationship of influence 77
  resulting 39, 108
  remedy or substantive institution 37
  subrogation 21, 176–7
  tracing 8, 57, 60–1

ultra vires
  company 36, 83
  institutional incapacity 36, 83, 112–13
  not a defence 36
  public authority *see* **public authority**
  tax 112–13
undue influence 11–12, 15, 75–9, 115–16
  acquisition of a right in property 75
  actual 76
  affirmation 153
  breach of fiduciary duty 77
  'but for' causation 76
  constructive notice 79, 115
  contracts induced by 78
  counter-restitution 129
  economic duress 75–6
  exploitation of weakness 81–2
  gifts 78–9
  illegitimate threats 75
  irrebuttable legal presumption 77
  limitation 148
  payment of money 75
  presumed 76–7
  proving 76
  reason/ present in the claimant's mind test 76
  rebuttable presumption of 78
  relationship of influence 77–8
  restitutionary rights 155, 162, 165, 167, 172
  third party undue influence 15, 75, 79, 115–16
  unjust enrichment and 40
  voidable transactions 75
unlawful obtaining or conferral by public authority, *see* **public authority**
unjust enrichment, *see also* **enrichment; restitution**
  contract and 151
  exclusion 151–2
  limitation 144, 147–9
  prevention of anticipated 7, 21, 40, 172, 175
    duress 40
    injunctions 40
    'prevention,' language of 40
    subrogation 7, 21, 40, 172, 175
    undue influence 40
  purchaser in good faith 131, 133–5
    equity 28
  when the enrichment is unjust 5–6, 9–16, 30–5, 63–116, *see also* **unjust factors**
unjust factors xii, 5–6, 31–5, 63–116
  see also **duress; exploitation of weakness; failure of consideration; fiduciary's lack of authority; ignorance; illegality; incapacity of the individual; legal compulsion; mistake; necessity; powerlessness; public authority; undue influence**
  benefit owed under legal obligation 6, 32–5
  consent (absent, impaired or qualified) 5–6, 31–5
  contrast with 'absence of basis' 31–2
  ground for restitution 31
  moral obligation 35
  over-indemnification 6, 35, 175–7
  policy-motivated restitution 32
  restitutionary rights 39, 162–70
  subrogation 176–7
usurpation of office 51, 96

value of enrichment 20, 37–8, 154, 157–8
  market value 20, 157–8
  subjective devaluation 42, 157
  subjective overvaluation 158
vindicating property rights 57, 131, 162
  restitution founded on continuing ownership 5, 25, 28
void contracts 35, 87, 88, 129
voidable contracts 35, 75, 87, 129, 133, 155, 169

weakness, *see* **exploitation of weakness**
will-making
  rectification of wills 162, 164
  unjust enrichment 29, 65–6
  Wills Act 1837 29

Index

Woolwich principle, *see also* **public authority**
benefits 111–14
change of position 117, 122
duress 71
limitation 146
restitutionary rights 39

unjust enrichment 34
wrongs
civil wrong 5, 25, 27, 71, 94–6, 121, 124, 136–7
illegality as a defence, *see* **illegality**
restitution for xii, 27
statutory wrong 27, 137